T0274755

THROUGH THE CRACK IN THE WALL

THE SECRET HISTORY OF JOSEF K

JOHNNIE JOHNSTONE
FOREWORD BY STEWART LEE

JAW
BONE

Josef K was about the heroic outsider suavely surfing across the fraught surface of their albino funk fracas. Haig sounds high on anxiety, finding an odd, giddy euphoria in doubt.

SIMON REYNOLDS, *RIP IT UP AND START AGAIN*

THROUGH THE CRACK IN THE WALL
THE SECRET HISTORY OF JOSEF K
JOHNNIE JOHNSTONE

A Jawbone book
First edition 2024
Published in the UK and the USA by
Jawbone Press
Office G1
141–157 Acre Lane
London SW2 5UA
England
www.jawbonepress.com

ISBN 978-1-916829-04-6

Printed by Short Run Press, Exeter

1 2 3 4 5 28 27 26 25 24

Josef K in Amsterdam, 1981.
Fran van der Hoeven

FOREWORD
BY STEWART LEE

My name is Stewart Lee. I am a fifty-five-year-old stand-up comedian. And I'm honoured to have been asked to write the introduction to Johnnie Johnstone's timely study of the Edinburgh post-punk pioneers Josef K. My tastes in both comedy and music were spawned by sub-bedsheet exposure to the John Peel show from 1979 to 1986. Ted Chippington. The Fall. The Frank Chickens. The Fire Engines. Eric Bogosian. Echo & The Bunnymen. John Hegley. And Josef K. But I bought my copy of *The Only Fun In Town*, on the fabled Postcard label, five years late, second hand from Garon Records in Oxford's covered market, in 1986, having handed my £2.99 to the shopkeeper, Rod Poole, an experimental guitarist tragically murdered in an LA parking lot twenty-one years later.

Back then you couldn't just snatch music out of the air like pollen or dandelion seeds, a point Johnstone himself drives home in the excellent book you are now being delayed from beginning. If you didn't pick something up when you first saw it, it might be gone forever. Nothing was available to be downloaded or streamed, and I still dream frustrated nightmares about the sides I remember seeing in Reddington's Rare Records but didn't buy as a teenager because I was too broke, too ignorant, or too cool for school. Vertigo swirls, two for a pound? No thanks, mate.

Hippie shit. But at least I had the sense to score *The Only Fun In Town*.

And now Josef K's 1981 debut was mine, and finally the songs I'd treasured, hissy and fading and taped from the radio five years before, were secured. 'Sorry For Laughing'. 'Crazy To Exist'. 'Heart Of Song'. All were as I remembered, the thin stringy serrated sounds of clever suspicious men in sunglasses after dark and second-hand suits, flirting with the Dionysian thrust of funk, but with Apollonian dog-eared Penguin paperbacks in their back pockets, as au fait with Studio 54 as with Franz Kafka, a dichotomy I aspired to embody. These boys were the people I wanted to be and, for a brief time before I discovered drinking, I almost was.

And yet I regretted having been, like Johnstone, just that little bit too young to have seen the group live. The singer Paul Haig, however, did once see me live. I wonder if he remembers? It was in the autumn of 1989 at the Red Rose Comedy Club in Finsbury Park. Don't look for it. It's not there anymore. I was twenty-one and doing an unpaid open spot on a bill with four real acts. I don't suppose I was very good, though the crowd's trust in me had already been diminished by the introduction I was given by that night's compere, the lugubrious bluegrass fan and magician John Lenahan, who brought me on with the uncharacteristically uncharitable words, 'And now the open spot, or as we call them, the running sores of the comedy circuit.' Cue half-hearted applause.

I don't remember how, or why, but a man with sharp hair and sharper cheekbones in the front row to my left started shouting things at me at some point in my set, I forget exactly what. He was not necessarily heckling but was perhaps trying to help or even to encourage me. 'What's your name then?' I asked, hoping to initiate a hilarious back-and-forth. But he didn't answer. Instead, the beautiful woman next to him shouted, as if on his behalf, such an exchange being beneath him, 'He's Paul Haig.' 'Paul Haig?' I said, 'From Josef K?' And it was indeed he, though his name meant nothing to anyone else in the room.

Thirty-three years down the line I would know exactly how to have had fun with this sort of situation. Why, only last year I got twenty minutes out of the fact that I found myself talking from the stage to the nephew of a member of the original line-up of Napalm Death. But I was less confident then, and to be fair, Haig's solo career hadn't set the world on fire, and the average person didn't know who the fuck Josef K were. Prophets without honour. If there'd been a glimmer of recognition in the audience, I am sure I could have got some mileage out of using phrases drawn from Josef K songs. 'Chance Meeting'. 'Sorry For Laughing'. Et cetera. But Paul Haig from Josef K's interruption, whatever it was, instead steered my set into a downward spiral from which it never recovered. I blame Josef K, for being forgotten, and me, for being shit.

Today, most people still don't know Paul Haig, or Josef K, the band he staffed alongside Malcolm Ross, David Weddell, and Ronnie Torrance. But they know the sound they helped shape, filtered through followers like Franz Ferdinand and The Wedding Present, to become scrawled all over the 6 Music orthodoxies of twenty-first-century twenty-something string-stranglers, discovering in the hungry beat of young post-punk Scotland a durable template for the nervous neuroticism of now.

In the war film *The Guns Of Navarone*, Anthony Quayle's Major Franklin is left behind by Gregory Peck's team of saboteurs after he contracts gangrene, but he later hears the explosion that destroys the guns from his hospital bed. His mission was, in the end, a success, though he was not there to see it. Is this what Josef K felt when they heard Franz Ferdinand's 'Take Me Out', twenty-two years after they disbanded?

Nowadays I know Haig's co-pilot Malcolm Ross a little, having met him through the fantastic Australian musicians Dave Graney and Clare Moore, whose work his guitar lines sometimes grace, and I see him for breakfast in the New Town every summer when I do my jokes at the Edinburgh fringe festival. Malcolm's modesty about the seismic impact his Josef K sound had on subsequent generations of guitarists remains ridiculous. If he didn't live five hundred miles away, I'd see Malcolm more often, but I am sure he would remain resolutely unconvinced of his own genius despite my best efforts. A fan since thirteen, I'm forever in his debt, but consider this introduction a part payment. As for Paul Haig? Well, the Red Rose didn't book me again for a year after I bombed that night. So I think he still owes me.

STEWART LEE

WRITER/CLOWN

STOKE NEWINGTON, LONDON

NOVEMBER 2023

INTRODUCTION
BY JOHNNIE JOHNSTONE

I don't dislike rock stars. I just don't want to be one.

PAUL HAIG TO JOHNNY WALLER, *SOUNDS*, 1981

The lifespan of every pop group is finite, and the decision about when to throw in the towel can be a calculated gamble. It's often about timing. What if that next single was 'the one', the song to bring them fame and fortune? Perhaps the breakthrough was only a few weeks away. There is a converse risk for those who stick at it for too long, that they might tarnish their legacy by refusing to call time. Some bands just go on and on, long after the lights have gone out. Oblivious to changing trends. Relentlessly recycling their greatest hits with rapidly diminishing returns. The decision is usually governed by one of three things: avarice, survival, or integrity. It can be a delicate balance to strike. But sometimes fate intervenes.

Almost every group who build a lasting legacy do so through the enduring appeal of the music they made. Irrespective of their level of commercial success, they must have had a profound social and cultural impact. But whether they stayed together for two years or fifty-two, the moment inevitably came when they ceased to exist. There are some groups, virtually ignored during their lifetime, who become increasingly influential after their dissolution. Take The Velvet Underground, for example. When they split up, few if anyone batted an eyelid, least of all the remaining members of The Velvet Underground, none of whom had been there at the beginning. During the few years they spent together, they barely registered much in the way of commercial or critical recognition. And yet, aside from The Beatles, there is arguably no group in the history of popular music whose influence has been as far-reaching. As for The Beatles, whatever one thought of their music, they changed everyone's lives, so that when the deed was finally done, as well as there being a huge outpouring of grief from fans, there was shock and dismay from almost everyone else. They were irreplaceable.

Like The Beatles, Josef K changed some people's lives. Ask Johnny Marr. Ask Alex Kapranos. Ask Phil Wilson. Ask Stewart Lee. Ask Douglas McIntyre. But very few people could tell you the name of a Josef K song, and the band's music is rarely if ever played on the radio. And likening Josef K to The Velvet Underground, as convenient and attractive as that might seem, is an analogy that's equally wide of the mark, for the Velvets left behind four albums that almost everyone agrees were peerless, sacred texts for every outsider with a guitar who followed afterward. It's reasonable to assume that everyone with even a passing interest in the history of popular music could name a Velvet Underground song, or at least recognise one from the radio or a television advertisement. Not so Josef K.

Scotland produced a disproportionately high volume of great bands in the late 70s and 80s, many of whom enjoyed a far greater degree of success: Simple Minds, Orange Juice, The Bluebells, Aztec Camera, and The Associates, for example. There were others who refused to hang around for long, but who nevertheless burned brightly and fiercely, and whose reputation has since mushroomed. The best of those was Josef K.

I first heard the music of Josef K on Christmas Day 1987, six years after the members of the band had parted ways. On the cover of the *Young*

& Stupid / Endless Soul collection, released earlier that year, the foursome looked debonair in their modish garb of slightly baggy suits and geometric haircuts. While they seemed reasonably cheerful, there was something a little solemn about their appearance. The smiles seemed a little forced. Almost as if they had little time for the burden of publicity shots. It is possible they couldn't really be bothered with all that stuff, that perhaps they had never anticipated someone might one day want to take photographs of them.

To my teenage self, the band's image seemed incongruous with the carefully cultivated slovenliness of the indie scene of the time. Not only did Josef K look smarter than those groups but they sounded smarter too. Many of the indie bands featured on the *NME*'s hugely popular *C86* compilation from the previous year seemed impossibly fey and their music insipid, virtually apologising for its own existence. *Young & Stupid*, by contrast, sounded cerebral and carnivorous, extremely agitated, yet at the same time had a suave air of sophistication. It was all those things the other music simply couldn't be.

Looking back, the C81 bands—Josef K's contemporaries—were arguably a braver and more imaginative cohort than the class of 1986. When I first heard *Young & Stupid*, it proved to be exactly the kind of thing I had long been searching for—the perfect Christmas gift. It became the catalyst for a modestly successful hunt for the band's fabled Postcard singles and their solitary LP, which had by then been unavailable for several years. Lord knows I had spent years trying and failing to find any sign of their existence in the LP racks of HMV and Virgin on Glasgow's Union Street. As things transpired, my younger brother would beat me to the punch with its capture, and while I was green with envy, the family home—much to my parents' disapproval—would vibrate to the glorious racket contained within for some considerable time.

I knew little about Josef K, but the allure of their music, like many of the bands and singers I discovered around that time, was emphatically reinforced by that dearth of information. Without the internet, one had to make do with the odd footnote in a rock reference book, little snippets in the weekly music press, or browsing between the staples of a patchwork indie fanzine where they might have been name-dropped by some other musician. Paul Haig's name would certainly pop up from time to time in *Smash Hits* or *Record Mirror*. And Malcolm Ross's face would certainly have appeared next to Edwyn Collins's in a multitude of glossy Orange Juice shoots from 1983. But that was it.

That necessitated a flurry of mix-cassette exchanging, essential to ensure you could wrap your ears around some of the rarer nuggets of the time. Usually, a friend (or a friend of a friend) was rumoured to have this album or that one. You might try to ingratiate yourself with a particular person, hoping to wind up at their house after a chance meeting at a gig, anticipating you might get an opportunity to peek at their record collection. Who knows what treasures you might find there? Maybe they'd even let you borrow a few. It's how I discovered The Electric Prunes, Lee Hazlewood, and The Television Personalities.

A stockpile of apocryphal stories would circulate about the musicians with whom you'd become besotted—tales exaggerated beyond all reasonableness, rumours that ached to be true. Some I particularly remember included the one that Jonathan Richman always instructed the bouncers at his shows to throw out anyone who was smoking cigarettes; that psych legend Skip Spence made his greatest record after miraculously tunnelling his way out of a mental hospital; that 60s band Love—dismissed as hippies by many—were actually Manson-like lunatics who kept a harem of sex slaves tied up in a haunted house; that David Thomas of Pere Ubu had been the first choice to play the role of Henry in David Lynch's *Eraserhead*. Like almost all rumours, there was usually a kernel of truth lurking beneath the surface (well, perhaps not the David Thomas one), but they were rumours, nevertheless. Unlike today, facts could not be instantly verified, and the world was all the better for it. Hours might be spent prattling frivolously over exploits of which there was little or no evidence. But those hours were not wasted. Rock'n'roll might be about sex and rebellion, but it's also about mystery, myth, and enigma.

Josef K encapsulated that mystery. For whatever reason, it seemed that no one was telling lies about Josef K. In fact, it was a struggle to find out anything about them. Back in 1980, I would have been quite happily rearranging the stickers on my Rubik's Cube in a ridiculous attempt to appear smart, or I'd have been happily transfixed by the otherworldly television repeats of *The Adventures Of Robinson Crusoe* on Saturday morning TV. Musical passions had yet to stir, but when they finally did (I was miles behind all the cool kids), all I could discover was that Josef K were from Edinburgh. Local boys, really. Few people could tell me anything other than what *this* or *that* member did after the group's demise. There seemed to be a collective amnesia about what Josef K had accomplished during their lifespan. Those evocative monochrome Harry Papadopoulos shots of the four blurred figures, poised at odd angles before classical and modernist architecture, added to the mystique. They looked like shadows melting, ghosts disappearing.

You could invent your own stories and legends, let yourself dream a little. When one or two of the older 'heads' at the indie nightclubs claimed to have seen the group perform live, I was mightily impressed. What were they like? Some recalled performances that were thrilling and incendiary, others positioned the band as guarded, awkward, even somewhat aloof. Me? I could only imagine. Every recollection, each printed word, suggested here was a band which obstinately refused to play by the rules. Nevertheless, what *was* immediately apparent was that the music they made was touched by genius. Josef K were modernists. Innovators. Unencumbered by expectations, their lightning-in-a-bottle 'career' produced five singles and one impulsively re-recorded LP. I had been told that they had made a solemn promise to record only one album and then quit. That wasn't actually true, but it was still the most punk rock thing I'd ever heard, making them yet worthier of my admiration.

—

I felt the need to write a book about Josef K because I believe they merit more than a footnote in a reference book or a website with only a few daily visitors. They seem forever destined to live in the shadow of other groups who may have seemed more significant or fashionable at the time. Surely, for once, they deserve the spotlight to themselves? Their story might be a hazy one—over forty years have passed since the fun and frenzy, and memories have grown thin—but what remains is a canon of intrepid sonic adventures and a tale of unfulfilled potential. More than anything else, however, the story of Josef K is a familiar one. It's about friendships going sour, and it's also about a few really bad decisions. Those are things that all of us can relate to.

Other books, even books about Postcard Records, play down their importance, but many people forget that Josef K were the only band to release an album for the label during that golden period. While Orange Juice, Aztec Camera, and even The Go-Betweens went on to enjoy a greater degree of success, Josef K remain the black-sheep fly-in-the-ointment existentialist-goatee-scratcher ace in the pack and the most talented and original music-makers of the whole bunch.

But by 1981, after only three years together, they were finished, their final denouement as shrouded in mystery as that of the protagonist of the novel from which they took their name. This book should shed more light on the real reasons for Josef K's demise, as well as afford proper consideration to the band's influence and legacy, but its primary purpose is to celebrate the wonderful music they made during their short career. I hope it does this.

1/15 | FIN /
NO GLORY

Don't concern yourself about anybody. Just do what you think is right.

FRANZ KAFKA, *THE TRIAL*

The Trial is one of the great works of twentieth-century literature, but it was never completed, and, like the author's other novels, remains a mystery unsolved. The ending of the published manuscript is startling and unsettling but, in some ways, deeply unsatisfying, if only because the reader can never be certain of the author's true intentions for the finale. It seems apt then that Josef K's career ended in such a similarly abrupt fashion, and it can be tempting to invent our own ending to a story that seemed to have only just begun.

At the same time, had Josef K made fifteen albums, there is every chance they wouldn't be remembered quite so fondly. That is one school of thought. Another might contend that Josef K could have been one of the most successful bands of the 80s. If only they had kept their nerve. If only the will had existed to keep going. If only. Consider how successful their contemporaries have been: The Cure, The Fall, New Order, Echo & The Bunnymen. Had things turned out differently, had Josef K succeeded in the conventional sense of the term, several books would probably have been written about them before now. But it is possible that—like, for example, Simple Minds—the members of Josef K would have their heads turned by the trappings of fame. Maybe then, something of their original essence, whatever it was that made them so vital and life-giving, would have been lost forever. It can be a long way back once you've lost all credibility.

The 80s and 90s were such strange decades for music—they did unusual things to many people, fans and musicians alike. Probably something to do with MTV. Or drugs. Or technology. Or all of those things. One can only speculate about whether or not Josef K had it in them to be one of the biggest bands of their generation, but even if they seemed perfectly designed for the 80s, there is little doubt their story is a much briefer one than it should have been. For, on August 23, 1981, a mere three years after their formation, Josef K came to an abrupt end.

The band's final concert hadn't gone to plan at all. Maestro's was located on one of Glasgow's steepest hills, Scott Street in Garnethill, on the northern fringe of the city centre. In the 70s, the venue had been briefly known as the Maryland, and younger folk might recall its rebranding as the Cotton Club in the late 80s and early 90s. It was a popular nightspot—the place to be seen for Glasgow hipsters, although particularly during the winter, when the streets were icy, it was a perilous occupation just getting there in one piece. As patrons made their way to the front door from Sauchiehall Street, their torsos reverted back into a vertical position, having been briefly locked at right angles. Fortunately, the venue was positioned only around a third of the way up the hill, just shy of the Art School, but that cockeyed clamber upward in some ways mirrored the band's own trajectory—a gradual ascent grinding to a sudden premature halt, the summit still frustratingly out of reach. To most casual observers at the time, Josef K's lift-off still seemed imminent. After all, their debut album had hit the shelves only the previous month. But the collective vision that had lent the music its impetus was slowly unravelling. Everyone had had enough.

Immediately, at the beginning of the set, Davy Weddell's bass string snapped. It had never happened before. The rest of the band closed ranks to improvise a version of Television's 'Little Johnny Jewel' while Weddell attempted to repair the damage. But the damage was already done. One can sense some of the growing weariness in Gary Barrett's muddy recording (he dumped his boombox next to the sound desk) from that ill-fated summer evening. Josef K's music was always too spine-tinglingly modernist to sound lethargic, and the sheer adrenaline rush produced by those switchblade guitars is still—for the most part—in evidence. But this rumbling instrumental take of Television's classic was unplanned, and it feels it. Malcolm's guitar snakes around corners looking for somewhere to settle—but everything suddenly sounds as if it is being undertaken grudgingly. And that night it was.

The opening track of any live performance usually dictates the audience's mood for the remainder of the show, but tonight the crowd remain enthused and appreciative. For the next twenty minutes, the band try to recover some momentum after the awkward start, losing themselves in the relentless rhythm and itch of 'Heart Of Song', but at times, such as on 'Chance Meeting', their twice-released 45, there are signs of fatigue instead of the customary effervescence.

The band were dressed in black that night, and it was a funeral of sorts. Listening retrospectively, one can detect dark clouds gathering. It is hardly that Haig sounds defeated, but the spark and smirk are absent. There's a numbness, hitherto undetected in previous performances. Perhaps he baulked at this very public trial, an act of virtual fratricide. Could it be that he felt himself the reluctant courier of the band's own eulogy? It might have seemed that way at the time, but in retrospect, he was perhaps a whole lot less bothered than most people imagined. He just didn't have the energy for it anymore, so much so that it might have felt like a moment of liberation instead.

The set ended with 'The Missionary', a song that should have breathed new life into Josef K's lungs, had the oxygen supply not already been extinguished. In terms of the overall performance, the musicianship is still exemplary, but the alchemy is no longer there.

The dressing room was like a wake that evening. As the band left the stage, the sell-out audience were generous enough in their appreciation, but the final curtain had descended. The decision to call it a day might have been made the night before. In one sense it seemed sudden, shocking even, but the writing had been on the wall for some time. Relationships within the band had become fractious, and nerves were tingling for release. If there was little appetite left for performing live, how much was being held in reserve for the next gruelling tour? What was the point?

What had happened? For a brief but beautiful moment, Josef K had been the most exciting band at the forefront of the post-punk scene. As a new decade dawned, here was a group with the hair and the threads, the wit and the intellect, the uncannily perfect calibration of melody and dissonance to herald a bright new future for pop. Fleetingly, they were every music writer's wet dream. But it wouldn't end that way. Any commercial success was transitory, while critical opinion had already started to shift. It seemed even those who had been their most fervent champions—most prominently Dave McCullough of *Sounds* and the *NME*'s Paul Morley— had turned their backs on them.

A review of their show at the Venue on August 15 by the *NME*'s Leyla Sanai, only three weeks before the Maestro's farewell, reflected an increasingly conflicted critical perspective. 'It's kinda funny but the . . . desire to venerate them was probably more of a hindrance to them than total obscurity could be . . . they have to live up to something, and they/the world/jolly Alan Horne are probably all baffled as to what this mysterious perkish delight is.' At the same time, Sanai continued, 'Technically, musically, atmospherically, there's nothing wrong, there's plenty right, their touch can be light or tight, dark or bright. They score quite highly purely on an entertainment scale —the fun 'n' frenzy of the merry jangling guitar attack, the suppressed power showing them to possess roots and reasons, the rare flashes of revelation, a certain hidden vulnerability, the intrigue and individuality of their passive stage presence—all these catch your eye, sharpen and focus your attention.'

It's an insightful review in so far as it identifies the paradox of Josef K's appeal—at its heart a falling between the cracks too-cool-for-school stubbornness. A refusal to play the game. Were they shy or just being rude? At least the '66 Velvets, backs-to-the-audience noir was a perfect match for the screeching cacophony it often accompanied. But with Josef K, there was a degree of expectancy among the audience, not only for combustible guitar noise—something they could produce easily enough—but also for suave and sophisticated pop music. For a memorable hummable chorus. That was anticipated of any Postcard release. It was also the way popular music was heading, even if no one was completely certain of that at the time. They could deliver on that front, too, if they were in the mood. Yet even when they did 'oblige' (it would never have been intentional), there was barely a smile and little or no engagement with the audience. Toward the end, instead of seeking to build some kind of rapport with fans, Haig played taped voice recordings between the songs. It made Josef K even more inscrutable.

At the time, Haig explained away this idiosyncrasy to Johnny Waller: 'I think Josef K is a very funny group. I'm always laughing onstage, putting myself in the position of being in the audience and watching us. I think it must look really silly, all those guys onstage with dark glasses on, it's absurd. I just can't bring myself to say anything onstage. We're there to play music, not to speak to the audience. I think it's much more interesting to use tapes to introduce our songs onstage.'

One needn't have to speculate what Alan Horne, Postcard's self-styled *impresario*, would have made of reviews like Leyla Sanai's. Doubtless, he would have been none too pleased. Walls would have been punched, insults thrown, the draft constitution of the label ripped in two and hurled into the nearest wastepaper basket. After all, he had a reputation to protect. And handling criticism wasn't one of his greatest strengths. 'I blame the *NME*,' he bawled upon the group's announcement that they were to break up, citing hyperbolic reviews and unrealistic expectations for creating tension between the band's members. Ironically, it was Horne himself whose relentless hectoring had hyped the media into virtual submission. His insistence that every song recorded pre-Postcard was an irrelevance. That kind of hubris was unsustainable, and his fifteen minutes were about to become a distant memory. Haig, meanwhile, sounded more resigned than resentful: 'We'd been together too long. There was no room for new ideas. I played the Glasgow gig, but I wish I hadn't. The PA was awful, and it was a bad way to end.'

Next morning: a collective hangover. It would be the bluest of Mondays, as the band began to ponder what life might look like post-Josef K. All over the world, the story was breaking of Mark Chapman's conviction for the murder of John Lennon. But in Haig's head, on a continuous loop, was the voice of Alan Horne, elastic and smug, cooing 'John Lennon's dead', as he recalled the moment the news of the assassination broke while the group was travelling by bus to London for a gig at the Rock Garden with The Fire Engines. That voice! It haunted him.

Soon, Haig was releasing a single under a different moniker (Rhythm Of Life) on the label of the same name. It was a move that suggested the end for Josef K was something he had been anticipating, even planning, for some time. A few months later, a C30 cassette called *Drama* also appeared. On the cassette case it stated that the songs had been recorded three days after the band's final show at Maestro's, but in fact Haig had recorded them at various times during the previous six months and had only tweaked them on the date in question.

Drama was totally different from what fans might have expected to hear from Josef K. It was still dark and brooding, but sonically a lo-fi slow burn of electronic ambience and tape loops. The biggest surprise was that it was almost entirely instrumental. It made one wonder if, by saying nothing, Haig was truly bearing his soul in the only way he knew how. 'Doing that stuff at home was a relief for my sanity. It gave me something else to focus on, rather than the darker stuff. And I didn't have to think about whether other people liked it or not. Not having to write lyrics felt liberating. *Drama* is incredibly lo-fi—although not necessarily by design!'

Who knows what might have happened had Josef K soldiered on? Haig wasn't yet twenty-one years old when the end came. The other three band members had only just reached that milestone. Twenty-one. They were still kids, really. Their legacy is protected precisely because it remains untarnished by the gated reverb production, the double live album, the major label sell-out, the ensuing gross fashion faux pas, the inevitability of growing old gracelessly. Instead, five singles and one album. Those evocative Harry Papadopoulos photographs freeze the foursome— young and stupid—in the prime of life, ensuring that, since the band's demise, they remain a ravishing enigma, with critics and fellow musicians consistently effusive in their praise.

I remember Ronnie and me going into Virgin on Thistle
Street to buy the new David Bowie LP on the day it came
out. We got Diamond Dogs and a hot pie for £1.50.

PAUL HAIG

Edinburgh Castle is built on an extinct volcano that elevates it above the city's theatrical landscape of gothic spires and steeples, charcoaled cobblestoned streets, and winding alleyways that slope down from craggy green hills to the port at Leith. Renowned for its chilly North Sea air, the wind in the main originates from the southwest, but when it blows in from the east it is decidedly more bruising. Just south of the city centre lies the leafy district of Morningside, famed for its much-coveted Victorian tenements and Edwardian villas and enlivened by its thriving upmarket boutiques and café culture. To its south are the less salubrious suburbs of Oxgangs and Firrhill. These areas are comprised mostly of Corporation-built public housing schemes, designed to replace the temporary prefab developments which were hurriedly constructed after the Second World War.

On the western edge of the Firrhill estate lies the local high school. It was here where four teenagers, brought together by their obsessive interest in pop music, would first become acquainted. None of the four actually lived on those estates, but Firrhill High School also drew a small proportion of its population from some of the more affluent adjoining areas of the city, making it a truly comprehensive establishment.

Those four teenagers were all born in 1960. The second half of the previous decade had been a period of relative prosperity for the UK, prompting Harold Macmillan to proclaim that Brits had 'never had it so good'. By 1960, the PM was making his famous 'Winds Of Change' address to the South African parliament, an early indication that the decade to come would be marked by a period of unprecedented social change.

Paul Haig was born on September 4, 1960, to parents Margaret, a short-hand typist, and Edward, an electrical engineer at the Ferranti plant in Granton. When Paul was just two, the family moved to a new home, closer to his father's workplace, on Lauriston Farm Road in Davidson's Mains. It was near the picturesque village of Cramond, which sits at the mouth of the River Almond and would have been a pleasant environment in which to grow up, with a long stretch of golf courses cutting off this suburban Shangri-la from the western edge of the city. Haig had a fairly conventional middle-class upbringing, with some memories more vivid than others.

The kitchen, 1963. Today is like any other day. Paul is sitting in his pram. Mum's doing what mum does. Paul spends most days sitting watching her potter about. Out of the blue (literally), a pigeon flies in the kitchen window. Paul's eyes dart around, following its movements. They can't keep up. And, in any case, his ears are now being put to greater use, as Mum is now screaming the house down. Paul's eyelids remain tightly fastened to his skull. He's so terrified he is unable to utter a sound. The bird refuses to fly back out of the window, but judging by its panic-stricken movements, it probably realises it shouldn't be in Mrs Haig's kitchen. Mum slams the kitchen door shut so the frightened creature can't extend its adventure throughout the rest of the Haig household.

For a few minutes—but what feels like an eternity—Paul is left alone with the bird in the kitchen while his mum races out onto the street, presumably to seek some assistance in the matter. But what if the bird flies upstairs and waits under Paul's bed? What if it's still there somewhere when Mum puts the lights out? Just then, a man Paul has never seen before comes into the house. He is wearing a chequered hat and a black suit with stripes on the sleeve. He seems calm and assured and speaks in a low tone that is entirely at odds with Mrs Haig's frenzied panting.

The next time Paul looks out of the window, he sees a small black dot fade from view. Then it disappears altogether. Mum is much calmer now. Even though the pigeon has gone, its flapping figure remains an unwelcome lodger inside his head. It is Paul's first psychedelic light show. Sensory overload. Indelible.

Perhaps this frantic commotion inspired in him a predilection for strangeness, discord, surprise. Who knows? But despite the family moving house a few times, Paul's childhood is characterised by a feeling of safety and security, and those close family bonds will remain unbroken. By the time he is six or seven, the family will have moved to a new address, a few doors down from his future bandmate Ronnie Torrance on Camus Avenue in Fairmilehead. Camus Avenue. Spectacularly prescient. Ronnie will go on to become Paul's closest childhood friend.

Born in Edinburgh on July 6, 1960, to parents Bill, a Technical Education teacher, and Irene, a part-time secretary, Ronnie and his older sister Sylvie emigrated with their parents to Adelaide when he was only a few months old but were forced to return from Australia around three years later when Bill became seriously ill with a rare tropical disease. Back in Edinburgh, Ronnie started school behind the wrought-iron fencing of South Morningside Primary on Comiston Road.

Meanwhile, Paul's formative education began at James Gillespie's, near the Meadows on Whitehouse Loan. 'I lived outside of the catchment area, so I don't know how I ended up there. I wanted to take the bus on my first day but was really annoyed that dad came to get me in the car.'

Gillespie's was situated adjacent to James Gillespie's High School, among whose illustrious alumni were writers Muriel Spark and Dorothy Dunnett and actor Alistair Sim. It was a similarly cushioned establishment to South Morningside, both offering scant preparation for the trials secondary school would provide. Nevertheless, Haig found it a chore just being there: 'It was a really austere school, steeped in old traditions—like something from an old black-and-white movie from the 1950s. It was an all-boys school. You had to wear shorts and you had to hold hands on the way in and out with one of your classmates. Mr Thompson looked like George Orwell, and he used to give you a good wellying with the belt. It was sore as fuck. The school dinners made me sick, so by the time I reached nine or ten, at lunchtime I eventually started going to a café. The café had a jukebox—it played stuff like "My Sweet Lord" and Badfinger. We used to buy a raspberry lemonade and a sausage roll—that is, two fried sausages on a roll. The girls' school was across the road, and we might occasionally meet a few of them in the café. So that was nice.'

Despite Paul and Ronnie attending different schools, the two families, as close neighbours, became good friends, and before long were regularly going on vacation together. But there was a more important factor that strengthened the pair's bond as blood brothers. Sandwiched between the family dwellings lived the most cantankerous neighbour imaginable, an elderly lady who found limitless occasions to vent her spleen at the young rapscallions living on either side of her. The downright impertinence of those boys sitting on her wall, boasting of their exploits to one another long into the evening, or zipping back and forward in front of her window, playing havoc with her peace of mind. That kind of behaviour might be acceptable in some other parts of the city, but not here on Camus Avenue.

'She was always on our case,' remembers Paul. 'She would call the police for anything.' The boys, eager to give as good as they got, provided as much ammunition as they could for their arch nemesis to discharge her frustration. At the very least, it was something to do. And they were always looking for something to do.

The end of the 60s was a boom period for some parts of the country, but life in Scotland at the time bore little resemblance to the nostalgia one might have today for some golden era of liberation and creativity. Scotland was a long way from being the *grooviest* place in the world. There was little evidence of the peace, love, and revolution the boys occasionally caught glimpses of on their television sets. Next to the stuffiness of middle-class suburbia, those kaftan-clad long-hairs seemed to inhabit a completely different cosmos. Many speak of the lost optimism of the Swinging Sixties, but there was little to be cheerful about in the Scotland of the time. Instead of flowers and love and peace, there was grime, crime, alcohol, and gangs. There's a famous clip of film footage from 1968 where 'Mr. Moonlight', Frankie Vaughan, visits Easterhouse, one of the most impoverished housing schemes in Glasgow's East End. Some dismissed it as a publicity stunt, but Vaughan had experienced a similarly deprived childhood in Liverpool, so he had a better grasp of what inner-city kids were going through than some were willing to give him credit for. His appearance was at least partially successful, facilitating a weapons amnesty and setting in motion a number of local community projects over the next decade or so. In any case, besides indicating how far Glasgow was trailing behind in the hipster stakes (Vaughan's glory days were essentially over), it bears witness to the dreadful reality of social deprivation at the time.

In stark contrast to both the peace and love generation and the urban deprivation of Scottish cities, Haig's was a typically conservative childhood. As he approached his teenage years, his father was already in charge of his own business—a fibreglass company—in nearby Dalkeith. That meant there was always food on the table, clothes when you needed them, a decent spread at Christmas. Those things were often taken for granted. Far more exciting than the trappings of material comfort, however, were the subterranean adventures Paul shared with his father at home.

Edward Haig leads his son downstairs into the cellar. It's a big space full of dad-type stuff. Everything there seems really old. Rusty ornaments. Ancient artefacts and contraptions. There are boxes full of unusual things—pieces of metal, stretches of cable, dark green bottles of liquids and white powders. When he's in the basement, Edward seems to come alive. A mad glint flickers in his eye; a mischievous grin spreads across his face.

Paul likes coming down to the cellar. It feels good to spend time alone with his dad.

'Close the door, Paul. You don't want your mum complaining again.'

Soon Dad settles down to work, and Paul is delighted to offer assistance. Dad calls it 'work', but it feels much more like playtime. Paul is already dreaming of the future. I'm going to be a scientist when I grow up.

Dad takes out a box of matches from his pocket. Paul prepares himself. Soon, liquids are changing colour and teeming shoots of froth spout from the tops of test tubes. Sometimes there's a flash of light. Sometimes a loud explosion. When Paul comes back upstairs, it looks like he's been sweeping chimneys all morning. Mum is not best pleased, but Paul isn't unduly worried. He's had the time of his life down there.

Home might mean security, but it's also a centre for new discoveries. It's where the fireworks happen.

As well as nurturing Paul's desire to experiment, Edward Haig made an even more impactful decision in 1972: to buy his eleven-year-old son a guitar. While thrilled, Paul looked at the curious object on his lap and worried that he might now have to learn to read music. As things transpired, that wouldn't be necessary. Haig was an autodidact: 'I learned how to hum a melody inside my head. That's how I attuned myself to other instruments as well.'

Two doors down, at almost exactly the same time, Bill Torrance had the same idea in mind for his son, Ronnie. Each took to their latest acquisition in the only way they knew how. 'He [Paul] went for lessons, but I couldn't be bothered,' says Ronnie. The next item on *his* list seemed a far less complex proposition. Surely bashing on a drumkit wouldn't require the same amount of discipline, nor as many hours of learning? It was a no-brainer.

Malcolm Jake Ross, their future bandmate, was born a long way away from Edinburgh on July 31, 1960. His mother Joyce (nee Elder) had been a history student at Edinburgh University before meeting his father, Andrew, a Church Of Scotland minister. Joyce would go on to teach children with special needs, while Andrew became a missionary in Malawi, at that time part of the British Central African Protectorate Of Rhodesia And Nyasaland. The Reverend Ross was stationed in Blantyre between 1958 and 1965 and was one of the founding members of the Malawi Congress Party, the political organisation that strove to achieve independence for Malawi in 1964. His support for democratic resistance and opposition to the oppressive regime of Hastings Banda proved far too vocal for some. There was always a risk that he was in way over his head. He later wrote a book about his experiences in the country, *Blantyre Mission & The Making Of Modern Malawi*.

Malcolm has many memories of Malawi—several of them somewhat traumatic, such as the day his 'pet' antelope was killed by a scorpion bite, or the frightening moment when a rhinoceros rammed into his father's Land Rover. But while these may have left him shaken, they pale in significance next to the death of his sister, Joselyn, in a car accident. Jocelyn was only six at the time, Malcom just two. In his apartment in

Leith there hangs a portrait of Malcolm and two of his siblings, Jocelyn and Gavin, taken shortly before his sister's death. Gavin was four at the time of the photograph. Malcolm remembers the photographer asking him to put down a small car he was playing with just before the picture was taken. Other than that, he has little memory of his sister, but it must have affected him profoundly, and the family were quite naturally devastated. However, it was not the unbearable heartbreak of losing their daughter but political circumstance that necessitated a hasty departure for the family.

It feels different this morning. Andrew Ross doesn't seem his usual self. There's a tense atmosphere around the house. He sets down before his son a pair of shoes. Malcolm has never worn a pair of shoes before. He glances back at his dad's face, looking for a sign. He puts them on but can't get used to how they feel, and ends up staring southward at his feet for the rest of the day.

After a short car journey, Malcolm emerges from the vehicle to find a sea of people making their way into a football stadium. He's now looking at hundreds of other pairs of feet. Some of them have shoes and some don't. The noise of the crowd makes him feel nervous. His jaw is clenched, and his heart feels like it has been pumped full of air. There's no sign of any football being played here today, or any other sport for that matter. Instead, on the PA system, a number of speeches peel from the speakers. Malcolm can't make out a word, but at the end of each speech there are rounds of applause and loud cries of approval. Everyone around him seems restless and excitable. Some are shouting and bearing less-than-friendly expressions. There is a skirmish a few rows behind.

Malcolm is very anxious, but he understands he has to wait patiently until all the speeches are over. He knows the last speech is finished when people around him start to make their way toward the exit points. He feels relieved, but the greatest relief—even more so than getting back home—is that he can finally remove these daft shoes from his feet.

A few days after the rally, some men drop by at the family home to speak to his father. The meeting is brief but seems important, decisive. The next thing Malcolm remembers is some suitcases being quickly packed and the car being filled up with the family's belongings. It's one of the last things he recalls about Malawi. Mum tells him they're going back 'home'. Malcolm has only the vaguest idea about what that means. This is the only home he's ever known. Soon after, he will come to a different land.

It is midsummer when he arrives in Edinburgh, this strange grey place, but as summer begins to shed its colours, Malcolm will feel the cold like he's never felt cold before. To begin with, he doesn't like going to school in this frightening new city. Everyone seems rather unhappy here, the building is grey and colourless, and there are lots of rules that don't seem to make any sense. But Malcolm has already learned that in life, circumstances can change in the blink of an eye.

Just as soon as the family returned from Africa, Malcolm was enrolled in class 2B at South Morningside Primary. It was there he would first encounter Ronnie Torrance and David Weddell, both of whom were pupils in the other class, 2A. Ronnie knew of Malcolm, but his first impression was not necessarily a positive one, as he says with a wry smile: 'He seemed far too intellectual for my liking.'

Meanwhile, back home, the Ross family grew in size with the arrival of two more sons (Diarmid and Alistair), and Reverend Ross withdrew from his duties as a minister, briefly becoming a warden at the halls of residence at Edinburgh University. Despite that, the family remained strong churchgoers until Malcolm was around fifteen, he notes, 'At which point my parents decreed I was old enough to make up my own mind about those things. My grandfather was very religious, and I suppose—possibly subconsciously—my dad may have sought approval from him by entering the ministry. My dad never had a parish, and soon earned a PhD before going on to work as a lecturer at Edinburgh University. So, it was a fairly middle-class upbringing, although I did go to the local state school.'

At Edinburgh University, Andrew Ross would work for a time alongside future prime minister Gordon Brown, then rector of Edinburgh University. He would later be very active in the Labour movement, as well as a vigorous opponent of apartheid. Those were principles that his son would undoubtedly share, but far more important to Malcolm at the time was his growing interest in music.

This interest would have been nurtured first of all by his parents, who prescribed viola lessons from a young age. Malcolm felt the discipline and formality of the lessons stifling. Clearly, he had not yet heard of John Cale. Had he, who knows, he may never have picked up a guitar at all. Instead of struggling with the instrument, he sought out time on his own. And time is in plentiful supply when you are ten years old. Just as well, because in the late 60s and early 70s, the Ross family spent a great deal of time moving around the city from house to house. They would never again move away from Edinburgh, however.

David Weddell was born on April 13, 1960, and, like his future bandmate, was brought up in Morningside, not a million miles away from Paul and Ronnie. Like Ronnie, he attended South Morningside Primary. Davy also lived relatively near to Gary McCormack, the original bassist in Josef K, who would play a prominent role during the embryonic stage of the band's career. The Weddell family lived in rented accommodation until Davy's father, George, an electrician, completed a course at night school in order to qualify as an electrical engineer and was finally able to buy his own home. Like his bandmates, Davy wasn't particularly fond of lessons, but he could stomach enough of them to enable him to pass his exams and train as a quantity surveyor. Mum and Dad weren't best pleased when he opted to give that up for a life of fun and frenzy.

—

It was at Firrhill High School that Paul Haig, Malcolm Ross, Davy Weddell, and Ronnie Torrance would come together for the first time. Opened by the Lord Provost in January 1960, it was a state-of-the-art landscaped comprehensive, completely incongruous with the bleakness of the surrounding environs, but it was already showing signs of physical wear and tear within its first decade. Of greater concern was the fact that its patrons were carefully cultivating the most inhospitable environment imaginable. The future members of Josef K would approach their enrolment with some trepidation.

'I remember the janitor at our primary school warning us about Firrhill,' Weddell recalls. 'It was a new school and had really good facilities, but it was terribly violent too.'

Ross concurs. 'The school was in a large council estate. None of us came from there, but eighty percent of the pupils did. If you weren't from the estate and you went to the school, it could be quite testing. I was there between 1972 and 1978. The 70s just seemed such a rough, violent decade.'

Having to share corridor space alongside a variety of miscreants and misfits is part of any teenager's everyday experience, and Firrhill, like schools anywhere else, contained its fair share of characters. There was the small gang of bullies who reined in support from those too fearful not to succumb to the dares, threats, and initiation rites; the spotty bespectacled kids who wore the wrong shoes and hid secret train sets in the attic; and inevitably there was always one small chap who liked nothing more than to dissect sparrows, melt plastic, and light his own farts. But, like most Scottish teenagers, most of the boys lived and breathed football.

'The four of us were all really into football, and I first became good friends with Malky in particular,' remembers Davy Weddell. As fellow fans of Hibernian, or the Hibees, they quickly struck up a firm friendship and went along fairly regularly to Easter Road. Ronnie likewise, was an avid fan of Leith, while Paul was the solitary Jambo (Hearts fan) in the pack. If not quite as successful a team as the early 1950s side boasting the 'Famous Five', Hibs still had a flair-filled side in the early 70s, boasting at various points the mercurial talents of Pat Stanton, Alex Gordon, Joe Harper, Des Bremner, and Alex Cropley. Paul, on the other hand, will remember peeking through his fingers in horror as his beloved Hearts were annihilated 7–0 in the 1973 New Year derby at Tynecastle, a result that encapsulated the gulf in class between the sides at the time. Outcomes such as that one probably helped the others forgive their accomplice his irksome preference.

If, as Ross says, the 70s was a particularly violent decade, there was an inevitability that it would find its way onto the football terraces. 'When I first started going to see Hearts, I was eleven or twelve,' remembers Paul, 'but when I got to about the age of fourteen, the violence got so much worse. I remember lots of fights, groups of fans being chased down the street in little towns you'd never been to before. I remember going to Hampden for a cup semi-final against Rangers. The van I was in came under fire from beer glasses, and all the windows got smashed in. The guy next to me got a big chunk of glass in his neck, and I thought, *I don't want to be near all this anymore*, so I never went back.'

Violence such as that was the 70s' most unwelcome companion. It lurked on every corner. 'It was a rough, violent time, but I learned to give as good as I got,' remembers Ronnie. 'We might have been singled out, but we weren't bullied because we stood up for ourselves and built a reputation for ourselves. Paul and I got into quite a few fights with others just to establish that we weren't mugs.'

As for lessons, they felt like a chastisement. Torrance was dyslexic but, even so, willingly obstreperous. 'I wasn't a model pupil,' he admits. 'I was very disruptive, and I spent an awful lot of time standing in the corridor. I got belted every day for some misdemeanour or other. I was suspended twice and was on a final warning before expulsion when I left.'

Ironically, the weapons of corporal punishment used to manage misbehaviour were manufactured just skelping distance away in the small town of Lochgelly in Fife. A challenge by Scottish parents (not Mr & Mrs Torrance) in the European Court Of Human Rights in the early 1980s proved a key step toward outlawing the heinous practice.

Each day, school was something simply to be endured in the same way as a power cut or an appointment at the eye clinic. Survival was the name of the game. When the desire to leave became overwhelming, Haig bailed out. 'As soon as I could leave school, I was off. It was just before my sixteenth birthday. While I liked art, music, and English, I hated everything else about it so much. Firrhill was a really tough school. Because we weren't from Oxgangs, we were considered *posh*. It wasn't too long after *A Clockwork Orange*. Everyone was wearing Doc Martens, carrying knives and screwdrivers. You would see people getting stamped on, people chasing one another across the different housing estates. There were lots of gang fights. It seemed a really menacing time. There was so much social unrest, austerity, budget cuts. The film *Control* captured that atmosphere of the times really well.'

As the 70s progressed, things would become even bleaker. From a socioeconomic perspective, it was possibly the darkest period the country had endured since the Second World War. The decade had begun with PM Ted Heath's regressive Industrial Relations Act, which led to a series of trade union strikes and eventually to the short-lived but ultimately disastrous three-day week, with its power cuts and suspensions of public services. By then, every household had a stash of candles in the sideboard drawer, and at times families couldn't afford to rely on street lighting. '*Make sure you're back before its dark or ye'll no get home.*' It also gave gangs extra license to terrorise local neighbourhoods. At the same time, there was a bubbling undercurrent of racist tension spearheaded by the National Front, a surge in football hooliganism (darts in the eye stuff) and domestic violence, as well as an escalation of the conflict in Northern Ireland following the Bloody Sunday outrage in January 1972, with the IRA bringing their campaign to the mainland. Although Scotland was never targeted and Edinburgh did not experience the sectarian divisions in the same way as people did in Glasgow and the West of Scotland, nobody could fail to notice the very public violence on their TV screens. 'There was a lot of global violence too,' remembers Ross. 'Baader–Meinhof in Germany, the Red Brigade in Italy.' Dark days.

Ian Rankin, author of the Rebus books, lived in Fife during the era but was a frequent visitor to Edinburgh. 'There was a sense that we were living in fairly depressed times. Edinburgh was slightly cushioned from that because it's not an engineering or an industrial centre, but there were lots of *For Sale* and *To Let* signs everywhere, so there were moments where Edinburgh did seem as depressed as anywhere else. And of course, the city is ringed by social housing schemes, which had all kinds of problems. All of that drip-fed into the feel of the city—all those issues that Irvine Welsh would go on to write about in *Trainspotting*: prostitution, drugs, unemployment, and poverty. It was a city pretending to be cultured and European but which was hiding a dirty little secret at the same time.'

As well as football, the boys sought other avenues for escape, and their shared love of music provided respite from the gloom of power cuts and Droog-inspired mayhem. That need to escape was shared by many teenagers, and it often manifested itself in a continuation of the distinctive mod subculture of the 60s, whose 70s manifestation was variously— although never on the same scale—skinhead, suedehead, or, slightly later, Northern soul dancer. These subcultures provided an antidote to the more mainstream 50s revivalism that had contaminated the pop charts. Although much of it was superficial pap (on these shores, Alvin Stardust, Showaddywaddy, Mud, Edinburgh's own Bay City Rollers; across the big pond, David Cassidy, The Osmonds, *American Graffiti*, *Happy Days*), it was, at heart, a lightweight precursor to the back-to-basics reset of punk, offering an innocent alternative to the excessive drugginess of the psychedelic and progressive music of the period. Nevertheless, for the more discerning teenager, the alien space rock of Bolan, Bowie, and Roxy Music provided a more glamorous alternative and promised a strange, seductive new future.

Even before Bolan and Bowie came along, Paul remembers being drawn to the sounds played in the Haig household. 'I remember hearing The Beatles. I was so impressed by their musicality. My parents also had Sinatra records, as well as this *Sergio Mendes & Brasil '66* album, which I used to play to death—it just seemed so glamorous. I liked The Doors, too—loved the depth in Morrison's voice.'

Everything began to change with the emergence of the glam superstars. 'I was mad about T. Rex and was into Marc Bolan really early on. We had a neighbour further along the street who was just a couple of years older, and he would play us his records. I heard Bowie and The Velvet Underground when I was a really young kid, before it became trendy. People think I'm making that up, but it's true. I was listening to Sister Ray at age ten. Bowie turned me on to Iggy and the Stooges too. When you heard The Velvet Underground, you realised how easy it could be to write music. Two or three chords could do it!'

'The first album I bought was *Let It Be* by The Beatles,' says Malcolm. 'Growing up, I liked The Faces, Rod Stewart, The Stones, and Bowie. I saw Thin Lizzy and Pink Floyd when they came to town but was unaware of there being any kind of music scene in the city at that time. Obviously, there was The Bay City Rollers, and everybody knew somebody who was one of the Rollers' aunties. There was Pilot'—of 'Magic' and 'January' fame—'but that was it. Most of the other bands who played Edinburgh at the time were just playing cover versions, so I wasn't aware of there being any kind of scene at all.'

Meanwhile, Davy's formative musical experience was in some way shaped by members of his extended family. 'My mum had four brothers and a sister. My aunt worked in a music shop called Band Parts on Leith Walk, and my uncles always had music playing in the house—Beatles and Stones, mainly. The first album I bought was *Electric Warrior*. I remember having *The Crazy World Of Arthur Brown* as well, but I tended to gravitate toward anything that seemed a bit different.'

In addition to the dark spells cast by the Velvets and Bowie, Ronnie had an ear for soul and funk music—an ingredient that would be deftly absorbed into Josef K's unique melange. 'Although Paul and I were into The Velvet Underground, Bowie and Alice Cooper, we also liked James Brown, and I really loved The Isley Brothers, Stevie Wonder, Earth Wind & Fire, and, later on, Donna Summer.'

With Ronnie and Paul spending most of their time alone bashing away on their new instruments, it was inevitable that they would try out together at some point. Paul remembers his first fumblings as an imaginary rock star. 'Ronnie and I had played in his attic, he on a really cheap drum kit and me on a cheap guitar. We did that on and off from when we were around thirteen. We'd play Led Zeppelin and Bowie covers and make a fucking racket.'

One unifying factor that solidified their passion for playing music was a shared love of a flamboyant new English outfit called Roxy Music. Haig recalls being totally spellbound: 'I'd heard they were an art school band who dressed in totally out-there glam gear and got shouted at when they played live for being too effeminate looking. Unfortunately, I was a bit too young to be going to rock concerts, so the closest I ever got to seeing them was when I was on the top deck of a bus going up Lothian Road and saw them get out of a black limousine to walk into the foyer of the Caledonian Hotel in Edinburgh's West End. They were wearing all their glam clothes and looked amazing, so it was a real bummer to miss the concert they played at the Odeon cinema. I first saw the sleeve for the second album *For Your Pleasure*, at Bruce's record shop in Rose Street.'

Short of pocket money, Haig had to make do with imagining what the record—with its glamorous sleeve and exotic song titles like 'The Bogus Man'—might sound like. He would soon find out. 'You can just imagine Eno's ostrich feathers being ruffled as he was playing it.' 'In Every Dream Home A Heartache' would be one of the first songs the embryonic Josef K—as TV Art—included in their repertoire. 'I have a vague memory of performing it in a cellar bar in Edinburgh and instead of attempting to emulate the flanged psychedelic finale of the original we stopped it dead after the famous climatic line, *But you blew my mind*. Probably a wise move. It's an amazing lyric for the time, a sinister monologue that portrays the dissatisfaction and ennui of the narrator over his self-indulgent living and vast wealth.'

Roxy, Bowie, and the Velvets had captured Haig's young imagination, but in truth, the pop charts of the mid-70s were crammed with the crass and the banal, and television entertainment reduced to three channels full of comedy/variety acts who seemed archaic, relics from a dying generation. John Denver, The Goodies, Gary Glitter, Gilbert O'Sullivan, Windsor Davis and Don Estelle, Paper Lace, Little Jimmy Osmond, Lena Zavaroni, *The Generation Game*, *Dick Emery*, *On The Buses*. It's little surprise the likes of David Bowie and Marc Bolan seemed a godsend when they made *Top Of The Pops*. But back then, most people just seemed to accept things the way they were. There didn't appear to be any alternative but to grow your hair long and sit in your friend's bedroom, smoking dope and listening to Yes and Genesis—a prospect that seemed even more hideous and defeatist. It made for legions of disaffected disenfranchised youth, with lowly prospects but plenty of anger and resentment. But it wouldn't be long before Edinburgh, like the rest of the UK's cities, prepared itself to be outraged by a new phenomenon: punk rock.

3/15 | SCHOOL'S OUT / EDINBURGH 1977

*I would never have made music had it not been for punk. I was
never going to be in a prog rock band or play blues guitar. There
were a lot of people who would never have made music if punk
hadn't happened. A lot of the best pop music is not made by great
musicians. Punk changed everything for us. But we were never punk.*

MALCOLM ROSS

Paul Haig left school in 1976, before Year Zero even began. He had
long harboured a desire to dispose of Firrhill's blue tie once and for all.
School had been a total drag. He managed to muster a little enthusiasm
for English, and he enjoyed going to art classes enough to avoid skipping
them, but everything else they taught you there seemed mind-numbingly
dull and pointless. It would be a pivotal year not only for him personally
but also for many of the UK's disaffected youth who, by then, bored
senseless by the flaccidity of mainstream entertainment and exasperated
by the deepening economic recession, had enthusiastically embraced the
nihilism and adrenalin rush of punk.

Punk was not a phenomenon that miraculously appeared overnight.
Rather, it had its roots in the fallout from 60s hippie culture, and it drew

much of its inspiration from other sources, such as anarchist philosophy and Situationist art. It had been slowly evolving throughout the early 70s when, during lengthy a period of economic austerity, its designers-in-chief, Malcolm McLaren and Vivienne Westwood, planted visual and cerebral landmines from the underground—or, more precisely, from their boutique on the King's Road, SEX. The shop successfully merged anarchist ethics with art, fashion, and pop music. Its shock-tactic branding may have attracted and repelled in equal measure, but the general public would soon be schooled by the tabloid media to nurture a sense of outrage and disgust.

Punk was liberal, contradictory, and, in its purest, most original form, highly disciplined in its undiscipline. It is something of a challenge to reject all social norms and constructs, and that conservative Middle England sought to suppress its advance only strengthened the prevailing sense of rebellion. Finally, here was something for young people to bleed for. Punk irritated all the right people. In its musical form, its brutal frankness and simplicity stood in stark contrast to the pseudo-intellectual theorising, unnecessarily complex time signatures and intolerable sonic bombast of the progressive rock music of the time. By extension, it seemed intent on tearing down the barrier that had built up between performer and spectator throughout the 70s. The prevailing sense of the rock star existence as defined by cocaine, fast cars, groupies, and sell-out arenas was challenged head-on by an inverted parallel vision: a new drug of choice (speed), faster louder songs, intimate sweaty venues, and a vigorously unapologetic streak of anti-establishmentarianism. In Britain especially, punk would possess a political dimension which was largely absent from its American counterpart. On these shores, it was undoubtedly more politically and culturally subversive, not merely some quirky affectation. Additionally, it was by and large working class and inclusive—of women, of gay people, of ethnic minorities. In America, it was still somewhat indebted to the bohemian art school aesthetic, and initially, at least, almost exclusively the product of white middle-class suburbia.

Countless numbers of young hopefuls recognised the possibilities generated by learning a few simple chords on their guitars. 'This is a chord. This is another. This is a third. Now form a band,' the *Sideburns* fanzine famously proclaimed in its first issue in January 1977. And, for a while, it really did seem as simple as that. In the UK, a chasm briefly opened up between punk and the establishment, but it didn't take too long to narrow, and punk itself began to be consumed—in both senses of the word—by the mainstream.

By the tail end of '77, punk had burned itself out as a creative phenomenon. That was inevitable. For how long can a shock shock? The consensus shifts, everything needs another jolt. Nevertheless, its initial vitality generated all kinds of new possibilities for bands and musicians. As well as women, gay people and other marginalised groups disenfranchised by the status quo, punk held a particular appeal for Britain's youth living outside of the capital.

Until the mid-70s, the Scottish music scene had been almost entirely masculine. Whether it was hard rockers like Dunfermline's Nazareth or blue-eyed soulsters like The Average White Band—both of whom had somehow managed to crack the American market—everything bore the stench of long hair, denim flares, and alpha maleness. The aim of most budding rock stars was—as well as avoiding a day's graft—to populate the dressing room with as much 'skirt' as humanly possible, and to perform churlish conjuring tricks like making more money than ordinary folk earned in a whole year disappear up your nose in a single night.

Even the country's most esteemed rock group was renowned for its flagrant machismo, but there was something about them that seemed a bit different. A dark undercurrent of violence, or the threat of violence, accompanied the Sensational Alex Harvey Band wherever they went.

With their raw misanthropic edge and sardonic sneers, they helped stoke unnaturally high testosterone levels, forging a psychological union between snotty young delinquents and middle-class dropouts. The taunting theatrical demeanour of Harvey and guitarist Zal Cleminson, as they cruelly surveyed the audience with their zombie stares, platforms parked on the stage monitor, was at once hugely intimidating, and very much prescient of the imminent punk explosion.

There had been a few Scottish acts that crossed over into the mainstream. Allan Campbell, who would later go on to manage Josef K, remembers the times well. 'Before punk, it was a totally different culture, but I don't think the Scottish music scene was as stagnant as people made out. There *were* successful Scottish acts. The Sensational Alex Harvey Band had been around for quite a few years. They had a punkish attitude. There was the Average White Band, Gallagher & Lyle, The Sutherland Brothers—not the most fashionable names I know—but these were acts who had considerable commercial success. Even Lena Zavaroni had chart hits. It's funny to think she was signed to Stax Records in Memphis!'

However, the dearth of homegrown talent was compounded by the reality that many of the more popular groups of the time tended to assiduously avoid Scottish dates. Campbell, like many other young people at the time, had to wait patiently for a rare alien visitation from the likes of David Bowie, Roxy Music, or Captain Beefheart & His Magic Band. Scotland wasn't quite East Germany, although in places it looked fairly similar, but finding an evening's entertainment beyond the traditional dancehalls wasn't easy, particularly for the more discerning music fan. There *were* nights out to be had in Glasgow and Edinburgh, but most of these involved having to endure the flatulent rock bands of the time, with infrequent but memorable exceptions.

'I remember Beefheart at the Empire in 1973, and also at Edinburgh University two years later,' Campbell recalls. 'That was a phenomenal line-up. Before the band's tour manager took it off me, I recorded twenty minutes of the bass player playing soprano sax, on a handheld cassette recorder. Then a friend and I went and sat with The Magic Band at a hotel next to the zoo in Corstorphine. He [Beefheart] did a drawing for me and just talked for four hours. It was just before punk, but it felt like a completely different era.'

Ian Rankin too remembers travelling across the Forth Road Bridge from his home in Carnenden in Fife in order to see some of the bigger names of the time. 'When I was at high school, we would sometimes get a bus together and go to a gig, but they were few and far between. I'd come over to Edinburgh to see Alex Harvey, Jethro Tull, or Genesis, but you'd usually miss the encore so you could get the final train back.'

There was no unifying sense of identity in the Edinburgh music scene before then. The city of course had produced at least one hugely successful act, The Bay City Rollers, but their commercial performance had peaked by 1976 and a steep decline in fortunes had set in. There was little to distinguish the capital from other smaller towns in Scotland, and as yet there was no identifiable social hub to provide a locus for those seeking encounters with similarly like-minded individuals. 'There weren't rock music cafes and bars where people could go and hang around,' Rankin recalls, 'and at the art school, people seemed more interested in becoming filmmakers, directors, or fashion designers.' It wouldn't be long before that would all change, but in '76, there was still barely a spark.

Refuge would be sought by the scabrous and unruly through the occasional Saturday afternoon drop-in to the handful of record shops in the city that could conceivably be considered cool. There, at Harvest on Bruntsfield Place, one might hope to catch an earful of some previously unheard nugget or bump into a semi-familiar face. The proprietors of a Greyfriars Market stall, on the other hand, had a reputation for offering short shrift to the uninitiated, although the racks of Ezy Ryder were sometimes treasure troves of rare Krautrock and other oddities. Meanwhile, the delightfully named Hell, at 45 Thistle Street, was run by Douglas MacFarlane and prided itself on being the cheapest shop in town—a great selling point, as it was located only a few doors down from Virgin—as well as boasting a badge-making machine.

For some, including Scottish musician Chris Connelly, the best place of all was Phoenix: 'The window [was] crammed with album covers, and the sleeves inside reinforced with cardboard so the spines would not bend: these guys took their business seriously, there was no natural light inside, and my memories of it are dark, in these pre-punk days, I remember buying a Henry Cow album and a lot of weird-looking jazz.'

But by some distance, the closest to a hipsters' paradise was Bruce's, which had three stores in the city and a clever marketing strap—written on the bags—that famously read, 'I Found It At Bruce's'. Brian Findlay had opened a popular and successful store in Falkirk in 1968, before younger brother Bruce opened the first Edinburgh shop on Rose Street the following year. Bruce had a shrewd mind for business, but he was also a huge music fan, so he was able to anticipate the forthcoming trends. He was particularly attuned to the emergent punk scene, and his mini-empire would flourish in the late 70s, with further shops opening in Dundee, Perth, Stirling, Kircaldy, and several other Scottish towns. When mainstream stores refused to display (and sometimes even stock) *Never Mind The Bollocks*, Bruce's seized the advantage through a window display guaranteeing the album's availability. The owners and staff were always well informed, and in their eagerness to stay one step ahead of the competition, they actively sourced ultra-rare imports as well as less accessible items. One staff member even recalled travelling through from Clydebank to the Edinburgh store to pick up a stylus for a customer. Now that's commitment.

By the late 70s, Findlay had already started his own record label, Zoom, which would give several local bands, including The Valves and the

Cheetahs, their first (and only) outings on vinyl. More significantly, Findlay would launch the early career of Simple Minds, becoming their manager in the process. His retail empire, meanwhile, was brought to a premature end in 1982. Before the Virgin and HMV megastores began to undercut the independent shops, one of Bruce's main competitors was Hot Licks on Cockburn Street. The staff there were equally knowledgeable, and they stole a yard on the other shops by having album launches and album signing sessions by the likes of The Damned and The Jam. One of the shop's most popular features was a bulletin board near the entrance. Aspiring musicians and artists could pin homemade adverts for new bandmates or simply search for like-minded souls. It was at Hot Licks where fellow Edinburgh hopefuls Scars advertised for a new singer and drummer.

One group that managed to straddle the seemingly insurmountable divide between the old ways and the new was The Rezillos, formed by a group of students at Edinburgh College Of Art in March 1976. The Rezillos were probably the first local band to accommodate the energy of punk, although they were never very comfortable with the 'punk' tag, preferring to label their style 'new wave beat music'. Their roots were in the 50s, and two of the founding members, Jo Callis (later of The Human League) and Alan Forbes, had initially envisaged a retro rock'n'roll sound, contriving together to form the short-lived Knutsford Dominators a year earlier. Punk's nihilism and political edge were entirely absent from the mix, meaning that not everyone took them very seriously. But they were lots of fun. Visually, they came across a bit like distant Scottish cousins of The B-52's, minus the Day-Glo sci-fi B-movie angle, with singer Fay Fife sporting mid-60s pencil skirts and on occasion a beehive hairdo. Despite or perhaps because of that, they would go on to enjoy a fair degree of commercial success, which was still relatively unusual for a Scottish band of the time. They even appeared on *Top Of The Pops*, and in the late 70s, that was the mark of having made it. They also had a huge impact locally, inspiring in younger fans a bold DIY ethic. 'If you went to the pub nearest the venue, you would see them having a few swift ones or bombing about town with their ridiculous cars,' recalls Ian Rankin.

Back on Rankin's home turf, just over the Forth Road Bridge, another bunch of snotty good-for-nothings were making similar inroads in Dunfermline and the surrounding areas of Fife. Skids would be one of the first Scottish bands to wholeheartedly embrace punk, and by the end of 1977, they found themselves playing regularly at the famed local haunt the Kinema. They possessed a cocky frontman in Richard Jobson and an eager and talented young guitarist called Stuart Adamson, later of Big Country fame, and had enough self-belief to catapult themselves into the public eye. Within six months they'd be supporting The Clash, and over the next few years they would be a key fixture on the Edinburgh gig circuit, scoring a Top Ten hit along the way with 'Into The Valley'.

Meanwhile, Another Pretty Face, formed the same year by future Waterboy Mike Scott, were one of the first local acts to make a name for themselves locally, although no vinyl was forthcoming until 1979. Their debut offering had been rejected by Virgin before they disappeared into obscurity. It turned out that the first Scottish new-wave band to get signed by a major label were Wishaw's The Jolt, who attempted somewhat unsuccessfully to bridge the gap between punk and mod revivalism. But their 1978 debut album flopped, and they've been more or less forgotten about ever since. Both examples highlighted the challenges still facing local bands who did not have the sort of representation/management to contend with the vacillating 'loyalties' of record company executives.

It may have been the Sex Pistols who blasted the doors off their hinges, but north of the border it was The Clash's performance at the Playhouse on May 7, 1977, that lit the touchpaper, ensuring Edinburgh would be the next UK city to undergo a revolution in its music scene. The Sex Pistols *had* played a Scottish show the previous October, at Dundee's College Of

Technology (now Abertay University) of all places. Their appearance was quite naturally the source of much excitement and bewilderment, with the audience giving them a characteristically mixed reception—something the band were already well accustomed to. A second Dundee Pistols show had been scheduled but was cancelled in the aftermath of the infamous TV interview with Bill Grundy in December, and Rotten & co would never again perform in Scotland. They did, however, appear at Virgin Records on Edinburgh's Frederick Street, where they signed autographs and LP sleeves for eager youngsters skipping school.

That event had been of little interest to Haig or Ross. Conversely, by the time The Clash arrived in Edinburgh, *they* were the hottest ticket in town, and Paul and Malcolm made sure they got their hands on a pair of tickets. 'Their performance at the Playhouse with Subway Sect was a major turning point,' Campbell asserts. In actual fact, four bands would play that evening, as part of The Clash's *White Riot* tour, with the full complement also comprising The Jam and The Slits.

Talking to David Pollock for *Record Collector* magazine in 2022, Ross recalled feeling 'shocked, uneasy. I remember being on the bus going down to the Playhouse and a Glasgow train had come in, so there were hundreds of these really scary-looking people rolling down Leith Street. But there was something about the *rawness,* the fact it wasn't a slick show.' That rawness—the sudden sense of informality—was completely transformative, and best exemplified by Slits singer Ari Up asking a member of the audience for a comb. However, it was another of the bands performing that night that would have a more enduring impact. Subway Sect, fronted by Vic Godard—who resembled a librarian—would unquestionably have a more decisive influence upon the future direction of the Scottish music scene than even The Clash. Similar seeds would be sown in Glasgow, too, following their performance supporting Buzzcocks at Glasgow Apollo the following year.

There was a special ingredient to Subway Sect that made them so important and life-affirming to budding Scottish musicians. Their Soviet Bloc chic lent them a mystique which, at first glance, seemed entirely unsuited to the spiky urgency of their sound. They weren't really punk, but neither were they pub rock, nor mod revivalists. Instead, they seemed caught in a no-man's land between literary 60s pop and the occasionally dull-witted pugnacity of the new music. They cultivated their own style ('We used to dye all our clothes grey in those days—in a big bath. We liked the colour,' said Vic Godard), they were deliberately contrary, and at times their meekness suggested something more effeminate. All of those attributes spoke to the poets, shy kids, and outsiders in the audience—those who were less inclined to launch themselves into the mosh pit and bravely absorb relentless arcs of sputum. Godard (one *d*—très important) eschewed leather, denim, and safety pin, opting instead for shirt, tight jumper, blazer, and Czech monkey boots, a sartorial choice that suggested bookish irony and probably, superior intellect.

For good measure, they merged the Velvets' twangy guitar sound to infectious rhythms and melodies such as 'Ambition', their breakthrough single, which boasted a floor-filling fairground organ riff. It went on and on, and you didn't want it to stop. Godard's words were more cryptic than say Pete Shelley's ('*I've been walking along down this shallow slope / Looking for nothing particularly*') but equally perceptive. By contrast, 'Ambition's aptly titled flip side, 'A Different Story', sounded like a hangover from some cockney jamboree, but its tuneful naivety in many ways anticipated the shambling indie scene to come.

Haig would draw some inspiration from the kind of oblique imagery contained in Godard's lyrics. They were enigmatic, slightly aloof. Sometimes, words communicate most effectively when one consciously avoids effort to decode their meaning. It is much easier to fall in love with a pop group because of their appearance. That first encounter always creates a lasting impression, and fortunately, Godard & co looked the part. Haig and Ross were taking notes, as were other local firebrands such as Davy Henderson, later of the Fire Engines, who identified the Edinburgh show as the moment things changed forever in the city. Subway Sect had made an indelible mark on the future direction of the Scottish post-punk scene. It is difficult to imagine the existence of Postcard without them, or even later spiritual descendants such as The Pastels, BMX Bandits, and possibly even Belle & Sebastian. But it would take a little time for their influence to ferment, and success—at least in a commercial sense—would remain elusive. The original band broke up under mysterious circumstances, having shelved their debut album, but they will forever be associated with the birth of the Scottish indie scene. Their later records were consistently good, but they were never quite able to recapture the original vitality of their first few singles.

—

While the fruits of the collective creative imagination were gestating amongst the city's youth, there were plenty of reminders about just why the new music seemed so important. A fortnight after The Clash show, the Queen visited the city as part of her Silver Jubilee celebrations. She opened a new terminal at the city's airport, did her customary round of meetings with provosts and clergy, and finished off with a banquet at Edinburgh Castle. If the young people needed any sort of reminder that they were still living in a deeply conservative country—even after three years of a Labour government—they needn't have looked any further. Yet their antipathy was heightened by the Sex Pistols' gloriously sardonic commentary on the national festivities. 'God Save The Queen', due to heavy censorship, would be denied its rightful place at the top of the UK Singles Chart, but despite—and perhaps owing to—that act of subterfuge by the 'establishment', a deep-seated mood of resentment continued to grow apace. In between, Haig was attending other gigs—such as Generation X, who were supported by Johnny & The Self-Abusers (later Simple Minds) on August 19 at Pantiles Hotel in West Linton. On that evening, the car he was travelling in crashed into a field, but fortunately, he wasn't seriously injured. Paul Mason (future Josef K roadie) had somehow managed to convince his mum to let him borrow her Mini. The journey to the gig was filled with trepidation and involved negotiating perilously narrow country roads with ludicrously sharp bends.

'Paul [Mason] was driving, and we both had a fag and a tin of beer in our hands,' Haig recalls. 'Paul was putting his foot down for most of the journey and as we approached this bend, I saw it coming. We went right over a fence and into a farmer's field. My hand got welded with my fag to the ceiling of the car and I got a massive burn. We sat for a few minutes completely in shock. We were stuck in this field in the middle of nowhere. What do you do? There was no chance of getting the car out. Somehow, Paul must have found his way to a phone box and then—it seemed quite soon after—his dad arrived. He was unbelievably angry: How could *you* let *him* have a drink and drive at the same time?! It's your fault as much as his!' Suitably chastised, Laurel and Hardy were given a lift back home courtesy of Mr Mason, and the car was retrieved from the field the following morning.

Incidents such as these illustrate the scarcity of live action. You just weren't going to miss a night like that. The rest of the time you really had to rely on football to provide occasional bouts of respite from the stifling sense of normality. A week after the Queen returned home, the Tartan Army made a journey in the opposite direction. During their adventures, they perfected a new art—uprooting squares of turf from the eighteen-yard box. They transported these/their herbaceous memorabilia back to Glasgow Central Station alongside an abundant supply of McEwan's lager on trains crammed to bursting point following Scotland's triumph over the Auld Enemy at Wembley.

By October, however, any pride about the national football team's recent triumphs—following their qualification for a second successive World Cup, courtesy of an extremely fortuitous 2–0 defeat of Wales at Anfield—was prematurely cut short by a grisly news story concerning the disappearance and murders of two Edinburgh teenagers. Christine Eadie and Helen Scott, both seventeen, had been found raped and strangled after leaving a pub in the Old Town on October 15. The case became notorious as the World's End Murders after the name of the pub where the girls spent their last moments. The killings shocked the city and would have had a particular resonance for Haig & co as the girls were fellow pupils at Firrhill Secondary. Like Paul, they had left school that summer. Indeed, at some point the previous year, Helen had briefly been Ronnie's girlfriend, although she and her circle of friends were generally closer to Paul—sufficiently so for him to later allude to her murder in the song 'Sense Of Guilt'.

Perhaps the news of the murders shocked Haig out of inaction, hastening the formation of the group. Often, in times like these—events that heighten that sense of one's mortality, of the fleetingness of existence— cradle a subconscious desire to reach out and seize the day, to make one's mark before it is too late. Who knows what impact the loss of his friend had upon him? Only a few years earlier, Paul had spent balmy evenings giving Helen rides on the back of his bike. Endless summer. Even allowing for the concomitant impact of punk, it seems more than coincidence that little time had passed after the tragedy before Paul and Ronnie took their first steps in forming a band. The more disquieting edge to the Josef K sound may have been rooted in the economic recessions of the 70s, but it was strengthened by World's End, which along with the as-yet-unsolved 'Yorkshire Ripper' murders south of the border contributed to a feeling of dread and malaise among the general population.

At the same time, pop had lost two of its biggest names in quick succession: Elvis and Marc Bolan. The punk generation wouldn't have been particularly bothered about the demise of the King—'*No Elvis, Beatles or The Rolling Stones,*' The Clash had sung defiantly in '1977'—but by contrast, Bolan had become something of a patron to the new music, taking on the role of virtual godparent, bigging up the Buzzcocks' *Spiral Scratch* EP and appearing with The Jam and Generation X on his short-lived TV Show *Marc*, made shortly before the car crash that ended his life. What's more, Bolan was a pop star Haig could identify with. He was the real thing. Even if the superstar lifestyle had taken its toll and his best days were behind him, he would always be a star. Both Haig and Torrance had been completely in awe of him. Would there be any other new stars to take up the mantle, or had those days now gone forever?

It was around this time that Paul Haig forged an important new alliance. His friendship with Malcolm Ross was immensely life-giving for both. They immediately recognised in one another a kindred spirit and soulmate. Ross, unlike Haig, had stayed on for a fifth year at school in order to complete his exams. By then, Haig was already attracting some female attention, as well as beginning to contemplate a career in music. 'Malky and I didn't know each other particularly well at school, but when I was around seventeen, I went to a party with my girlfriend, and Malky was there. It would have been just after punk, and we started talking about music and quickly discovered we had loads in common. In particular, both of us were totally knocked out by the first Talking Heads and Television albums.'

It was Haig who took the initiative. 'Malky didn't really play guitar much at that point, but I soon went round to his parents' house and showed him some of the things I had worked out on guitar, and that's how we began playing tunes together. We learned by ear, picking out notes and chords. That helped attune your ear to the melody, and over time we began composing our own tunes.'

Malcolm was equally smitten by his new acquaintance. 'When I became friends with Paul, the two of us immediately agreed it would be a good idea to start a band—to become musicians, rather than actually having to work. I was still at school, and Paul had just left. His parents knew a guy who was into playing social clubs or working men's clubs, so we would go along to a couple of these concerts to watch some of the bands. I think that was Paul's parents trying to give him a hand, and I remember on one occasion Paul getting up with the band and playing on a couple of songs.'

Haig still gets the shivers recalling the moment. 'I remember borrowing Malcolm's Rickenbacker that night. I was totally petrified.'

More than anything, however, Ross reckons the pair's mutual admiration of The Velvet Underground was the key to cementing their friendship. 'For Paul and me, the main thing was definitely the Velvets. That was how we started, doing Velvet Underground covers, so they were immediately the biggest influence. Their music seemed *so* important. In fact, I loved the whole New York scene that followed on from that. We both did. Television and Talking Heads were huge influences as well. I liked Robert Quine and some other guitarists as well, but I particularly loved Tom Verlaine's angular style, which was always so interesting rhythmically. Then it had that discordance as well.'

There was still another group with whom Malcolm had recently become obsessed. 'If I'm being honest, at the time I met Paul I probably just wanted to make music like Pere Ubu. They were a really big influence for me, and of course Subway Sect, who just seemed more intelligent than the other bands. But it was definitely the East Coast American art-punk scene that attracted us the most, and we really kind of saw it as an extension of The Velvet Underground.'

The parallels between Ross's skidding chalk-on-chalkboard guitar—like metal lacerating glass—and Tom Herman's scorching guitar lines on the early Pere Ubu records are straightforward enough to detect. More importantly, it was indicative of Malcolm's determination to shake off punk's reductivism, for which he harboured deep mistrust. He was suspicious of both its puritanism as well as its technical shoddiness. 'At heart, I was a modernist. Punks were dirty. None of us had ever played in bands before and that probably gave us a clean slate. You could tell the bands who had been making music before punk—they would throw in rock guitar clichés here, there and everywhere. We made sure we never did. Paul and I were always striving to be, if not experimental, then at least not clichéd. I wanted to maintain some kind of dignity.' Accordingly, Ross and Haig sought a wider selection of ingredients for their sound, determined as they were to retain punk's vitality and spirit while ensuring there would be no accusations of musical incompetence.

As much as 1977 was the apex for punk, it was also the high point of disco, with the soundtrack to *Saturday Night Fever* topping the album charts for almost five months (six in the United States). For most self-respecting punks, disco appeared to be the enemy. But while many of the hits which peppered the charts, such as those churned out by Boney M, were unashamedly imbecilic, others—such as the seamless streak of hits by Nile Rodgers and Bernie Edwards of Chic—contained an energy and economy that attracted punk's more enlightened wing. In many ways, Rodgers's chop-chord guitar style even mirrored the flippancy and directness of punk musicians, although technically he was clearly a far more accomplished player. Chic would eventually become a key influence on many post-punk bands. And Josef K would be no exception. 'There was always an element of disco and funk in our sound,' Ross acknowledges. 'My dad was a soul fan and had records by Curtis Mayfield, Stevie Wonder, and other artists. I often listened to them, but at that time you couldn't tell anyone at school that you were into soul music or someone was liable to kick your head in.'

Ross wouldn't have been the only one to exercise a little caution in his purchasing habits. Even before 1978, people had felt obliged to take sides between the old rock establishment and the burgeoning new wave scene. For young punk hipsters, reggae was in; prog and blues were out. Across the barricades, 'serious' music fans discerned in punk little more than a racket made by talentless charlatans completely devoid of any musical prowess. Of course, they were right about its amateurishness but that was precisely one of its great strengths.

Allan Campbell recalls the battle lines being drawn. 'Terms like post-punk or new wave now sound a bit archaic, but there's always a line-drawing exercise, where very often if you are doing something different it becomes necessary to refute everything that came beforehand. But things don't spring up without roots. The classic example was of course the Pistols. John Lydon saying *Never trust a hippie*, then it emerges that he is a really big fan of prog bands like Van der Graaf Generator. But that's part of the game—dismissing some bands as being completely out of date and irrelevant was a way of defining yourself. It's easier with hindsight to see how things fit together. It's that *new generation* thing, teenagers ritually refuting their ancestors.'

There were some skeletons in the Haig closet, too, but despite his fondness for Led Zeppelin (Malcolm would later admit to being a convert too, though for the time being they were strictly *verboten*), he and his new associate clicked immediately. By natural extension, the pair were joined by Paul's longstanding sparring partner Ronnie. The three were very briefly joined by Robert and Graham Russell, both of whom soon disappeared. No one really remembers why.

'I started off playing guitar actually,' Torrance reminded Johnny Waller in *Sounds*, 'but I was really bad, so I started beating skins to get all my aggression out. I still do that—I have an old kit and I just smash it. I used to smash windows, punch holes in doors, so I thought I should channel that aggression elsewhere.' Ronnie's guitar 'apprenticeship' goes some way to explaining why, in the band's early days, he kept time with the guitar chords. But there was another simpler reason for that anomaly. As yet, they didn't have a bass player.

Three quarters complete now, the 'band' quickly sought to recruit a new face. 'We auditioned a few guys, including a rock dude with a monster Rickenbacker bass and a huge eagle iron belt, and he started to jam heavy rock stuff,' recalls Haig. But Malcolm already had someone else in mind—a gangly looking beanpole by the name of Gary McCormack. 'None of us knew Gary very well,' divulges Paul. 'Malky just said that he had noticed a guy walking around Morningside who happened to look pretty punky, so it was actually that simple. Malcolm just walked up and asked, Hey, do you want to be in a band?'

The only problem was, McCormack was yet another guitarist (that makes four), but he immediately gave his assent to the proposition that he switch to bass. 'I think Davy [Weddell] probably recommended me to Malcolm,' he recalls with a hint of irony. 'He knew I played guitar—that I didn't play bass. I'd known Davy for a while. We hung about the same locale, the same parks, since we were around six or seven.'

McCormack, born in June 1961, was a year younger than the others. He was brought up in Bruntsfield, not far from Morningside, but unlike his bandmates he wasn't a Firrhill pupil, attending instead James Gillespie's High School. The youngest of four children, he had been nourished on a diet of Bowie and T. Rex singles by his older sister. Bolan's music in particular had knocked him off his feet. Next to 'Metal Guru', his big brother's Status Quo and Nazareth albums began to reek of staleness. One of McCormack's earliest memories is of going to see Wizzard at the Odeon in February '74. No harm in that whatsoever, of course. Anyone who had followed The Move in the late 60s would know that Roy Wood had it going on. But in October of the same year, at the same venue, he found himself going along to see Mud, an occasion about which he still feels faintly embarrassed. Perhaps he shouldn't be. As Jon Savage has astutely pointed out elsewhere, Mud ought to have taken some credit for providing the template for Steve Jones's guitar sound. Jones drew from those records as much as he did from James Williamson on *Raw Power*, although would have been more reticent to admit that. But as soon as McCormack heard the Pistols, there would be no more Mud concerts. McCormack immediately identified himself as a hardcore punk. 'I loved all those bands: The Damned, The Clash, The Stranglers. I used to go to all of the punk gigs. The thing I remember was that everyone in the audience seemed to know each other—it felt like the scene became massive really quickly. There was so much going on. And then an even closer brotherhood developed among the bands that formed in Edinburgh.'

With McCormack on board, by the summer of 1978 the first incarnation of the band was complete. Three guitarists to trade, and a drummer who'd started as a guitarist. Unworkable, of course, but as envisaged, McCormack was earmarked for bass and was happy to switch over, picking a few tips from Ross about how to keep rhythm. A more pressing issue, and the cause of some anxiety, was the realisation that some poor soul would have to take on the role of lead singer. It was almost as if the possibility hadn't ever occurred to them until that moment, and in many ways that was true. But supposing one day they might be expected to perform in front of other people? Until now, Paul and Malcolm had been sharing vocal duties during rehearsals, but surely they needed a lead singer and frontman? Talking Heads had one, Television too. The time to decide had come.

To everyone's surprise, there was total agreement. Haig was the unanimous choice, if a slightly hesitant appointee. 'When I first started dabbling in music, I was interested in experimenting with sound, playing two cassettes together simultaneously, that kind of thing,' he recalls. 'I loved the Velvet Underground track The Gift, which I'd known from an early age, so I decided to play all the music through one speaker, and I imitated—in my best Welsh accent—John Cale's monologue. I first played it back to a few friends (possibly the Russells) and they couldn't believe it was me. They were convinced it was the actual record itself. But it was never my intention to be a singer. I just wanted to play guitar. Because I recorded the John Cale tape, I was often asked to sing, but I did so quite reluctantly. I've been doing it for a long time now, but even today it feels slightly alien to me. I'm definitely happier writing instrumentals.'

One could hardly claim Cale's (and presumably Haig's) performance on 'The Gift' to constitute 'singing', but without doubt Haig underestimates his gift. There was a strength to his voice, a sonority and composure, that made up for any apparent lack of melodiousness. He could sound flat, but his tonsils were supple, flexible—'lustfully ingratiating', as Paul Morley would note in a live review from early 1981. Yes, his voice may have lacked the range of someone like Billy Mackenzie's—whose didn't?—but he could croon, swagger, and jab as he saw fit. The effect was a combination of Lou Reed's deadpan aloofness and the assuredness and panache of Sinatra or Scott Walker.

'After we cut back on the cover versions, Malcolm and I both wrote music and lyrics to begin with,' notes Haig, 'Malcolm's first song was called "Good Time Girl". It didn't seem that Malcolm was entirely confident about writing lyrics. Neither was I to be honest, but we both knew it was essential to try.' At this point, their eyes were on local faves Scars, who were already performing exclusively self-penned material. 'We tried to write "Good Time Girl" together,' recalls Ross, 'but it came across as a kind of a Lou Reed pastiche. Something that might have been on *Sally Can't Dance*. Or maybe it was maybe more like Mink DeVille. It was a sleazy New York junkie hipster affair. We just abandoned it—we didn't even play it with a rhythm section. It was completely cliché-ridden.'

From the beginning, Haig and Ross wrote independently. 'I would try stuff out in my bedroom at home, using two cassette players. I'd get the main chords down and then try out a bassline over it. The lyrics were thereafter always mine, and Malcolm would often write complete tunes himself. I would take the tape away and write lyrics to them. I always found it easier to write by myself. I had all the parts in my head anyway, and I always felt I was able to visualise things.'

By the middle of '78, both sets of parents would have to patiently endure the ungodly sounds drifting downstairs from their sons' bedrooms as the embryonic fourpiece attempted to chisel their ideas into some kind of identifiable shape. They were reading avidly, too—classic European and existentialist fiction mainly—seeking inspiration well beyond the dreary slogans and white noise.

Now it was time to decide on a name for the band. It almost seemed like an afterthought. Often, a band's name is the first thing agreed upon. An important decision. Even before they've written a line or played a note, they may have already imagined their name on a bill poster or a record sleeve or splashed across the *NME*'s front cover. Sometimes, the choice of name is a statement of intent, a manifesto for the future. Possibly, it might contain a more subtle or discrete reference to seduce those of a similar disposition, or it might cultivate an appropriate air of mystique. In truth, for Ross and Haig, naming the band was the furthest thing from their minds. They were too busy learning how to play their instruments properly and write songs for it even to occur to them, and while it might not have mattered to begin with, it would soon begin to matter a great deal, provided their aspirations went beyond excitably thrashing away in Malcolm's bedroom or Ron's parents' attic. So, when the conversation arose, a few ideas were floated, but it wasn't Josef K they chose. In fact, the only meaningful suggestion came from Paul, who was determined to ensure the word 'art' featured in the name. The others were unconvinced. Despite that, they acquiesced with Paul's suggestion, TV Art. Before long, however, even Haig began to have doubts.

'We were always struggling with the name,' Ross reminisces. 'There was never anything all four of us were happy with. Paul wanted *art* in the name. Ronnie didn't like that. I suppose TV made us sound modern, futuristic. You don't expect a band called TV Art to be serving up blues music. But at the same time, there was already Television, and Alternative TV, so it probably wasn't the best idea!'

TV Art. It was their name. For now.

4/15 | VARIATION OF SCENE / CHANCE MEETING

We just didn't care about other people's opinions.
It was us against the world. Nothing else mattered.

PAUL HAIG, LINER NOTES TO *ENDLESS SOUL*

July 1978. If you tuned in to Radio One for more than ten minutes, almost inevitably you would catch a song from the biggest movie of the year. The pop charts were stuffed wall-to-wall with Olivia Newton-John and John Travolta hits as *Grease* fever gripped the nation. Filmgoers would flood out of the exits only to find the end of the queue for the next screening—a phenomenon not unlike the previous year's big movies, *Saturday Night Fever* and *Star Wars*. For the general public, such feel-good fare provided a welcome antidote to the malodorous spectre of punk, although in truth there wasn't much left of that. As far as the Sex Pistols were concerned, the game was up. Both as a creative entity and by virtue of the fact that their personal lives were beginning to unravel, they were a spent force. Then came their ill-fated Thames boat trip, an event that triggered an even more concentrated effort by the establishment to silence them altogether. Publicity was denied unless it was bad publicity. And there was plenty of that. The tabloids took delight in printing articles sensationalising the band's personal misdemeanours, presumably to spark even greater outrage. Just ban them and shut them up. So, as far as radio and television went, they were kaput.

While there were many other bands eager to carry the baton, by now their chances of mainstream success were diminishing. Any supposed threat of youth rebellion appeared to have subsided too. The best a teenage misfit could hope for now was an occasional television appearance by Buzzcocks or Magazine or, during particularly lean periods, Elvis Costello.

However, a more insidious and enduring revolution really was underway: one less to do with safety pins, slogans and crass gestures or the politics of anarchy and chaos, and more to do with forging completely new sonic territory. Like any significant musical and cultural phenomenon, punk's original purity had become bastardised and homogenised through affectation and imitation. There always exists that brief moment where the possibilities seem infinite, for example the idealism of summer 1966 in Haight-Ashbury—the *real* 'Summer Of Love'. By 1967, it was all over, although the charts told a different story, and every magazine was still hyping the dream. Alas, the dream had already turned into a nightmare, the energy diluted through the commodification of 'product' and recast by the establishment and the mainstream in a more palatable form.

There had been exceptions—Germany in 1970, for example—where it seemed a unilateral decision had been taken never to look again into the past. The result? Songs without words. Songs without endings. Songs that weren't, in any conventional sense, even songs at all. Cue a complete rejection of tradition, a total embrace of the new. 'Krautrock' was one— admittedly disparate and eclectic—movement that seemed to transcend any tendency to amalgamate with the mainstream. The punk explosion fell somewhere in between, yet despite the bubble bursting, the ripples spread far and wide, long after the initial shock fizzled out. It made a new and exciting future a distinct possibility.

By July, John Lydon was in the studio recording 'Public Image', a declaration of intent if ever there was one, and one of the greatest 45s ever made. But life, at least at surface level, continued as normal. In Scotland, that meant depressingly familiar stuff. The national football team had just disgraced themselves at the World Cup in Argentina, losing to Peru and playing out a woeful draw with Iran. They then did what Scottish teams traditionally do, overcoming all the odds when it no longer matters, beating eventual finalists Holland 3–2. But one sublime moment of magic from Archie Gemmell couldn't disguise what had been an ignominious failure. It was a time, too, when Callaghan's Labour administration seemed unable to provide a psychological lifeline for the nation's youth. The government was in terminal decline. The so-called 'Winter Of Discontent' was approaching, with its profusion of strike action by public sector workers. Even now, the spectre of Thatcher's Britain was looming.

Somehow, in in the most trying of circumstances, artistic creativity can be especially fertile. In a *volte face* from punk's sonic assault, guitars, rather than being employed as surrogate cudgels, reinvented themselves as brushes, knives, scalpels, machines. Everything was in a state of flux, primarily due to the emergence of bands like PiL, Magazine, and later Joy Division. Then there was Wire—they had always been working on another level, '[taking] the axe to rock'n'roll and leaving the 'n'roll out,' as Colin Newman put it.

The 'progression' in the sound of the British bands—from Buzzcocks to Magazine, from the Pistols to PiL—was remarkable. Yet despite the heightened artistic aspirations of their British contemporaries, Malcolm and Paul still felt a greater affinity with the more artful sounds emanating from across the Atlantic. When it came to being artful, there was one particular problem: Gary McCormack's natural preference for the 'one-chew-free-foah' approach to noisemaking. That contributed to a growing sense of unease rather than an unbearable tension. At first, this was more than compensated for by the unbridled enthusiasm of simply creating music together. And McCormack was a good bass player. For a short time, at least, the eagerness to get up onstage would mask any personal differences in taste and temperament.

Malcolm had somewhere in mind. And he was confident the arrangement would be relatively straightforward. TV Art's debut performance would eventually take place at Pollock Halls, the Edinburgh University halls of residence. Malcolm's family had stayed there until he was in his early teens, as his father—before he began lecturing at the university—had a job at the time as a warden, so he knew the place well. Nevertheless, it was still quite a daunting experience for a bunch of shy introverts to play in front of forty or fifty students and friends for the first time. The occasion, a party for a friend of Malcolm's brother Gavin, meant it was a typically low-key first show containing its fair share of false starts, bum notes, furrowed brows, and indignant exchanges, as the band tried to negotiate shaky covers of 'Psycho Killer', 'Prove It', 'Be My Wife', 'What In The World', 'Sweet Jane', and 'I'm Waiting For The Man'. In a way, it had felt like going to the dentist.

'We were so nervous, but we got through it,' Ross recalls. More importantly, that tortuous combination of dread and anticipation was now out of the way, and, to their credit, they had even mustered enough courage to try out one of their own compositions—possibly 'Romance', although no one can quite remember. One can only imagine what might have been going on in their heads that night: Malcolm zig-zagging around awkwardly with his hunched Wilko duck-walk; Gary, eyes scanning the room, locking stares with anyone who felt bold enough to reciprocate; Ronnie knocking empty bottles and cans over behind the drum kit in the vain hope of finding something that might still be half-full; Paul playing it supercool, shades on, stretching the larynx, watching the girls gaze in admiration—but, inside, absolutely shitting himself. It was a first bittersweet taste of the fun and frenzy to come, with Paul and Ronnie celebrating in style after the gig by indulging in a knockabout fight. With tables and chairs strewn all over the floor, Torrance, with his customary disregard for prudence, thought it would be a sensible idea to scoosh foam from the fire extinguishers over all and sundry. 'I was always the problem child,' he laughs.

Once that sense of relief beds in, it is frequently accompanied by a newfound surge in confidence and a concomitant desire to perform again. A sweet taste. The thrill of it all. Lining up the next gig became the absolute priority. While they would return to play Pollock Halls a second time—this time alongside The Dirty Reds and The Cubs—they would grace another few venues first of all, including the White Hart Inn on the Grassmarket, and the Wig & Pen. 'We were seventeen or eighteen in the summer of 1978,' recalls Ross. 'The Wig & Pen was where the punks used to hang out. The landlady there was pretty happy to let the punks in, and she eventually allowed bands to come in too. There was no PA or anything, but groups could bring their own equipment if they wanted to play.'

The Wig & Pen (today the Malt & Shovel) was located halfway up Cockburn Street, a picturesque crescent crammed with clothing boutiques, gift shops, and pubs that still connects the High Street to Waverley train station. It had already played host to a number of other local punk and new wave bands, including Switch and The Cheetahs, by the time TV Art began to frequent the premises. At the Wig & Pen, friendships would be forged among the embryonic local musical contingent. There, Haig and Ross would meet The Dirty Reds, led by Davy Henderson, who would later mutate into The Fire Engines, as well as Scars. At that time, Davy Weddell was a close friend of both Malcolm's and Gary's. Weddell had seen Scars perform at Balerno Scout Hall a few months earlier, but their show at the Wig & Pen in August of 1978 was a revelation, particularly for Ross. 'When we saw them play, it was just so inspiring. They had a whole set of original material. *God, look at them! We could do that!* It definitely encouraged us to begin writing our own material. Scars were hugely important. They showed us the way.'

Scars, formed by brothers John and Paul Mackie in early 1977, were already one step ahead of the chasing pack, one of the first groups to prove that scruffy young upstarts from north of Hadrian's Wall could get up and do it for themselves. And get noticed too. That gave their peers something to aspire to. The line-up would be completed by two other members recruited by the Mackies after they placed an advert in the window of Hot Licks, the record store on Cockburn Street. Bobby King became lead singer while Calum Mackay got the nod as the band's new sticksman. King had gallons of punk attitude—his admiration for Bowie, Steve Harley, and Alex Harvey was self-evident, and his distinctive look turned heads. An acre of curly hair—more Tim Buckley than Graeme Souness—framed his handsome boyish countenance. It was an image that, whichever way one looked at it, went totally against the grain at a time when most new bands were desperate to mimic The Clash's chopped crop. King's flailing expressionistic arm movements also caught the eye. He sang with passion and conviction, but equally impressive for wide-eyed onlookers was the band's accomplished musicianship. These guys could play. Paul Mackie (aka Paul Research) probably drew elements of his sound from the Banshees' John McKay, but he was a terrific guitarist in his own right.

By late 1978, Scars had signed to the Edinburgh-based imprint Fast Product, one of the most promising UK independent labels. Founded by Bob Last and Hilary Morrison, Auld Reekie's very own Malcolm McLaren and Vivienne Westwood, the label was operated from Last's flat on Keir Street. Fast boasted an impressive roster of talent, including The Human League, Mekons, and Gang Of Four (all Yorkshire-based), and its use of ear-catching monikers ('difficult fun' / 'mutant pop') and penchant for smart graphics would inspire Tony Wilson and Rob Gretton to forge ahead with their own vision for Factory. While they were based in Edinburgh, most of Fast's releases were by English bands, so it wasn't necessarily representative of the local scene. But they still boasted Scars, who whenever they performed—which for the most part was in Edinburgh and its immediate environs—bristled with an energy and confidence rarely seen before in the capital.

The story of Fast Product is explored in greater depth in *Hungry Beat*, an oral history of the Scottish music scene of the time, and its predecessor, *Big Gold Dream*, a 2015 film made by the book's co-author, Grant McPhee. Suffice to say, Last showed near to zero interest in TV Art. 'Socially, we fitted in better with Scars, Dirty Reds, Cubs, Associates,' reflects Haig. 'We played stuff to Bob, but he didn't show any interest.'

'He thought we were crap,' admits Ross. 'He gave us advice, but there was never any prospect of us joining up. The other bands had probably known each other a bit longer than us. We were maybe a bit more abrasive. Bob felt he knew better than us. He thought he was a generation ahead. Later, when we became part of the Postcard scene, that maybe led to feelings of resentment, that we in some sense had a foot in both camps.'

Last was an important figure. There was a feeling among the Edinburgh bands who were coming through that it was vital to get him onside. 'His position within that group of musicians was curious' says Allan Campbell. '*What would Bob think?* seemed to be the collective feeling. I remember when Josef K played the Nite Club, and they used to leave bits of paper and pens for people to comment. Bob wrote something along the lines of, *Play more cover versions of "Louie Louie".*'

'There was a cliquey thing at Fast,' Haig insists. 'Bob Last had come to see us and wasn't impressed with Ronnie, who was using a Syndrum. *Those Syndrums are bloody over the top!* he said. But I don't think we took *them* too seriously either, although everyone else did. We weren't involved with the label apart from once or twice, when we packed singles and the *Earcom* thing for them. We were supposed to pack up these concept pieces in order to obtain some extra cash. We were so young. We always laughed at that. *It's a concept!* Fast Product were so into the concept. Everything was a concept—let's put sandpaper in! So, we just thought, *Let's put in a bit of orange peel, maybe a fag end or two*, because we found it all so funny. We were like naughty boys, throwing crisps in and everything.'

The city spawned a cluster of other bands, some with a connection to Fast (The Prats, The Flowers) who had formed around the same time and were now feeding off one another for inspiration. 'We'd all come out of punk at the same time,' says Haig. 'You could relate to the others whom punk had affected. It was a sense of us against them, the bond strengthened by being on the receiving end of people shouting abuse at us in the street!'

'There was a close community of bands,' remembers Torrance, 'although the stale smell of heavy rock still hung in the air, so we were fighting against the tide a little. We hung out at Virgin Records on Frederick Street with The Cubs, The Flowers, and The Dirty Reds.' Among the staff at Virgin were Dave Carson (of Boots For Dancing fame) and Angus 'Groovy' White. Friendships were formed there and strengthened in the pub on a Friday night. 'All the cool guys would drink at the Tap O' Laurieston in Tollcross,' adds Torrance. 'It kind of became our local. It was next to Edinburgh College Of Art so was always full of musicians and students and had a great atmosphere.'

'It was the place to go, but it was really a manky old pub—an old man's 70s pub, completely unglamorous,' adds Haig. 'Your feet would be stuck to the carpet. There was a saloon bar and a lounge bar. There was a downstairs part with a fag machine and a games machine in the corner. People used to queue up to play the Asteroid game on there. It was dingy and drab, but it was full of artistic and creative people, so it was always buzzing. There was a high quota of pseudo-intellectual poseurs too, and many of the bands wanted to appear well read with their Penguin paperbacks stuffed into the side pockets of their suit jackets.'

As well as the Tap, three of the four members of Josef K would regularly frequent the city's bookstores in search of stimulating fare. 'Ronnie had a completely different aesthetic,' suggests Ross. 'We had to accept that, but the rest of us would go to the bookshops and try to track down books by Herman Hesse and Camus. We were just so interested in life. Wanted to find out as much as we could.'

That sense of adventure meant that, in common with most teens, as soon as Friday came around the eagerness to escape the parental home was irresistible. 'Davy didn't work on a Friday, and I don't think Paul did either,' says Ross. 'I used to go to Davy's mum and dad's house, and we would grab some lunch before Paul would pick us up in his mum's car. We'd drive into town and go and have a look round the record shops. There wasn't a lot of drinking. Instead, we'd go to a café, have a few cups of coffee, drive round a bit and then usually end up back at mine listening to LPs. We went to the cinema a lot too. The Film House and the Calton Studios. We had a fondness for the kitchen sink films of the late 50s and early 60s, but also European cinema. I remember Davy and I going to see a Fassbinder season, and then we took in a season of Buñuel films. We loved Buñuel's surrealism and absurdity.'

As well as hanging out with the rest of the band during the weekend, Paul and Malcolm solidified their friendship by travelling beyond the city limits to see some of their favourite bands perform live. One of the first gigs they attended together was in Dunfermline, where they saw The Clash on July 6, 1978. 'The Kinema had an upstairs area with a bar,' says Ross. 'Downstairs it was a stalls area, where under-eighteens could get in. There wasn't a bar there, but it had a stall selling Mars Bars.' He and Haig had come with a few other friends to see the support act that night, New York duo Suicide. 'We thought they were brilliant, but they just got so much abuse from the audience,' recalls Haig. 'I remember them being totally covered head to toe in saliva, literally dripping in gob.' Ross remembers

Alan Vega looking like he'd 'had a shower when he came off stage, covered in big lumps of Mars Bar and phlegm.' When the pair went backstage to apologise for the treatment the duo had received, Haig's jaw dropped at Vega's response: 'Hey, man, what do you mean? That was great. I loved it. We play New York and they just sit and clap politely.' Haig met up with Vega a number of years later in New York: 'They were a huge influence, in much the same way as the Velvets. Suicide's music was great. We totally loved that first *Suicide* album—it was completely off its nut!'

The pair would continue to look out for other bands and sometimes had to travel south of the border for the privilege. Talking Heads had famously played at Strathclyde University in May 1977, supporting the Ramones. The night before, it had been two other New York groups, Television and Blondie, playing at Glasgow Apollo. A New York weekender! But both gigs were missed by Haig and Ross, who would have to make do with taking in their first Talking Heads show in London, at the Electric Ballroom, in December 1979. They also headed for the capital to see Joy Division at the ULU the following February.

'The thing about Edinburgh at the time,' states Steven Daly, 'was that there were some groups who spoke a similar musical language and had the same sensibilities: Josef K and The Dirty Reds in particular. They had a pub they would go to and venues they would play. Edinburgh was probably more Bohemian, more artsy. They could play art theatres and so on. People like Davy Henderson and Malcolm were quite New York-centric. They weren't trying to be punk. It was too late for that. People were setting out in different directions, but I suppose the New York thing was a common aesthetic.'

———

While the Edinburgh music scene had burst to life, forty-five miles west along the M8 there was another band threatening to rival the impact of Scars and the East Coast scene. The Nu-Sonics had been formed by two school friends from the affluent north Glasgow suburb of Bearsden. Budding pop stars James Kirk and Steven Daly would soon recruit their fellow pupil Edwyn Collins to the group. Collins looked the part, all right—boyishly handsome, foppish, smart—but Daly and Kirk harboured reservations about some of his artistic and literary preferences and felt dutybound to alter one or two questionable habits, such as his weekly purchase of the *Melody Maker*. That was a no-no. In their eyes, the *Melody Maker* was blatantly uncool, and they pledged to re-educate their new friend in ways noble and true, which at the very least meant buying the *NME* instead.

Like the members of Josef K, Collins was Edinburgh-born but had lived in Dundee between the ages of six and fifteen, attending school at Morgan Academy alongside fellow Scots musician and future Postcard artist Paul Quinn. By fifteen, his family had relocated to the west coast. It was at the local high school, Bearsden Academy, that the group first came together. Initially a quintet, the line-up was completed by Edwyn's friends Alan Duncan and Geoff Taylor. Both would be jettisoned in 1978 to make room for Girvan-born David McClymont, who brought to the mix a pungent dose of bong-smoking hippieness (and, no doubt, a few Yes albums), but these impurities would soon be eliminated—and the old clothes discarded—as he took up his position as the Nu-Sonics bassist.

Daly sang lead during the band's early performances, including their debut show at Paisley's Silver Thread. But he soon made way for Collins to take over as lead vocalist, reverting to drums instead. Like TV Art, The Nu-Sonics—named after Collins's Burns guitar—had been inspired by the Clash tour the previous May and now possessed sufficient confidence to give it a go themselves, despite regularly being heckled in public for their somewhat effeminate appearance. Indeed, at one early performance they resorted to playing Showaddywaddy songs to appease a crowd of drunken baying meatheads. By then, they had rechristened themselves Orange Juice. It seemed a delightfully contrary move, defiantly at odds with the prevailing macho culture.

Unlike Edinburgh, Glasgow had highly unusual licensing laws at the time, meaning that those seeking to witness their favourite bands often had to travel beyond the parameters of the city. Occasionally, that might mean a short trip to Paisley, or perhaps even traversing the M8 to reach the capital. A massive programme of regeneration was underway in a city still blighted by its reputation for violence, knife crime, football hooliganism, and alcoholism, and physically the city was an eyesore. Its bleak industrial heritage painted every façade black. Town planners and politicians sought to overturn Glasgow's reputation for violence, and alongside a proposed structural transformation, they were keen to tackle some of the underlying issues. Alcohol was identified as the chief culprit. For some time, then, the local authorities shied away from promoting any potentially antisocial events that might aggravate its razor capital image. No mean city no more. After a riot broke out at a Stranglers concert at the City Halls in late 1976, 'punk' bands were banned by the council, so Glasgow lagged well behind other Scottish towns and cities, where there was a greater willingness to take advantage of a potentially lucrative upsurge in nightlife the new music might provide.

'In the city centre, you didn't have clubs with live entertainment or venues that served alcohol,' Daly recalls. 'You couldn't charge at the door. You could have pub rock bands that didn't get paid any of the door takings. Even groups like The Adverts, Generation X, or The Prefects couldn't play in Glasgow, but they were able to play at the Silver Thread in Paisley. The Silver Thread was a hotel with a ballroom and reception room, but because it was outside Glasgow's city limits, they could have a bar and charge ticket prices. You could play the Apollo, but not many bands had that pulling power at the time. Anything below that, and there was nothing. It was terrible at the time in Glasgow, completely hopeless.'

The good people of Glasgow were, however, able to watch some of the bigger stars play the city centre, and it was at David Bowie's June '78 Apollo gig that Edwyn Collins first met Alan Horne, an odd, bespectacled, Saltcoats-born fellow of lofty ambition. There was a self-belief and conviction about Horne that at times bordered on arrogance, and occasionally stretched a few miles beyond that. Nevertheless, Collins felt an instant connection, while Horne saw his young protégé as a conduit to actualise his plans as some kind of Svengali figure. Horne could quite easily have been dismissed as a crank, but he had a habit of wearing others down through his relentless wittering, commanding their attention by vocalising his often-absurd delusions of grandeur. The seeds of Postcard Records were sown here, but there would be another chance meeting of greater significance to the embryonic TV Art.

Clouds (later called Coasters Roller Disco) was a popular venue in Edinburgh's Tollcross area. The location had been a hub for ballroom dancing since the 1940s, but in the late 70s it would play host to a series of legendary gigs. The Clash performed there twice in 1977, with established punk and new wave acts following in their footsteps, including the Ramones ('the first time I ever saw people pogoing,' says Haig), The Damned, The Saints, The Jam, Buzzcocks, Generation X, and Magazine. On August 18, 1978, however, the venue was scheduled to host Siouxsie & The Banshees.

'The Banshees had skipped Glasgow, like many bands,' remembers Daly, 'and they clearly weren't prepared to play these shitty wee hotels in Paisley.' So, Daly opted to make his way through to the capital, and when the enthusiastic young fan arrived a few hours before the show with a faint hope of meeting the band, he encountered a likeminded soul with whom he locked stares as they loitered conspicuously outside the entrance to the venue. It seemed entirely natural that they introduce themselves to one another.

'I went on the afternoon of the gig to look around the record shops, then went up to the venue to listen in to the soundcheck,' Daly remembers. 'I met this guy hanging around outside. We got talking. He told me he was in a group too, and we decided to stay in touch. The guy was Malcolm Ross.'

For Ross and TV Art, the meeting would be a hugely fortuitous one, although neither of the pair could possibly have envisaged how tightly their careers were about to intertwine.

5/15 | HEADS WATCH / CRAZY TO EXIST

We were like a gang. We would all hang about together. We didn't like talking to promoters as much as possible from the music business. We just thought that they weren't in the gang or on the same wavelength. I suppose we were quite puritanical. And we didn't like sexism or laddishness.

MALCOLM ROSS

Becoming famous was never the main priority. But by making music they loved, TV Art hoped that for a time at least, they could escape the dreaded rat race. The alternative seemed pointless. There is little that unsettles the teenage mind more than being knee deep in a dead-end job, gradually beginning to resemble everything you've ever despised. Becoming a cog in the wheel, like all the others. Bank clerk, sales assistant, office party, in tray, overtime. Avoiding that is a challenge, and for those with aspirations to carve a career out of making music, it can be a delicate balancing act, particularly at the beginning. Mums and dads are usually only willing to help out in the short term. They expect to see results. That might have to do with financial considerations, perhaps nurturing a sense of responsibility, possibly even a slight degree of jealousy: '*I* worked, I did *my* time. Why should *they* be allowed to get by without paying their dues.'

TV Art might have fancied their chances as much as the next band, but they were thoughtful and considerate of their parents' feelings and knew that holding down a job or attending lectures were duties they had to undertake. All the same, those things ate into valuable band time.

Haig had a variety of jobs after leaving school, firstly at Craighall Studios in Granton. 'It was a real slog. I had to get up really early, and it was about an hour's bus journey each way. The company owned a record shop too—and I was *demoted* there. It had been my dream to work in a recording studio. I was told I would be trained up as a tape operator, but I was only given one session—to record the Scottish folk band The Whistlebinkies. That was a long day! I didn't take a break from morning 'til night. In fact, it was almost always Scottish folk or dance bands that recorded in there, so obviously it wasn't what I liked. I recorded some classical music for them at the Usher Hall too. But I learned a little about mixing there—pushing up the bass and putting the guitar where you wanted. All of that seemed so exciting.'

The first thing Haig and Torrance ever committed to tape was at Craighall. 'The owner's son Jeff got us in one night—his dad was away somewhere—and along with Ronnie we made some absolutely awful music. But it was the first time I had written and recorded anything.'

By the time TV Art got together, Haig had taken a job, briefly, in Jeffrey's Audio House on Earl Grey Street, having missed out on a place at Glasgow School Of Art through a stroke of ill fortune. On the day the admissions interview was scheduled, he required wisdom tooth surgery. Having missed out on the opportunity to grace the corridors of that hallowed place, he found himself scrambling about for some source of income. Eventually, he took a job working in the archives department of the Lothian Health Board. 'I got the job through some employment scheme. It involved micro-filming one-hundred-year-old records of people's illnesses.'

If Haig later felt haunted by ghosts and an ongoing struggle with anxiety, perhaps the roots of his malaise lay here. 'I ended up trawling through these old crinkly photographs of these terrible illnesses from the Victorian and Edwardian era, which had been retained in these decrepit folders. They needed to destroy all the paperwork, so everything needed to be transferred onto microfilm. It was really grim.'

Haig's mental health had always been rather fragile. He was flirting with anorexic tendencies, brought on by spells of depression and obsessive concern about his physical appearance. His weight had dipped below eight stone, and at times he resembled a skeleton wrapped in clingfilm. His archivist job no doubt accentuated the sense of doubt, the spirit of hopelessness that was growing inside him—so much so that the world's problems seemed to weigh more heavily upon him than ever before, almost as if they were all crammed inside the pointed edges of that haircut. In some ways, they were. Haig possessed a near-fatal tendency to overthink everything. The upside of that was that it fed his creative instincts. There, in the dark recesses of his heart, the lyrics presented themselves more readily.

'One of the first songs Paul wrote was about Helen Scott, and some of the lyrics for the song would later be incorporated into 'Sense Of Guilt'.

At the same time, Malcolm—preparing as any reasonably conscientious seventeen-year-old should—enrolled at Stevenson College, hoping to achieve a Higher in music. He wasn't entirely sure what alternative career he had in mind but thought a music qualification would give him something to fall back on. Meanwhile, Ronnie had begun an apprentice at Brian Drumm Hairdressing, an upmarket boutique among whose regular clientele were certain members of the Royal Family when, for whatever reason, their regal canoodling took them north of the border to Balmoral. Ronnie had good reason to believe he was being groomed by the company's artistic director for a new salon due to open the following year in Los Angeles—an opportunity he was excited by—but as soon as the band started bagging a few more gigs, he felt obliged to decline the invitation.

Practicalities. For a short spell, TV Art dragged their gear around from house to house, firstly from Ronnie's to Paul's (the shortest of journeys), before eventually settling at 27 Colinton Road in Morningside, where Malcolm's parents were happy to allow them space to rehearse, as frequently as they wanted, upstairs in the attic (Malcolm's bedroom). There, step by step, they worked out the sounds that intrigued them and began—tentatively at first—to write their own songs. 'We made too much noise at my folks' house, and Malcolm's parents came to the rescue,' recalls Torrance.

After their first few live appearances, TV Art would gradually introduce more of their own compositions into their sets, but for the time being, performances would still contain a sprinkling of Bowie and Velvets material. The repertoire of covers was important in laying down a marker. It gave the public a sense of the 'purity' of the band's influences, as well as helping them navigate a pathway toward something distinctive of their own. Many of their predecessors and even some of their contemporaries had found it difficult to completely shake off macho posturing and cliched riffing. The 'rock' tag was something they desperately wanted to avoid. Even if Haig and Ross entertained some variation in their musical sensibilities, both were equally determined to avoid any association with that. With Vic Godard and Subway Sect, the emphasis had always been to ensure 'no babys, no yeahs' in the lyrics. With TV Art, it would be to avoid anything whatsoever that might smack of 'rock music'. With that in mind, they reasoned, a change of personnel might guarantee faithfulness to that maxim.

Replacing Gary McCormack turned out to be an uncomfortable business that caused Haig and Ross no shortage of anxiety. But the 'band of brothers' mentality would never really exist until he was gone. McCormack was a good musician and a larger-than-life character, but he wasn't really part of the gang. One thing that united the remaining three band members was their disapproval of McCormack's unwavering Stranglers fixation. His penchant for leather jackets—a sartorial choice too stereotypically 'gobshite punk rock' for what TV Art had in mind—was the clincher. Josef K had been inspired by punk but didn't need to wear a uniform to prove it. All that punk clobber was a turn-off, and much of the music McCormack found appealing was too crude and unsophisticated. Haig and Ross observed that punk was hampered by a regressive puritanical streak—a creative straitjacket that made little allowance for improvisation and experimentation. There was always a risk that it would become the very antithesis of what it had set out to be.

Certainly, as far as McCormack was concerned, there was a shared feeling between the two guitarists that he wasn't quite the right fit. But how to go about telling him? Ross and Haig have only the vaguest recollection of this event. Haig claims it was Ross who pulled the trigger. 'Malky just told him that I wanted him out, as a way of getting him out, but it was definitely Malky's idea. Having said that, I was in full agreement with him.' It just wasn't going to work.

'We found it very hard to replace Gary,' Ross admits. 'We didn't have a big circle of friends at the time. Ronnie probably did, but he mixed in different circles. He regularly went out northern soul dancing. He had loads of girlfriends too. Paul and I didn't know how to talk to girls. We asked some other people who we thought might fit in, but we didn't want to make the same mistake twice.'

In McCormack's place, Davy Weddell would become the band's new bassist. Weddell had been conscripted to help set up the band's equipment for some of their early shows, so he was well-known to the others, but there was one problem: he couldn't play. He had also known McCormack for some time, and this made things somewhat awkward. Crucially however, Weddell possessed the kind of sober and affable temperament Haig and Ross admired. They were willing to overlook his lack of prowess, given that his musical sensibilities were more attuned to their collective vision than McCormack's had been.

'Gary could play bass really well, but his style wasn't quite what we needed,' Haig reflects, 'whereas with Davy, we could teach him what to play, as he was only learning. So, we were able to add really melodic basslines into the mix. Joy Division were doing a similar thing. Anyway, I remember Davy knocking a pint over our guitar amp one night, so maybe he really wasn't cut out to be our roadie!'

As one half of the rhythm section, Ronnie immediately expressed reservations, fearing momentum would be lost if they had to 'train' a new bassist. 'I was really pissed off because to begin with, Davy couldn't play, so we couldn't really jam together in the same way. There was a disruption to the rhythm section, a disruption to the flow.' Ultimately, though, the change of line-up would prove to be a shrewd move. Nick Currie remembers Davy bringing a whole new dynamic to the band's sound. 'He seemed to possess the cheapest bass ever made. It was as if it had been strung with elastic bands. If you listen to those records now—it's a completely unique sound. To my eternal chagrin, when we later made an album together as the Happy Family, he took his money to buy a new bass. That was a shame because his bass sound was no longer the Josef K sound I loved.'

'We showed Davy a few things on the bass,' says Ross, 'and for the first time we felt happy that everyone was going to get on, that there would be some kind of unity there at last, as he was part of that small circle of friends.'

McCormack, meanwhile, took the news of his sacking surprisingly well. 'It was the first band I'd ever been in. I loved the whole thing about being in a band, showing off and all that. It would have hurt at the time, but I've no regrets at all now.' All perfectly understandable, as he would soon go on to have a successful stint as part of anarcho-punk outfit The Exploited before eventually switching to the big screen. An encounter with Irvine Welsh after *Trainspotting* led to a role in the next Welsh adaptation, *The Acid House*. Later, he was able to secure parts in films such as *Valhalla Rising* and *Gangs Of New York*, where he found himself working under Martin Scorsese.

'When we filmed *Gangs of New York* in Rome, at Cinecitta, he [Scorsese] would [pointo over to me and] say things to the cast like, *I like this guy here. He's ok!* So, I ended up as one of the henchmen to Daniel Day-Lewis. Daniel stayed in character for the whole nine months. We'd be talking about day-to-day stuff, and he'd still converse in a New York accent! But as for leaving the band, to be honest there was no acrimony. It seemed quite harmonious because I wanted to move on to something else anyway. My mates were playing the Pistols and The Damned, and I was definitely more into the British side of punk than Paul and Malcolm were.'

As it turned out, those sleepless nights endured by Haig and Ross had been wasted, all that anxiety misplaced. For now, both had enough to worry about holding down jobs and attending classes, though Haig would have an uncomfortable encounter with McCormack a few years later. 'He came up to me in a club and asked, Who have I got to thank about never having got to play in the *real* Josef K? He was staring at me as if he was about to headbutt me! I thought, *This is going to kick off.* I couldn't tell how angry he really was. Thankfully it didn't!'

—

When Davy Weddell joined the band, he was training to be a quantity surveyor. By all accounts his prospects were very bright. Now, he was faced with the onerous task of informing his desperately disappointed parents that he was putting a 'proper career' on hold in order to take up with his bandmates. Weddell was first and foremost a fan of the group, and he could hardly be blamed for passing up the opportunity. Quite naturally, his parents blamed him anyway. To begin with, Weddell experienced a measure of 'imposter syndrome', but before long he was able to settle into the groove.

'I had been sitting in at rehearsals, doing the sound for them,' he recalls. 'Paul had a bass he used to write stuff on, and he lent it to me. I couldn't really play, so I had the basslines written for me. I knew how good Paul and Malcolm were and wouldn't have had the confidence back then to do things differently from how they had suggested. But, thankfully, they were brilliant.'

There was a sense of newfound harmony, all four enthusiastically sharing similar musical sensibilities. Ideas were solidifying about TV Art's sense of identity. Haig and Ross were thick as thieves in that regard. As Haig would later tell Simon Reynolds, 'As soon as I heard things like Television, the *No New York* compilation, Talking Heads, maybe Wire, all of that just sounded like a huge step forward from just thrashing it out,' Haig suggests. 'I thought, *That's how you play guitar*. I much preferred Television's clear crisp sound to the blasting of The Clash and the Pistols.'

'When I first heard *Talking Heads 77* and *Marquee Moon*,' he adds, 'I thought, were I to craft a sound, it would be based on those records, but of course your own sound becomes more a mish-mash of various influences.'

From the outset, Ross felt it imperative to move away from distorted guitars. 'Everyone was using a fuzz box. We wanted a clean, trebly guitar sound. We were interested in trying to take that idea to its extreme. More angular and jagged certainly but there was always a rhythmic dimension to the sound.' Speaking to Reynolds, Ross noted, 'It was just a matter of avoiding distortion and turning the treble up full. We liked playing really fast rhythms, and you needed a really sharp sound for that to work. Using distortion meant you would lose the effect.'

Haig and Ross hoped people would notice that they 'were both more rhythm guitarists than lead guitarists. We were interested in expressionism, in modern art. We were modernist in outlook. We didn't want to be repeating music from the past. Paul had read a Lou Reed interview where he said that lead guitars were rubbish. So, we both thought, *Yeah, let's just go with two rhythm guitars.* A lot of what Josef K were about was as much to do with what *not* to play as with what to play. Josef K could never have anything rootsy, no blues scale. We were always looking for the *modern*, European versus American. We saw Television and Talking Heads as New York bands, not American bands, however strange that might sound. New York meant something different from mainstream American music.'

As for how they should look, the pair were equally struck by the image of Television on the inner sleeve of *Marquee Moon*. 'We decided we needed to have their guitars, their amps, their shoes, everything,' Haig admits. At no sense were they even mildly anxious lest they be led astray by the 'showy' musicianship on the aforementioned album. That dividing line was a thin one for other people caught up in the punk scene, some of whom took great exception to the lengthy guitar solos that miraculously blended the excursive sound of Quicksilver Messenger Service with the cleaner surf-like sound of the early 60s. Not so Paul and Malcolm. Ross started off with a Rickenbacker but soon after elected to play a Fender Jazzmaster in imitation of Verlaine. Paul, meanwhile, started off with a Columbus Gibson copy, the guitar Lou Reed brandishes on the cover of *Transformer*, but soon 'upgraded' to a Fender Mustang, which he managed to get at trade price while working briefly at Varsity Music, a musical instrument shop on Nicolson Street that still exists today. Haig was probably impressed more by its patronage by David Byrne than its clean, twangy bite, although that too was part of the appeal.

'We used those guitars purely because of Television and Talking Heads,' he accepts. 'Tom Verlaine and Richard Lloyd had those guitars on the inside cover of *Marquee Moon*. David Byrne played the solo on "Psycho Killer" on a Fender Mustang when Talking Heads were on *The Old Grey Whistle Test*. I just loved the sound of the guitar on *Talking Heads 77*. Just about every single indie band today uses a Fender Mustang.' Those tedious hours spent working at Varsity Music had at last paid dividends. 'When I was leaving, the owner said, You'll never make it unless you learn how to play "The Dashing White Sergeant" at weddings. Him and his co-pilot in the shop were always poring through the music press. Six months later, I would have been in those pages, the little upstart who had the audacity to pack his job in.'

Solos were out, so Ross and Haig overlaid their rhythm guitars, eventually conspiring to create a propulsive, jagged dynamic quite unlike Verlaine and Lloyd's virtuosic soloing. Two rhythms, not two leads. Lou Reed would have been chuffed. 'I don't think we sounded too much like Television,' claims Haig. He's right. Television, for all their uniqueness and their accommodation of the spirit of punk, looked over their shoulders at the past in their idolisation of Moby Grape and the San Francisco sound, which they valued as equal to The Velvet Underground. By contrast, notes Haig, 'We were listening to Chic, Teenage Jesus & The Jerks, and Stockhausen. I was always trying to get Ronnie to play a 4/4 beat. We wanted people to dance. To make a marriage between abrasive punk and getting people to dance. Disco was a bad word at the time, but if you used the beats in the right way, you could get away with it.'

—

In the beginning, there was little that was remotely 'danceable' about Josef K's sound, no sign of a glitterball suspended above the dancefloor. The first TV Art demo was recorded in a converted laundry in March 1979. It goes down as a very primitive attempt to lay down sketches of their first songs, but it turned out to be a huge disappointment. All four had raced home in anticipation, clutching those cassettes like winning lottery tickets, only to find themselves crushed. Seconds after pressing play, hearts sunk, the moment of supreme expectation evolving into an excruciating hush of vacant stares and painful grimaces. All that was discernible was a muddy gloop of noise, completely devoid of the high-octane sound they had anticipated. In the summer, TV Art would go on to record a full set of songs at Mike's Studio on West Saville Terrace, but the first attempt was a wholly disheartening experience.

It could have knocked the stuffing out of them, but they regrouped. Friendships were strengthening, and, with the prospect of the odd live show, they were determined to put things right. 'We would go into town on a Saturday,' says Ross. 'There was a little café called De Marco's above a little shop on the Royal Mile where we hung out drank coffee and smoked fags. It was like an old London caff from the 60s. You would order your milky coffee in glass cups, along with your Tunnock's Caramel Log, head up the rickety stairs and, over a packet of Lucky Strikes, plan out the future. Ron would never buy anything—insisting that the coffee was a rip-off—so he'd make do with tap water!'

Rehearsals were almost always on Wednesday evenings and during the day on Sundays. Nothing else to do on a Sunday in 1979. As they practised more regularly, alchemy and confidence were growing, and, before long, the cover versions began to ebb away.

'The way Paul and I collaborated on stuff was that more often than not I always came up with the music,' suggests Ross. 'Paul would then take the cassette away and go away and compose lyrics and sing. It wouldn't be changed much. Only occasionally we might get fed up with some of the lyrics. Paul would regularly cannibalise the lyrics or play around with song titles. We didn't over-analyse anything. We played what we wanted to play. Paul wouldn't tell me to change anything, and we wouldn't tell Ronnie to change anything.'

'Yes, I renamed things from time to time, just to mess up my PRS!' jokes Haig.

As we have already established, the band's image was hugely important. They were undoubtedly inspired by Subway Sect's 60s kitchen sink / Left Bank aesthetic, although one member of the band was rather more self-conscious than the others. 'I always wanted to be different,' admits Torrance. 'I was into designer clothes from boutique shops, but I also shopped in Oxfam. The others were more serious and wore grey, but I liked colour in my clothing. I wasn't that punk rock in my outlook, but I still wanted to get up people's noses. Paul and I even got suits tailor-made for ourselves. I associated a bit with a London crowd, too, so I always felt like I was six months ahead of the others in the fashion stakes. I always had my own style. There was a little spell where all the guys decided to wear the same coloured shirts, but I was never going to go along with that. No way!'

'Ronnie, being a hairdresser, was more of a flashy geezer,' says Steven Daly. 'He was a good laugh, but maybe not as much of a music devotee as Paul and Malcolm were.'

'I used to love 60s fashion but had been too young to wear all that cool stuff,' accepts Haig, 'although I did used to alter my dad's old suits from back then. We weren't deliberately trying to be different or to provoke a reaction, we were just wearing what we liked and could afford!' The objective was definitely to look clean and modern. Sharp haircuts and pressed shirts were the order of the day.

At the same time, Steven Daly had made good on his promise to keep in touch with Malcolm, and each would update the other over the phone of their latest adventures. With impeccable sense of timing, Daly advised Ross that Orange Juice were scheduled to play a concert at Glasgow School of Art on April 20, 1979. Coincidentally, TV Art were due to play the night after at the student union of Edinburgh's Art School on Teviot Row. Daly, at Collins's behest, suggested the bands might fill in as support acts for one another, a reciprocal arrangement that offered an opportunity for greater exposure. The Glasgow date would be the first time that TV Art had ventured outside of their home town to perform. At the same time, the close connection between the bands set in motion an insidious rivalry that, while never enunciated, would impact upon the contrasting trajectories the two bands were about to trace.

'Steven was funny, witty, organised, and efficient,' affirms Ross. 'All four members of Orange Juice were very clever people. Probably too clever for their own good to work as a unit. Steven could definitely get things done. He in particular was very organised. Orange Juice probably wouldn't have done any gigs if it wasn't for him. He could write letters, speak to people, and he didn't surrender control to Alan Horne. At the same time, he could be quite abrasive. I remember him confronting David McClymont about where he had acquired this pair of old late-50s/early 60s boots, and David saying something like, I stole them from an old woman. I remember Alan and Steven wrestling with one another in the back of the van. Orange Juice definitely had good songs, even if their playing was a bit sloppy. We were definitely better-rehearsed and much tighter at that point in time.'

Ronnie had other concerns. 'I was quite apprehensive about going to play in Glasgow. The city still had a real reputation for hostile audiences. So, I brought a few cars full of mates, in case there was any trouble, and instructed them to stand round the stage and prepare themselves to expel anybody who needed ejecting! But, thankfully, they weren't required. Instead, I think we went down quite well.'

Their companions had a tougher shift, as Alan Horne later recalled to James Nice: 'It justified the general belief that Glasgow was not yet attuned to the Orange Juice sound. Edwyn had beer thrown over him, fights broke out, and the audience's behaviour was so bad that it was decided to ban groups henceforth.'

The same month, April 1979, also saw the release of Scars' debut single for Fast Product, 'Adult-ery' / 'Horrorshow'. Bobby King's snarling vocals and the stinging swell of Paul Mackie's guitar made it hugely popular locally but also ensured that the band were regularly featured on John Peel (recording two live sessions for him in the process) as well as receiving greater attention from record labels down south. Within six months they had been signed by Charisma. It seemed an odd match. Charisma had built its reputation through the release of albums by progressive-rock bands such as Genesis and Hawkwind, but like many other labels at the time, they were eager to dip into the new-wave market. By 1981, Scars had moved to London, where, following an ill-judged image makeover—halfway between *Aladdin Sane* and Adam & The Ants—they released a decent album, *Author! Author!* Within months their swagger suddenly deserted them, however; King walked out before the band disappeared into obscurity. They split in 1982, destined for cult status rather than the top of the charts.

Orange Juice had also undergone a temporary change in personnel, and this proved to be the catalyst for the launch of TV Art's career. Inspired by the success of Fast Product and Scars—and increasingly frustrated by what he saw as Horne's psychological grip on Collins—Steven Daly felt impelled to act. 'Alan and Edwyn and David McClymont were hanging around with acolytes from the art school,' he says. 'The people who were around Alan at the time were so Warholian. The constant cry was, *That's great, isn't that fabulous?!* It was all so self-congratulatory, and we hadn't even done anything yet! I was painfully aware of how much needed to be done, very aware that nothing was *great*—not yet, anyway. Things came to a head, and I just left. After school, I had been working in Listen Records. Then I worked in the DHSS on Maryhill Road, so I had saved up a bit of money. I had no intention of starting a label, but I did want to put out a couple of records.

'One of the groups I'd seen at the Silver Thread, among other places, was The Backstabbers with James King. In any other city, they would have probably had a pretty decent record deal, but Glasgow was so backward. They were definitely in the same league as the bands who were getting deals in London and Manchester, but because they were from Glasgow it was clear they were going to get nothing. So, my idea was to do a record, just to get something released by them. I thought they were great. I think the drummer didn't want to go along with it, so I ended up playing on it. But that was a one-off record, and the idea was simply to break even.'

The record in question was Fun 4's 'Singing In The Showers', the only release on the short-lived NMC label. It was everything that Orange Juice weren't—white sheets of noise, moronic lyrics—but received minimal airplay, got little promotion, and died a quick death. Undeterred by this disappointment, Daly tried again. This time, his hand was forced to launch a new label, Absolute. It is possible that James King—for whatever reason—wasn't happy to be on the same label as Josef K. By the time a third double bill with Orange Juice had been arranged for June 30 at the Netherbow Theatre, Daly was no longer occupying the drum stool. As he watched from the sidelines, nearby in the audience was Allan Campbell.

Campbell was already building a reputation as a promoter. He was slightly older than Daly and had started out writing reviews for the student newspaper at Edinburgh University around 1974–75. 'I could remember as far back as the Stooges and MC5,' he recalls.

'He had a Pete Wyngarde-type moustache and called himself Duke Piranha,' recalls Haig. 'We would approach him and ask, Duke, have you got any gigs?'

Alongside running nightclubs and putting on bands, Campbell was trying to hold down a job as a secondary school teacher. It was a chaotic, breathless existence, but somehow he managed to remain clear-sighted, astute, and professional about it all. Duke was a 'fixer', capable of pulling strings and finding solutions to little problems which might materialise. One of his 'projects' was the Aquarius nightclub at 40–42 Grindlay Street, tucked in off the main road behind the Usher Hall. He was convivial, with a keen eye for new talent and a good sense of perspective, and was eager to make his mark in any way he could.

'I was generally enthused by what was happening,' Campbell recalls. 'I definitely wasn't a punk. I was a music fan. I had been buying records since the mid-60s, but I was genuinely excited by whatever might arrive on your doorstep. Some people thought, *I'll start a band*. I suppose I thought, *I love music, but I'm not musical. How can I be an enabler or participate in some way in something I think is great?*

'The most obvious way I could think of was to put on small gigs. You don't go into it thinking, *Right, now I'm going to become a promoter*, but rather, *Where can I put on these small groups?* I didn't approach it from a business perspective. It helped that there was a strange air of altruism and personal contact with the bands and singers. There seemed to be a lot of people wanting to get involved in some shape or form.'

Campbell was enthusiastic but nursed doubts about whether or not he could make an impact. 'I didn't have a clue about what a manager did,' he admits. 'I had begun to put on touring bands like Teardrop Explodes, Echo & The Bunnymen, Orchestral Manoeuvres In The Dark, The Monochrome Set, and The Cure—bands who were just establishing reputations for themselves. But it was entry-level stuff. One of the very first things I did was the Tuesday night at the Aquarius. There, I put on a few bands for a pound a head and hoped enough people would come to ensure I avoided losing a lot of money.' One of the first bands Campbell put on was The Associates. 'They had something special,' he insists. 'It was their first ever show. There was hardly anyone there!'

The Associates would become—alongside Simple Minds and Orange Juice—one of the most successful Scottish bands of the 80s. Formed in Dundee, the duo (singer Billy Mackenzie and multi-instrumentalist Alan Rankine) would spend much of their first year playing the Edinburgh gig circuit. They quickly released an unauthorised Bowie cover as their debut single. Remarkably, the very first person in the world to buy a copy was Malcolm Ross.

It's late afternoon and Malcolm has sneaked off early from college. He's regretting going in at all. The longer evenings of summer are over, and he doesn't want to spend the last few hours of autumn daylight in a classroom. Wasting away an hour or two mulling around the record shops seems a far more attractive option. Might be able to pick up a few singles. After popping into Virgin on Rose Street, he walks around the corner and nips into Bruce's. As the door closes behind him, his ears are seduced by a tune that's somehow familiar yet infuriatingly difficult to identify.

'What's that you're playing?' Malcolm asks shyly.

The sales assistant smiles wryly at the hunched figure in trench coat and beret leaning over the counter.

When Malcolm offers to buy the record, he feels for reasons unbeknown to him, that he has momentarily become the object of ridicule.

'I suppose that's your mate, then?' the sales guy asks, eyes darting sideways. He clearly believes Malcolm's presence is part of some carefully choreographed routine.

'Huh?' Malcolm is now even more confused. At that moment, the penny drops, and he suddenly recognises the song that is playing. It's a really weird rendition of a Bowie song, but Malcolm likes it. A lot.

'Well, can I buy it?' he asks again, still puzzled.

The beret-topped figure at the counter gesticulates to an acquaintance who disappears briefly from the shop.

Malcolm waits patiently, browsing through the vinyl racks, and feeling decidedly awkward.

I'll give it five minutes, then I'm out of here, he thinks.

Then the sales assistant puts him out of his misery.

'It's this guy's single,' he remarks, nodding at the dapper-looking fellow at the counter. A few seconds later, the fellow's acquaintance returns with a handful of copies of the record, and Malcolm rummages through his pockets for some loose change.

Then he has the record in his hand. The Associates, 'Boys Keep Swinging'.

The first Associates single. The first Associates sale. So, here was another new Scottish band with a record deal. Maybe it really was possible! *We* can *do this*, he thought.

A few weeks later, an equally strange coincidence. In between classes at Stevenson College, Malcolm gets talking to one of his fellow students, who discloses that he too is a member of a band.

'Ours is called TV Art. What's your band called?' Malcolm asks.

'Oh, we're The Associates,' comes the reply.

'Really? You're kidding? I just bought your record at Bruce's the other day.'

'Pleased to meet you, man. My name is Alan Rankine.'

Small world, et cetera.

Rankine and Mackenzie would establish themselves as one of the most inventive of the new wave of shiny pop bands of the early 80s. Peel got a hold of their first single, affording them some instant exposure. Their early material (in particular, *The Affectionate Punch* and *Fourth Drawer Down*) created a uniquely languorous Cold War-style electronica, but before long they had transformed themselves into an ostentatious cabaret of poperatic delights. The pair would have their faces plastered over the covers of glossies and inkies alike, and they would go on to perform regularly on *Top Of The Pops* and other TV shows, scoring a top ten single ('Party Fears Two') and album (the era-defining *Sulk*) in the summer of 1982. That seemed a long way from their debut performance, three years earlier, at the Aquarius, to an audience of only fifty people.

The gig had been arranged by Campbell after he had acquired a copy of The Associates' demo tape. Suitably impressed, he offered them the gig, recalling with delight that 'Billy arrived for the soundcheck wearing an electric green suit. You looked at him, then heard him sing and thought, *Oh my god! I don't know what this is, but it's absolutely amazing!* They went on far earlier than they were supposed to, as at the time they had a drummer from the local boys' home who had to get back to his lodgings by ten o'clock! But even on a Tuesday night, people would come out because they sensed there was something happening. Metropak, Another Pretty Face, The Flowers. It was really exciting.'

More exciting than any of the others, though, was TV Art. That night at the Netherbow Theatre on Edinburgh's High Street convinced Campbell he ought to make a move. 'I just thought there was something really exciting about them. You felt that whatever it was they were doing was beginning to form already. They had a certain sound, they had a certain appearance. They had intuitively started to work out what they were doing. In the vaguest terms, I just thought, *I want to push this—I've got to get other people to hear this!*

6/15 | THE TRIAL / ABSOLUTELY FABULOUS

It's hard to forgive dear
When you shot all the things that we loved…

JOSEF K, 'CHANCE MEETING'

TV Art recorded a new demo of songs on Saturday, July 14, 1979, at Mike's Studio with engineer Gordon ('Nobby') Clark. Clark had been the original lead vocalist with The Bay City Rollers but had left in acrimonious circumstances, completely disillusioned with the direction in which he felt the band was heading. Unbeknown to him, a commercial breakthrough was imminent, and global superstardom would follow for his estranged bandmates. After leaving the Rollers, Clark had released two unsuccessful solo singles but had a strong desire to remain in the music business, prompting him to open a rehearsal space/studio on West Saville Terrace. At the time of the TV Art demo, he was also heavily involved with The Associates.

While the new demo was an improvement from the first tape, the songs remained, for the most part, unrefined and ill-defined. However, if finesse was lacking, the band's identity was beginning to crystallise. One's first impression is of the weight of the world beginning to bear heavily on Haig's shoulders. Musically, there are only occasional flickers of the acicular intensity to come, but the demo provides a sonic barometer of their progress. The predominance of the electric piano—similar in style to Yvonne Pawlett's on the early Fall records—already sounds a little out of place, but the angular guitar shapes are beginning to form. One could grumble that the execution seems a little sloppy, but here is a band striving for an authentically unique sound even if they are still lacking complete conviction.

What *is* impressive is the sheer abundance of ideas. The recording shows great promise. In his notes about the band, James Nice recalls how they had harboured high hopes the demo might arouse the interest of 'a credible boutique imprint such as Radar, Dindisc, or Rough Trade', but disappointingly it did nothing of the sort. Instead, the session captured TV Art during an important moment of transition. In fact, within a week of committing these songs to tape they had abandoned the name TV Art. They would also jettison the spooky electric piano. Instead, Haig and Ross were intent on transforming their guitar partnership into something far more dynamic and original. And they did. From now on, their sonic canvas would alter radically. But the demo remains an important document, not least because two of the songs would become, in their rawest form, the band's first single—something they could not possibly have foreseen at the time.

Scattered throughout the tape are seeds that anticipate the thrilling urgency characteristic of the band in full flight. Ronnie's percussion on 'Final Request' is terrific, effortlessly mixing up the tempo alongside Malcolm's falling-backward-down-the-stairs guitar. Torrance would be furiously stripping layers from his sticks twelve months on. It is clearly a song they valued highly, as it would later become the flip side to 'It's Kinda Funny'.

'Night Ritual' features some spasmodic shape-throwing, a first awkward lunge onto the dancefloor. By contrast, the two minutes and twenty seconds of 'Heads Watch' contain all the ingredients of the future Josef K sound. Best of all, though, is 'Sense Of Guilt', which comes fully formed, almost identical in structure to the version recorded for *Sorry For Laughing*. All that's missing is Malcolm's inspired viola—in its place, some weird electronic noodling—and the Syndrum pow-wow. Paul's vocal is cold, mechanical, possibly a little John Foxx-ish. It's tremendous.

The template for 'Terry's Show Lies' was clearly Talking Heads, and with its chopped chord riff the song represents the closest the band ever came to reggae; the rhythm and keyboard-led melody is slightly discordant, although it is completely unlike the convulsive hiccupping later version of the song, with which it bears no resemblance whatsoever. 'No Glory' shows greater urgency and could be a cast-off from The Fall's recent *Live At The Witch Trials* LP. But it was 'Romance' and 'Chance Meeting' that would be selected from the demo by Steven Daly to become the band's first 45.

Although he was developing as a songwriter, Haig was still in thrall to Bowie and The Velvet Underground, lending his lyrics a pessimistic, slightly sinister, dystopian tone. He was also full of admiration for Joy Division, whose sombre architectural precision and use of European iconography captivated his impressionable young mind. Other groups such as Magazine and Wire were mining similar territory. Both shared a similar sense of foreboding in their lyrics, and Wire in particular the same mathematical imprecision in their music.

The other key influence was literature. Haig and Ross were knee deep in early twentieth-century existentialist fiction. 'I was reading an awful lot,' Haig later told Grant McPhee. 'Kafka, Albert Camus, Knut Hamsun. There was this recurring theme of alienation that ran through all of their books, and that had a big effect on my lyrics.'

'Either Davy or Malcolm had a copy of *The Trial*, and I completely psyched into it,' he remembers. 'I could really relate to the main character.

It felt like I had the same kind of feelings as he had. It was a bit like discovering something that was already there. All of us had a go at reading it apart from Ron who, to this day, says he can't get past the first page. But I was deeply influenced by it. I loved that book.'

Unlike Josef K or the unnamed protagonist of Hamsun's *Hunger*, who roams the streets of old Cristania forced to sell buttons for bread, Haig grew up in comfortable middle-class surroundings. Nevertheless, he shared Kafka and Hamsun's sense of entrapment. What was this thing called life? What was the point of anything, really? Around the same time, the BBC aired a three-part dramatization of *Crime & Punishment* starring John Hurt. The series was much admired, winning BAFTAs and a Golden Globe. Coincidentally, much of it had been shot in the cobbled alleyways of Edinburgh's Old Town—a location considered suitably bleak for the novel's action to unfold in. All these literary reference points would be hungrily absorbed into Haig's *weltanschauung*, as he explained to Mark Brennan in *Melody Maker*:

'It just happened the way things evolved. It all came from the books Malcolm and I read. And the people we were. It was all totally honest and natural, never a forced image. There's always a danger of being categorised. I suppose in a way, Josef K evolved a certain image and we were expected to live up to it. I think people took us too seriously. They expected us to be dark, sombre, unsmiling. But really there was a streak of humour through the whole thing. It was always slightly tongue-in-cheek, but people didn't grasp that.'

Haig agonised over his lyrics, and even today he can be unforthcoming in his discussion of them. He would later acknowledge that it pained him to listen to the early songs as they transported him back to what was a psychologically traumatic time. To many, that might appear strange. His band were beginning to make a name for themselves, and by all accounts he was greatly admired and respected by his fellow musicians both within and outside the band. Gary McCormack has suggested that 'Paul was a stud—the girls were mad for him', though Malcolm's comment that he and Paul 'didn't have a clue how to speak to girls' suggests Haig may have been troubled by a lack of confidence. It would have been many a young person's dream to have stood in his shoes—up there onstage, receiving all the attention as lead singer.

Paul Haig was on the verge of releasing his first record and was travelling all over the UK to see his favourite bands. Before long, he would be touring the country with his own band. Here we had a suave young intellectual with a penchant for music, art, and literature, but there was something deeply wrong. Spiritually, he was probably more K than Raskolnikov, and the level of introspection and soul-searching involved in writing songs had the potential to tip him over the edge.

At this point, Davy Weddell was still a nervous wreck when it came to performing live, even going so far as to hide behind the PA stack when they played at the Teviot Row with Orange Juice. But his confidence was slowly building. When the band opened for Adam & The Ants at Clouds on July 20, they would take to the stage for the first time under a new name. Ant (Stuart Goddard) had been heavily involved in the early punk scene, playing bass for Bazooka Joe, who supported the Sex Pistols at the first ever gig at Central St. Martin's College of Art & Design in November 1975. He had also done a bit of acting, starring as Kid in Derek Jarman's *Jubilee* in 1978. Despite that, his band were hardly media darlings. Many found their fetishist lyrics and paraphernalia off-putting. They had just released their second 45 ('Zerox') and were trialling songs from their debut album *Dirk Wears White Sox*, but to decidedly mixed receptions. Few could have predicted that within eighteen months, Goddard would be the biggest pop star in Britain, inspiring a brief but unsustainable spell of Bolan-like hysteria.

In the week leading up to the Adam & The Ants gig, Daly was adamant that the band change their name for their forthcoming 45. If he was going to the trouble of releasing a single, under no circumstances would it be by TV Art. Ross had first suggested Strawberry Switchblade, a name James Kirk had dreamt up for a fanzine that would never materialise. Malcolm was very keen, the others unsure, but at the same time, Ross remembered an old friend of his had briefly used the name Josef K in a school band. By now, Ronnie aside, all were devotees of *The Trial*.

'We were sitting in a café with Steven one morning,' Ross recalls, 'and we all agreed to go with Josef K.'

The handbill for the Ants show simply read 'Plus Support'. Disappointingly, while there is a grimy recording of the Ants' show, no audio recording remains of Josef K's 'debut' performance. 'I remember the audience gobbing on us,' says Ronnie, 'and thinking, *Thank fuck I'm a drummer and I'm sitting way back here*. I repositioned my cymbals to give me a little more cover. I remember we were meant to pay the hire charge for the PA system, and we disappeared without doing that. I think we got away with it. Result!'

Malcolm's most vivid memory of the occasion was locking his eyes upon the mirrors at the opposite end of the hall. 'It was the first time I'd been able to see the group as we played. We had our Oxfam suits on, and I thought we looked really great.'

Meanwhile, Daly was keen to issue something on vinyl quickly, but as far as the band were concerned, for a first record, it was a hugely underwhelming first experience—no record contract, no advance, no high-tech eighteen-track studio, no big-shot engineer. All the same, to see your music pressed onto vinyl was still every young musician's dream. Perhaps through a combination of self-doubt and low expectations, they acquiesced.

'We took the best two tracks and Steven pressed them up as our first single,' remembers Ross. The intention had never been to release the songs—at least not in this rustic form—and they neither captured the frenzy and euphoria of the band's live shows nor were they sufficiently pristine or polished to possess much commercial potential.

'Romance' was the first song Haig had ever written. 'I remember writing it when I was very young. It was definitely channelling my inner Iggy Pop. I was thinking of *The Idiot* and *Lust For Life*. It was so simple, minimal. I still really love that song.' By contrast, 'Chance Meeting' was more melodious—extremely hummable if somewhat sluggish. The interesting work here is happening in the background—the two rhythm guitars scratch out little arcs of funk but are outmuscled by Malcolm's electric piano, which is afforded centre stage. Ronnie's percussion is steady, Davy's bass subdued, while the unusual shift in tempo midway through sounds like a mastering glitch.

Daly took responsibility for arranging the pressing and distribution before going to Portland Place Studios to have the recording mastered by George Peckham. 'I remember Alan Horne was pretty helpful with it all,' he says. 'I drove down to London with him, and we went round the record shops. He was just starting out with Postcard at the time. I think we put the record out at roughly the same time as Orange Juice's "Falling And Laughing". They were reviewed during the same cycle.'

In actual fact, Josef K's first single appeared at the tail end of 1979, pipping Orange Juice's first release for Postcard. On its front cover was a grainy image of four solemn visages caught at twilight (Paul's face almost completely hidden by shadows), leaning back against the Leamington Lift Bridge, which sits atop the Union Canal. Various other photos, credited to Geoff Cropley and roadie Paul Mason, adorn the reverse. On the run-out groove to ABS001 was scrawled the words 'Strawberry Switchblade'. There was just one problem. Before the first few copies left the city's record shops, Steven Daly was back behind the Orange Juice drum kit, his Absolute adventure at an end. So, what now for Josef K?

Virtually synchronous to the single release, Allan Campbell took over as the band's *de facto* manager. It was one of the few occasions in the Josef K story where there was any clarity about a business arrangement. Over the next two years, there would always seem to be a degree of uncertainty about everything. Yet Campbell was definitely a steadying influence.

'I think Josef K sensed that I might be of some use to them,' he says. 'But I had been very impressed by them too. When you see a band for the first time, it is genuinely exciting. You can't quite articulate what it is that makes them special. And it really felt like they had something special. They had just put out their first single with Absolute. It eventually sold out, but it didn't do that well really. I got on board before Postcard got involved.'

The band played a few gigs during the remainder of 1979, including a blinder at George Square Theatre on December 8, alongside Scars, Another Pretty Face, and The Visitors. Josef K were fourth on the bill. Dressed in black, they wore their hair slicked back, taking to the stage accompanied by blinding light and a soundtrack of Psalms.

A little over three weeks later, Josef K—along with everyone else—waved goodbye to the 70s. A new decade dawned, and soon they would have a new label and a new sound. Their time had come.

7/15 | TORN MENTORS / THE ADVOCATES

Postcard had this quality that it was local but also international.
You could recognise the markers; there was some Velvets in there,
some Tamla, Chic, some Buzzcocks, but it was wholly itself and
it was great. Horne's mission statement was there immediately—
why isn't Postcard music on Top Of The Pops? It had a sense of
humour, a sense of provocation, a sense of play and a sense of
seriousness as well. style, personality, and a vocabulary of its own.

PAUL MORLEY, *HUNGRY BEAT*

The general consensus of the music press was that Orange Juice had produced a better debut 45 than Josef K. Objectively speaking, it was impossible to argue. 'Falling And Laughing' tickled a collective sweet spot. It was witty, charming, immediate, and elicited from press and public alike a considerably more enthusiastic response than 'Chance Meeting'. Housed in a bright pink sleeve, it pictured the boys—with Edwyn's mile-wide grin— looking impossibly cute. It was Postcard's very first release, and a triumph.

The success of 'Falling And Laughing' would have encouraged Josef K, who at that stage would probably have regarded themselves as not only superior musicians but also more sonically adventurous. It wasn't a competition—not at that point—but it's possible that, at this moment, something within Haig and Ross hardened. Throughout their short career, both would consistently express a cool diffidence about the music press and whatever it might have to say about their music, but after the first reviews of 'Chance Meeting' appeared in print, their disdain definitely grew. Their attitude toward the *NME* and *Sounds* would never really change—even later on, when those publications were briefly united in exaltation, recklessly gushing out streams of praise. Even then, they refused to take it all very seriously. Crucially, however, they didn't allow it to affect their sense of self, far less dictate the musical direction they might follow.

At that time, Josef K still found it faintly surreal that their names were in the *NME* and *Melody Maker* at all. It all seemed rather ridiculous to them, in much the same way as it did a year or so later when the fans who hung about backstage after shows asked for autographs. When that sort of thing happened, they didn't know where to look. *You want me to write my name on a bit of paper? Really?* How odd it all was. In that sense, the members of Josef K were decidedly different from Edwyn Collins and Alan Horne, who slavishly devoured the attention of the media and enabled it—at least to some degree—to influence the end product.

'Falling And Laughing' was *Melody Maker*'s Single Of The Week in February 1980. By contrast, 'Chance Meeting' received a decidedly lukewarm reception: 'Serious Edinburgh band put perfect Lou Reed voice on top of a pounding drum/bass motif and juicy guitar/keyboards noises— mainly to indifferent effect.' The *NME* was equally pithy: 'More wigs and hats. This time a passable Lou Reed. Energywise, this is just a shade up on The Stranglers' million-seller "Don't Bring Harry". I'm reminded of the late Joyce Grenfell's immortal cry, Effort! St. Swithen's, effort!'

It was from an unlikelier source—*Sounds*—that the critical trajectory began to shift. Dave McCullough saw through the greasy production and amateurish delivery: 'Josef K come clean with effective Reedian spookiness, enhanced by some winning keyboards that remind me of vintage Fall circa Yvonne Pawlett. I've a tape of Josef K's and that suggests the same thing: this is a band of potential.'

Before it became a rather feckless glossy booklet stuffed with pin-ups of Simon Le Bon and John Taylor, *Smash Hits* provided a much-needed blast of colour and style to counter the occasionally po-faced intellectualism of the *NME*. It boasted some quality journalism too, and—with cover stars such as The Specials, The Jam, PiL and X-Ray Spex—a variety of insightful features. Of 'Chance Meeting', the magazine was even more enthusiastic than McCullough: '[It] is certainly something different. A slow deliberate beat, distinctive toy organ sound and gruff voice combine to highlight a good melody line and a catchy hook that sneaks in and refuses to leave, and there's a neat speedier instrumental close. The B-side "Romance" is equally good: more modern dark pop plus more beat and good guitar work, but still keeping the low intense atmosphere. Gets better with every play. Buy this one.'

In the meantime, the band received a huge boost when they were given a chance to open for The Clash at their show at Edinburgh Odeon on January 20, 1980. It was customary for Strummer & co to try to give a leg up to local bands by offering the third slot on the bill, and it would be a memorable night for several reasons. The Clash were on tour to promote their current tour-de-force, *London Calling*. Second on the bill, for the whole UK Tour, was Mikey Dread, with whom Josef K were asked to share a dressing room for the evening. That resulted in a series of comic interludes as Davy Weddell's thick Scottish brogue clashed with Dread's languorous Patois.

'That was a good night,' remembers Davy. 'I remember talking to Mikey but I couldn't remotely understand anything he was saying!'

Allan Campbell, however, was able to cut through the language barrier to make a surprising discovery. '*What's your name?* Mikey asked me. I said I'm Allan Campbell, and he laughed and said, *My* name is Michael

Campbell! It resonated for some time later—there are so many Scottish names, from the slave plantations.'

Meanwhile, Ross remembers Paul Simonon and Joe Strummer coming into the band's dressing room immediately before the show. The room had a window that faced out onto a lane behind the theatre. 'They opened the window up, and all these teenage Clash fans without tickets climbed in the window and raced through to see the gig.' It was such a Clash thing to do, almost beyond parody. As for Josef K's performance, it was typically magnificent, but not everybody was equally enthused, as Johnny Waller reported in his review of the show for *Sounds*, where he claimed the band were heckled as 'mod revivalists'.

'We wore suit jackets, but I wouldn't say people saw us as mod revivalists,' Ross suggests. 'We wanted to reject the rock'n'roll leather and denim stereotypes. Vic Godard had spoken out against Americanisms in music. That didn't make us mods, but some of the audience might have been annoyed with us. They possibly saw us as arty-farty, but the bottom line is that we weren't The Clash, so we were always going to get at least some abuse. In fact, I remember it being a good night. We got a reasonably good response. Well, nobody threw anything at us anyway!'

Davy recalls things rather differently, suggesting there were in fact a few missiles hurled in the band's direction: 'Malky was taunting the audience, saying, You can throw glasses at us all night, but in the morning your girlfriends will still love us!'

With Daly having put his pet label project on hold, Josef K had found themselves, for the time being, homeless, and without a record deal. Even before the release of 'Falling And Laughing', Daly would have understood intuitively that Orange Juice had what it took to succeed. That feeling was so deeply ingrained in him that he couldn't quite bring himself to make a once-and-for-all break. Not just yet anyway. Nevertheless, Daly had seen enough of Josef K himself to believe they'd be a good fit for Postcard, and he immediately sought to twist Alan Horne's arm. To say Horne remained unconvinced is at best an understatement. He misconstrued in the Edinburgh quartet a wearisome solemnity—a characteristic he had openly derided in Joy Division ('an awful bore').

Naturally, Josef K were in awe of Joy Division—so much so that Malcolm even traded in the wonky keyboard he used on 'Chance Meeting' and the early demos to buy bus tickets for himself and Paul to go and see the band play at the ULU in February 1980. The pair ended up spending an uncomfortable night wandering about London in the middle of the night before roughing it at Victoria Station until the earliest bus to Edinburgh turned up. They had barely managed to scrape together enough money for the concert tickets, so booking into a B&B for the night was out of the question. Some doorways were inspected for sanctuary, as they gravitated toward the stale limp air of the odd convector heater, but in those private and cramped spaces, they ran the risk of attracting some undesirable attention (and there was plenty of it), meaning they resigned themselves to finding a decidedly colder if slightly more public location.

With Daly leaning heavily on Horne's shoulder, it was only a matter of time before a resolution was found to Josef K's predicament. By then, Campbell had become the band's manager. That would complicate things. While Horne swithered, Campbell was faced with the challenge of finding a label for his young charges. 'We sent out loads of demo tapes to record companies. They didn't react. It was naive of us. Malcolm is a realist, but in a positive way. He was reluctant to send out too many tapes and would say things like, *I mean, who wants to get rejection letters anyway?* I suppose they were creating art and waiting to see what happened. That requires a certain amount of confidence. But their models and inspirations were mostly others who hadn't exactly stormed into the charts with a bullet— The Velvet Underground, and Television—music with an absolute value, but not necessarily Top 20 music.'

Nevertheless, from a distance, Ross harboured some admiration for the independent spirit being nurtured at Postcard. He and Haig would definitely be open to offers. All it needed was for Horne to reciprocate.

As well as the Aquarius Club, Campbell was running Valentino's, formerly the old Palladium on East Fountainbridge. It was an extremely unusual venue with a sizeable capacity of around six or seven hundred. Set up as a discotheque, it featured wall mirrors and had a dancefloor that lit up, while there were Mondrian-coloured split squares on the floor. The club was set up over two levels, and it had a giant video screen where people could watch films on ancient thick U-matic tapes before the bands came onstage.

'It sounded more like a New York club,' Campbell says. 'I liked the feel of the place. I had to get a stage built for it. I tried to weld part of it together on my own and almost blinded myself! I must have got someone else to finish it. I don't think there was anywhere else like it in Edinburgh, or in Glasgow for that matter. There was a bar upstairs too called JJ's—and occasionally we would put on a much smaller act up there. Later, Blue Orchids and Strawberry Switchblade played there. It's now a Job Centre.' (Valentino's even boasted one bill that, over forty years later sounds like an impossible mismatch—U2 and Fire Engines—but few would have raised an eyebrow in 1980.)

Meanwhile, with Orange Juice's first single receiving the plaudits, Alan Horne's swaggering self-belief intensified, and his eagerness grew to strengthen the Postcard 'roster' through the acquisition of another 'signing'. But despite Daly's suggestion, it wasn't Josef K he had in mind. Instead, he set his sights on an up-and-coming duo from Down Under. The Go-Betweens had been formed by Robert Forster and Grant McLellan, two immensely talented young songwriters who had met after enrolling on an arts theatre course at Brisbane's University of Queensland in 1977. The pair had already released a few singles back home, including an affectionately twee tribute to actress 'Lee Remick'. Smart and savvy, their ambition was matched by an enterprising streak that saw them set off for the UK in November 1979 with a plan to sell their songs at record company offices up and down the country. Horne and Collins had heard the early songs, and while on a lightning-quick trip to London, they slipped a note under the hotel room door of the Welcome Inn at Sussex Gardens, where Forster and McLennan were temporarily resident. It was a typically audacious act, but Postcard's public personae were capable of bold, even obnoxious gestures, such as the famous occasion when they blustered their way into the BBC studios brandishing a copy of 'Falling And Laughing', which they proceeded to wave under John Peel's nose before urging him to 'Wise up, old man!' The great man—fearful of a second visit—duly obliged by playing the song on his show that evening.

Mission accomplished, The Go-Betweens—suitcases crammed with vinyl to unload—were lured north of the border and soon agreed to record a 45 for the label. Horne was instantly smitten with them, so much so that he even sought out the wisdom of his two bewildered Aussie troubadours regarding the prospective signing of Josef K, virtually frightening them off for good at the same time. Fortuitously, however, Horne overheard Malcolm Ross playing 'Dock Of The Bay' during a soundcheck, and, with characteristic contrariness (Stax must have been *de rigueur* that week), he finally succumbed.

It might not have happened, but it did. They were going to make music on Postcard. 'We had some interest from labels before then,' claims Haig. 'Arista for example. But because everything was new and the scene in Scotland was growing stronger, we went with Postcard.'

Horne had conferred upon his label a pinkish athletic motto: 'The Sound Of Young Scotland'. It certainly suited Orange Juice, but it felt incongruous with Josef K's darker edge. Reflecting upon the decision later, one senses Haig might have been a little regretful that they didn't follow another path. 'Everything about The Sound Of Young Scotland was a copy—a microcosm of New York, West Coast and Motown, with Horne trying his best to imitate Andy Warhol. It all moved very quickly from Absolute to Postcard. Nothing was ever concrete, no terms discussed. It was always just, *Let's do the next track.* I don't think we really wanted to be on a big major label, so we just went along with what was on offer at the time, and that happened to be Postcard. People everywhere were churning out very low-budget records. You could go buy them all at Bruce's and Virgin. It was great fun. Malcolm later came up with the title of that compilation which perfectly described who we were at the time—*Young & Stupid.*'

By contrast, Ronnie Torrance felt a little uncomfortable with the band's new label. 'It was quite awkward with Postcard to begin with, because we weren't necessarily jingly-jangly happy people,' he says. 'We did our own thing, and we wanted to be different. We didn't seek to please people. If people liked us, they liked us, but we really didn't care if they didn't.'

Almost overnight, there were three bands on the label. While The Go-Betweens were in Scotland, they made the journey through to Edinburgh, where Horne requested Malcolm invite them to use his parents' house—Josef K's primary rehearsal space—in order to prepare for two concerts he had lined up featuring the entire Postcard roster. The first showcase was scheduled for April 11 at Edinburgh's Nite Club, the re-match at Glasgow College of Technology on the 24th. Flyers and bill posters for the second show featured the tagline 'Funky Glasgow Now!' The two concerts have become near-legendary 'I was there!' moments in the history of modern Scottish music. Before long, the impact would ripple outward, with vibrant centres in Glasgow, Paisley, and Bellshill following in its wake. If it didn't quite have the fist-to-jaw impact of punk, it was equally important in its own way.

The Go-Betweens opened on both nights, with Orange Juice and Josef K alternating as headline act, in accordance with their earlier gentlemen's agreement. At the second show, Josef K took to the stage in psychedelic

Day-Glo shirts, tailor-made for them in a Morningside boutique. The choice of attire no doubt bewildered a few folk and was decidedly at odds with the noise being made on the stage. They wore the shirts on at least one other occasion—in Paisley—prompting a pithy review in *Sounds*, where the writer dismissed them as 'about as psychedelic as a tube of Smarties'.

'They cost us ten quid each,' laughs Haig. 'The shop had a big roll of material and they cut from that.' Ronnie was less enamoured with the idea; Davy may have worn his for a short time after the others had abandoned them. After that, their only function was to brighten up their wardrobes.

Meanwhile, Daly doubled up on drums for The Go-Betweens, who would headline a few additional gigs of their own—at Glasgow School of Art and the Bungalow Bar in Paisley—before they returned south of the border with lighter cases, but plenty more admirers.

—

Now, with Allan Campbell as manager and Alan Horne biting off the ears of the music press, Josef K had two quite singular advocates for their talent: the cool, methodical, pragmatic Campbell, and the wilfully perverse Horne. 'Allan Campbell wasn't punk at all,' remembers Malcolm, 'but he was just so knowledgeable about music. Back then, if you were interested in a band from the 60s, it was so hard to get any information about them at all. Obviously, there was no internet then, but in actual fact, there weren't many books about rock and pop music either. It was even difficult to find old newspaper and magazine articles, so Allan was really useful as an information provider. But despite Allan's knowledge, Alan Horne was definitely a bit bitchy about it all. He probably didn't like the idea of Allan being Josef K's manager.'

Campbell himself, like many others, found Horne's Marmite abrasiveness off-putting at times, although he admired his remarkable ability to get things done, and his quick wit and sense of humour. 'You sometimes felt there were two Alan Hornes. The spiky slightly irritating Alan Horne, who would pronounce on things—he had that very punky attitude. Josef K were huge Joy Division fans, but I have vague memories of Alan pontificating, saying disdainfully, *Hmmm ... Joy Division. Yes. Baaaad model*. On any given week, he would make these pronouncements—you know, *Elvis Costello is rubbish* or some such. He clearly was of a mind that by putting someone else down, you strengthen yourself. I remember a few years later, being on an interview with him on BBC Radio Scotland. It was a three-way conversation between Alan, myself, and Greil Marcus, who was on the phone from San Francisco. We were talking about post-punk and new wave, then at one point down the line, Greil offered his own thoughts on the British post-punk scene, or whatever it was. It was followed by a long pause and Alan—in that old, careworn kind of way— saying, *Oh Greeeeeil, you're toooo old and toooo far away*.

'The other Alan Horne was very uncertain about things,' Campbell continues. 'If one or two people said something even remotely negative about a Postcard record, he would quickly lose confidence. It's exhausting to keep up that front all the time. He liked to wind people up. It was a control thing. When he set up London Records, much later on, he had a dentist's chair there, and he would elevate and lower it, saying things like, We can build you up and we can let you down. If you stick your neck out, you're going to be very divisive. I got to like him very much. He was great with put-downs. I interviewed him later for an STV series called *Out There*, and when I put it to him that some people called him a genius, he replied, Count to ten and add VAT in the music business, and you're a genius! He would sometimes phone you up and be perfectly sweet. Normally, that's when he wanted something: *Can you drag this box of singles round the shops in Edinburgh?* He had problems with Bob Last of Fast as well. Alan considered what Bob was doing to be diametrically opposed to what *he* was doing. They had very different ways of dealing with things. I'm sure Bob would have seen Alan as an upstart, creeping into his territory.'

Horne had initially hoped to be in a band with Brian Taylor (later Brian Superstar of Pastels fame), with whom he shared dwellings at 185 West Princes Street. Modelling himself on Andy Warhol, he earmarked Collins as his Edie Sedgwick, his Joe Dalessandro—a pretty face who would be a conduit to fame and success. It was all rather fabulous, darling. He envisaged his patronage of a hip and happening new sound as something that had the potential to revolutionise the music business. He oversaw the label's low-budget cottage-industry aesthetic, nurtured a small coterie of helpers and hangers-on, and flirted with art and mixed media ventures such as *The Postcard Brochure*, a luxurious forty-page label manifesto. It was filled with photographs, lyrics, and loose narrative sections, while its delicate calligraphy (by Krysia Klasicki) lent it a sense of bespoke mystique.

'Alan had known Orange Juice a lot longer than us and obviously preferred their music,' admits Ross. 'But it could change at any time, what he thought was good. You would go up to his flat and he'd be playing a soul record, saying it was the best record ever made, insisting that the whole label should be making soul records. The Sound Of Young Scotland idea must have originated from one of those soul days. But then, the next day, he'd be playing a country & western record, and he'd be trying to find out how to get hold of a pedal-steel guitar for James Kirk and working out the best way for Orange Juice to go full-on Country.'

Horne's capriciousness was the stuff of legend. Bowie was God, Bowie was a hideous bore. Punk was where it was at, punk was for thugs and Neanderthals. And despite his fondness for Orange Juice, there was an element of friction and tension and teasing with Edwyn. 'Sometimes, he would even praise Josef K, just to get at Edwyn,' suggests Ross. 'He'd use lines such as, *You know, they were much better than you the last time you played together—the audience loved them more*.'

Although they were inseparable for long spells, Horne played on Collins's sense of vulnerability. 'Edwyn always wanted to sound very professional and slick,' adds Ross, 'but we were young and inexperienced. He was quite insecure. For instance, a little later, when Aztec Camera released their two singles on Postcard, Alan pronounced Roddy a *boy genius*, and that definitely compounded Edwyn's feelings of inadequacy.'

That is possibly one reason why Orange Juice never got around to recording an album for Postcard. Instead, their debut album would appear on Polydor in 1982. 'When we were first getting ready to do the record, we began to realise that Alan was losing his focus a bit,' remembers Steven Daly. 'There were new groups coming along that he was interested in. His mind worked very fast. Orange Juice had only been around for a year and a half, but we had established the label as a name. Before the first album, Edwyn had accumulated all these songs he had written. Everything was ready. But we were worried—in spite of the quality of the songs—that things could fall flat if Alan didn't put enough effort into promoting it because he was so likely to be distracted by other things. I mean, it was only him at the label. There were no other managers, just Alan. So, we went off to the major label, let them pick up the tab, released it through them, and then paid Geoff Travis back.'

Horne probably did 'lose focus' as he allowed his idea of an ever-expanding empire to cloud much of his decision-making. The loudest noise in his head, even louder than 'ka-ching, ka-ching', was the voice that told him he was a god among men. Sometimes, the only voice to find room in his head was Alan Horne's voice. While Edwyn was a trusted confidante, he was surrounded by sycophants, so there was always a danger he could lose control of things.

One constant remained—Horne's steadfast cynicism about Josef K. 'Even today, Alan Horne says he *never* liked us,' says Ross. 'He just needed another band for the label. He and Paul always had difficulties. He found

Paul's song titles and lyrics pretentious, and of course Paul, quite rightly, didn't think Alan should have any say at all in these things. Neither Paul nor I would allow Alan to dictate to us, nor would we have allowed Bob Last or anyone else to do that either.'

Despite Ross's suggestion of unity, it is likely that Horne unintentionally created, or at least deepened, an existing fault line within Josef K itself—one that undoubtedly impacted adversely on the group's gang-of-brothers mentality. Putting it somewhat crudely—although the truth is never quite as simple—Malcolm and Davy, who had always been very close friends, remained on relatively good terms with Horne, while Paul and Ronnie, still thick as thieves, found little to admire in him but plenty to mistrust. 'Syuzen [Buckley, Malcolm's then-girlfriend and future wife] and I would stay at West Princes Street a lot,' remembers Ross. 'David, Alan, and Trisha [who did the artwork for the singles] all stayed there. David moved out and Brian Taylor [Superstar] of The Pastels, moved in. It probably didn't help Josef K that I was pretty friendly with Alan and Orange Juice. Paul and Ronnie weren't at all. In fact, it's not an exaggeration to say that Ronnie hated Alan, and equally, Alan hated Ronnie.' This left Ross in an uncomfortable position, trying to keep the peace. 'I always tried to see both sides of the argument,' he adds. Torrance's dislike of Horne outweighed even Haig's. 'He was a lying bastard. I had no time for him,' he says bluntly.

Haig concurs with Ross's view that Alan's main concern was Orange Juice, rather than Josef K, but possibly felt this 'slight' more acutely than Malcolm. 'We were just another selling angle, whereas Orange Juice were a dream to him—a perfect mix of Tamla Motown, The Byrds, and a good bit of that West Coast sound. We were a bit more like The Velvet Underground compared to their Byrds. Orange Juice were definitely his thing. Josef K was just another band for his label. He didn't like me either, so we never got on together at all. To me, he was just a loudmouth. He wasn't averse to putting the boot in at times. I remember on one occasion, walking along past the university in Edinburgh. It was just Alan and the four of us. At the time, I was feeling really nervous and had a small rash on my chin, which I'd become pretty self-conscious about. Alan turned round and said snidely, Well at least I don't have a bad rash on my chin due to drug abuse. Malcolm gently admonished him, saying, Paul doesn't take drugs, Alan. But I never forgot that.'

Haig has alluded to the awkward relationship elsewhere, telling Simon Reynolds, 'Alan had this vision for Orange Juice all along—to turn them into a great pop band, but he found Josef K far too abrasive and dark.' By contrast, Malcolm and Davy made frequent trips through to Glasgow, where they found Horne's company as congenial as their bandmates did querulous. No doubt that aggravated some of the tensions between the two pairings within the group, and these would later grow from tiny fissures into cracks and cavities that would become impossible to fill.

However, despite their differing perspectives, there is little doubt Horne performed a crucial role in bringing Josef K's music into the public eye. 'Unlike Liverpool and Manchester, Glasgow didn't really have a Bill Drummond or Tony Wilson, anyone like that,' notes Steven Daly, whom history records as having had several bust-ups with Horne. 'To be honest, I don't remember rolling about on the floor with him very often. Maybe only once!'

Inarguably, Horne pushed the band into making some great records. 'To give Alan his due,' says Douglas McIntyre, 'he had great taste in music. The re-recorded version of "Chance Meeting" is absolutely fantastic, so if that was the result of him cajoling or bullying the band into doing it, then it was the right thing to do.'

Even Malcolm, who remained fond of Horne, recalls him having some 'madcap ideas. I remember one week he was all excited because he was writing to Elton John: We were thinking Elton John may just want to put up £20,000 for the record label, he said. He always wanted to make us feel like we were on the verge of much greater things. I remember too when "Radio Drill Time" had been out for a short while, Alan saying something like, Grace Jones is thinking about doing a version of the song for her next LP. Then you would speak to the guy at Rough Trade about it, and he would say, What?! Nah, I've just put it on a tape, and sent it to her.'

'Like Bob Last, Alan was very controlling,' says Ross. 'It was always a struggle to get things done without having to hand over too much control. Alan might have liked Television, but he hated Talking Heads, and he would never entertain a band like Pere Ubu. He would have identified them as prog-rock, so we were always at odds with Alan's aesthetic in a way that Orange Juice weren't. He had a postmodern *magpie* aesthetic. It worked well, probably because no one else was competent enough to do it in any way that made it seem identifiable.'

Unlike Horne, Josef K were realists. They wanted to create great music, not change the world. 'I was always puzzled by this desire some people had to 'change' the music industry,' reflects Ross. 'I don't know, do shoe designers want to change the shoe industry? But that was the plan for Alan, Bob [Last], and Stevo at Some Bizzare. The *Animal Farm* idea—the pigs getting up on their back legs, but with the best intentions. But the whole British post-punk thing had little relevance in the States. It had more relevance—due to its artiness, I suppose—in Europe, but even there, the person who sold the most records in Germany in the 1990s was David Hasselhoff!'

The nearest to a genuine mentor figure for the young band was certainly Campbell. He had a good knowledge of music, knew all the right reference points, and understood how to organise and advocate effectively. Listening to him recall his role as the band's manager, one immediately detects the fatherly guiding instinct absent from Horne's psychological makeup.

'Like a lot of great groups, Josef K knew each other from school, but they connected well as people and worked together as people—a friendly falling together,' Campbell says. 'Malcolm taught Davy to play bass, for example. The best groups are often small gangs. They understand one another and protect one another. And with Josef K, their personalities definitely complemented one another.'

Campbell was instrumental, too, in securing lucrative support slots for the band, some of which were vital in fermenting their reputation as an electrifying live act. 'They were a force of nature,' remembers Mike O'Connor. 'The interplay between Haig and Ross was incredible. There was a burning frenzy about them, and Paul in particular was just mesmerising. They looked like they were from the future—the band who fell to earth.' Even so, occasionally things might not work out quite as planned, as Campbell recalls: 'I remember negotiating a support slot via an agent for a show in Grangemouth supporting Echo & The Bunnymen. Less than two hundred people turned out and the band had to change in the toilets! There was never any grand plan, but there was definitely a shared excitement, and that propelled things forward.'

Even so, Campbell had several competing commitments, and a more burning question for the band remained—could Josef K really afford to pay a manager? 'I was holding down a job as a secondary school teacher, putting on bands, and managing another band called The Delmontes,' says Campbell. 'It was completely crackers. When Josef K got a distribution deal with Rough Trade, I stopped working with them. Malcolm was a practical guy. They weren't really making any money from the records, whereas I had a number of other jobs, so it made sense to let me go. The band had to begin looking after themselves. Whatever money was coming in, they would have to live off that. I had no argument with that.'

Campbell's departure was arguably of more significance than anyone realised at the time. The absence of his avuncular presence left them at the mercy of Horne. Nevertheless, despite his apparent indifference, the Postcard imprint would pay dividends for the band—at least in one sense.

It meant their names and faces were now splattered all over the music press. There was little or no money coming in, but the world now knew their name and people were listening to their music.

From his legendary sock drawer, Horne hoped to mastermind the future of the music biz. And, with three bands on the roster, his plans seemed to be reaching fruition. The silver-tongued devil even managed to wangle a lucrative distribution deal with Geoff Travis at Rough Trade. To begin with, Rough Trade had reckoned Josef K's demo tape to sound 'unprofessional' and were extremely reluctant to get involved. Now that the band were on Postcard, Rough Trade were fully on board and soon trying to fix up a UK tour. Horne's plan was to release three singles—one by each act—at the same time: The Go-Betweens' 'I Need Two Heads', 'Blue Boy' by Orange Juice, and Josef K's 'Radio Drill Time'.

Postcard might have seemed like the happening label of the moment, but the reality was somewhat different. In fact, it was always a fragile proposition. 'Compared to Factory or Fast, Postcard had no capital,' insists Daly.' You got a sense that those labels were able to expand but Postcard never had any money. Alan only had as much money as the next record. It was very hand-to-mouth and extremely fucking unpleasant. That's the funny thing about indie rock—people think it's happy-go-lucky and whatever, and I'm sure it was for some of the bands which came after into a pre-existing format. But actually it was really unpleasant. It wasn't run like a business. It was all a bit excitable and haphazard.'

'The amateurishness of the label wasn't deliberate,' suggests Malcolm Ross. 'Subsequently, many labels have been deliberately amateurish. I've never liked that.'

Josef K's liaison with Horne would never be the marriage made in heaven that some made it out to be. Nevertheless, along with Orange Juice, Josef K were now The Sound Of Young Scotland, and for the moment, at least, Postcard—that most dysfunctional of families—was home.

8/15 | NIGHT RITUAL / FUN 'N' FRENZY

Josef K's very raison d'être was to combat tired, clichéd ideas about rock'n'roll—in the parlance of the time, they were anti-rockist. They rejected the age-old notion of the musician as degenerate hedonist, and played music that was terse and smart, all bursts of energy and no solos. They didn't do drugs (at least, not at this point), they hardly drank, and they weren't womanisers or groupie magnets.

PAUL LESTER, *RECORD COLLECTOR*, 2007

To obtain optimum value for money, Orange Juice and Josef K were booked in to Castle Sound together on April 30, 1980. Orange Juice recorded 'Blue Boy' and 'Lovesick' in the early afternoon before Josef K followed them to lay down 'Radio Drill Time'.

The B-side to the single, 'Crazy To Exist', was recorded in Wilf Smarties' living room. Smarties was the frontman of local outfit Mowgli & The Doughnuts and was a familiar acquaintance of both Allan Campbell and the band.

Thung-thung-thung-thung-thung-thung-clang-a-clang-a-clang.
(Brrp brrp brrp brrp brrp brrp brrp brrp)

There's so many pathways that lead to the heart
The records were letters, the wrong place to start.

Lyrics that communicate uncertainty. One observation about Paul Haig's role as a lyricist is that he unfailingly sought to treat the listener with respect. Like an adult. An equal. He may have been a teenager himself, but Josef K's songs were never intended to be singalongs for the school playground. It wasn't that they were obscene or dealt with adult themes. But they presumed the audience was intelligent enough to interpret them in their own way, in much the same way as, for example, Bresson, Bergman, or Tarkovsky made films. None of those directors would have been remotely inclined to direct the viewer toward a predetermined conclusion. Let the viewer work it out for himself. Why explain anything? 'A book read by a thousand people is a thousand different books,' the Russian director once said. Likewise, Haig was not one for being deliberately obtuse, but his songs were borne out of an overwhelming sense of the absurdity of everything, and he did not possess an ego sufficiently large to impose upon others his sombre worldview. 'That's definitely what I hoped to convey,' he says, 'although there are still parts of some songs that are very personal.'

The lyrics to Josef K's first Postcard 45 were at least partly inspired by the sleeve notes to Lou Reed's 1975 act of folly (or genius, depending on your own worldview), *Metal Machine Music*. 'Radio Drill Time' would establish Josef K as one of the most exciting bands of the era. Its modernist element comes in part from its tight mathematical precision, but also from the *wrrblllwwwoooyeooouppp* radio signals that lend it its disorientating atmosphere. 'It was one of only a few occasions I was in the studio with them,' recalls Allan Campbell. 'They were completely in control over what they were doing. They knew exactly what they wanted. It was all done very quickly in one half day.'

The two records were produced by Alex Ferguson, who also produced Alternative TV, and were released in hand-coloured sleeves that folded one way then another. Josef K's 'side' was drawn by Robbie Kelly. 'You folded it in half, printed on one side, and hand-coloured with felt tip pens,' says Ross. 'Lots of hangers-on would drop by at West Princes Street and they would each take a few sleeves to colour in.' The photo on the reverse was taken—once the last customer had been seen off—in the hairdressing boutique where Ronnie worked, Brian Drumm.

'Radio Drill Time' confirmed that since their first outing for Absolute, Josef K had evolved into a more formidable and far more adventurous unit. Synchronous to their sonic progression was an acceleration of commitments, with live dates becoming more frequent, but imagination and confidence were flowing freely, and the band's youthful ardour meant there was bags of energy for it all.

Before long, Josef K had begun to outpace other more well-established Scottish bands—at least in a creative sense—and the two sides of their first Postcard 45 provided an archetype for the sound they were looking for. Next to the slightly gawky 'Chance Meeting', the shrink-wrapped guitar and jagged rhythmic intensity of 'Radio Drill Time' was far a more robust proposition, a double-breasted Italian suit—buttons tightly fastened, cufflinks glistening, posture straightening—next to its predecessor's slightly slovenly corduroy, 'art teacher' feel. Instead of mimicking Joy Division's near-military precision, the unorthodox hi-hat timings add layers of strangeness, later accentuated by the warbling radio signals. John Peel played it regularly on his show throughout the autumn of 1980. It became something of a firm favourite, and it wouldn't be too long before he tried to get the band in session.

The oblique solemnity of the lyrics would become something of a trademark of Haig's. Like Camus laying 'his heart open to the benign indifference of the universe', he would agonise over those verses more than his bandmates could possibly imagine. It was a responsibility that gave him sleepless nights, and he remained eternally dubious of their merit, concerned about how they might be interpreted or scrutinised—by the listener, by his bandmates, by anyone who might actually sit down to read them. Perhaps they would think him naive, or worse pretentious?

Alan Horne's indifference wouldn't have helped. Writing music was usually a collaborative occupation, although Malcolm would sometimes take the lead with it, but the lyrics were entirely Paul's business. He was—and remains—guarded about their meaning, partly because they were at times so acutely personal. 'Paul would never have discussed his lyrics with anyone,' says Ross. 'They were quite ethereal. Song lyrics don't have to be poetry. They weren't conventional love songs. Edwyn wrote songs like that and always did. With Josef K, we wanted to write the sort of songs that hadn't been written before.'

'The lyrics always started from the music,' says Haig. 'A couple of chords or notes gets me started. I would visualise things and then the subconscious stuff would emerge—memories and so on. I always was at pains to capture the way I was thinking at the time. It was important to be economical, but having to condense everything made it even more difficult. I was quite taken with Japanese Noh texts, which encouraged me to try to get things communicated in a tight form.' It's something he managed expertly on 'Radio Drill Time'.

Despite its title, the flip side, 'Crazy To Exist', was a far more upbeat affair, boasting a super-elastic bass riff—possibly lifted from The Fall's 'No Xmas For John Quays'—alongside guitars so trebly they sound like a boxful of broken bells. Haig, in peak Knut Hamsun mode, sounds characteristically fatalistic ('*Oh, this is your life, this is so small / Sleeping in doorways, corners and halls / Sometimes I know, it's crazy to exist*'). Musically, the song shifts shape around two minutes in, the tempo gradually beginning to de-escalate. It remains one of the singer's most impassioned vocal performances, and he sounds near delirious as the song reaches its climax, aided and abetted by a surging icy racket of feedback.

—

Josef K had reinvented themselves, but despite the huge sonic leap forward, 'Radio Drill Time' / 'Crazy To Exist (Live)' initially received a lukewarm response from the music press. For *Record Mirror*'s Chris Westwood, who interviewed the band at the time of the release, it was 'a loose attack on music media "sensitivity", a positive understated tugging of flat colourless guitar and enthusiastic rhythm: a shoddy useful pop record.' Paul Rombali of the *NME* concluded, 'Songs about the radio seem to be born either out of a desire to get played on the radio or a desire to get revenge for not being played on the radio. It would take a deft sardonic touch to mix the right amounts of praise and put-down and create a record that numbers the faults of pop radio at the same time as it fits all its bills. This is likeable enough for several other reasons, but it's not that soldier.'

If early reactions were muted, reviews such as Rombali's prompted *Sounds'* Dave McCullough to come to the band's defence. 'The cruds who've pissed over this singular gem for the past two weeks in their own glibly dim way, ought to be kennelled and then put down with a large unpleasant needle. Suffice to say, "Radio Drill Time" is soulfully mournful and vitally modernistic, it is up to date and beyond that.'

Shortly before this review, McCullough had penned a feature about the new wave of Scottish bands entitled 'Postcard From Paradise'. *Sounds* had been the first of the weekly music papers to shed the spotlight on Horne's exciting new label. 'Scotland seems to have digested punk-and-after like no other area in the country,' he exclaimed, before contrasting the 'shiny-faced and maddeningly eclectic' Orange Juice with Josef K's 'unsmiling music—intense and unhappy ... absurdly modernist.'

Along with Paul Morley, McCullough had been one of Joy Division's greatest champions. With the death of Ian Curtis, a chasm opened up, and the pair were intent upon 'discovering' the next big thing. In what turned out to be a revealing interview, McCullough sought to meet separately with the two bands. Naturally, perhaps, Horne positioned himself with his Glasgow protégés, even going so far as to confess to McCullough that Josef K 'were not really my cup of tea'. The writer, meanwhile, considered his audience with Josef K to be one of the strangest interviews he'd ever undertaken. A series of uncomfortable silences were punctuated by the occasional allusion to literature ('Have you read Herman Hesse?') and admissions to collective feelings of inadequacy at, well... giving interviews. At the end, the writer left bewildered.

'Josef K make me feel superstitious and ready to, as is fitting in the context of their Kafka name, leap out of the next window,' McCullough quipped. Nevertheless, it is interesting to note that his article predicted Josef K would ultimately outsell and outlast their Glasgow counterparts. Who knows upon what basis his prediction was based? At that time, there was a plethora of ersatz Joy Divisions springing up all over the place, and possibly he reckoned Josef K's music a closer approximation to that archetype, and to futurism, than Orange Juice's. If so, he was right about that, at least, if well wide of the mark with his prediction.

Shortly after, Haig would be inspired by Curtis's passing to write Josef K's next 45. On the night after the singer's suicide, Malcolm Ross was informed of the grim news backstage at one of the earliest shows by the newly formed East Kilbride outfit Aztec Camera. Despite his shock, he was immediately struck by the fresh-faced precocious talent of the band's singer/guitarist, Roddy Frame. It wouldn't be long before he made an approach, hoping to persuade him to 'sign' to Postcard.

Initially, at least, Frame appeared reluctant—he had already sent a demo to Zoo Records, clinching his band a support slot with The Teardrop Explodes—but having by now convinced Horne, Ross persisted.

He perhaps oughtn't have. With the cruellest of ironies, it was a liaison which would spectacularly backfire for Josef K, given that Frame's arrival—following a second recommendation, this time courtesy of The Bluebells' Robert Hodgens—prefigured their own relegation further down the pecking order as any kind of real priority for the label's owner. From the moment Horne's 'boy wonder' arrived, Josef K were barely an afterthought.

1980 was the year Josef K perfected their sound. It was also a year of increased media exposure. But they appeared to be taking it all in their stride. They had little time to think, reflect, or plan ahead, and for the time being, at least, they were happy to live in the moment. They had their feet planted firmly on the ground, even while they were carving a reputation as a terrific live act and as what Ian Rankin calls 'pioneers of a new glacial European music. We'd gone through punk and we came out to something that seemed to be a little bit more cerebral, a little bit brainier. The performances, the staging, everything was monochrome, very stylized, very European. I think folk had been looking at Kraftwerk, and there was a sort of uniform that bands would wear, with nobody really standing out or showing off. They had those white shirts buttoned up to the collar. The notion of the frontman disappeared a bit with Josef K. It was like every member of the band had equal billing. The frontman as spokesperson— they didn't seem to be into that at all. If you didn't know the band and you saw a photograph of them in *Sounds* or *NME*, you would be hard placed to point to one of them and say that's the singer. They didn't play that game.'

Audiences were won over by the verve and taut energy of Josef K's performances. In 1980, they were almost always on top form. The late drummer Ian Stoddart, who played with several Edinburgh bands, most notably alongside Davy Henderson in Win, recalled seeing them on February 22, 1980, at the Nite Club: 'It was a great venue, right above the Playhouse on Leith Walk. They had photos at the top of the stairs and you would look out for yourself to see if you had made it on there—eager to find out if you were part of the in-crowd! There were bands on all weekend. I remember the first night I went there. It was the first weekend after the place opened. What a great bill: Josef K and Scars! I remember walking in and seeing these four guys on stage in white shirts looking dead cool. I was a huge fan of Josef K. I preferred them to Scars. There was just something about them—a postmodernist thing. It was really coming from The Velvet Underground, but via Joy Division and Talking Heads. Josef K were fantastic. They had great chemistry onstage.'

It was as a live band that Josef K really began to enhance their reputation and standing. 'I remember playing a gig in London,' says Torrance. 'We were headlining, and after the soundcheck we left the venue to go for a bite to eat. When we came back, they were queued round the corner. It suddenly felt like we'd arrived.'

'On form, Josef K were unstoppable,' claims Allan Campbell. 'However, sometimes their guitar sound couldn't be replicated live. They were reliant on sound engineers who didn't always understand what they were looking for. Early on, I would try to speak to the PA guy and try to explain what they needed, but the sound balance was definitely not as good as it could be at times.'

Steven Daly remembers witnessing a series of sonic assaults. 'It was a full-on attack. I remember "Crazy To Exist"—songs like that were very tightly wound. There weren't a lot of highs and lows, no light and shade, little variation in the dynamics.' David McClymont concurs. 'In a live setting, when the alchemy was there, their performances could be electrifying. They were one of the best live bands you could see.'

—

'I tried to see Josef K live as many times as I could,' says Nick Currie. 'I saw them at the Edinburgh Art School's Wee Red Bar, then at the

Astoria supporting Magazine—a dream bill for me.' Currie had been a music writer, writing reviews for the Aberdeen student paper *Gaudie*, and was mesmerised by several of the early post-punk bands. 'I particularly loved Wire and Magazine and The Passage. I remember going to gigs by people like Simple Minds, Magazine, or The Slits and finding only about twenty people in the audience, in places like Robert Gordon's Institute Of Technology in Aberdeen. There was a massive indifference on the part of the public, even to bands that were getting a certain amount of hype in the national press. But I got very excited by Postcard Records and latched onto Josef K in particular because I liked their artiness. I was also a huge Kafka fan.'

Toward the end, Currie's enthusiasm engineered his access to the band's rehearsals, and he grew closer to them personally. 'I was in utter awe of them. I remember running to a rehearsal and tripping in my frenzy, ripping my baggy waiter-style New Romantic trousers!' he recalls in the liner notes sleeve to the *Endless Soul* compilation album. (Before going on to become a critics' favourite as Momus in the mid-80s, Currie would front the first post-Josef K offshoot, Happy Family, alongside the band's rhythm section and, albeit very briefly, Malcolm Ross. They would sign to 4AD, but their impact was minimal.)

The night at the Astoria to which Currie alludes occurred on April 28, 1980. Josef K were once again—like at January's Clash gig—third, and un-named, on the bill. Bauhaus made up the triumvirate, playing in between. Prior to the gig, Haig and Ross had hardly been avid fans of Pete Murphy and co, whose vampirish stench and vacuous proto-goth they found unbearable. Sharing a bill with them—and those ugly stacks of black hair in the audience—confirmed their worst suspicions.

The Astoria—at Abbeymount, close to Holyrood Palace—had formerly been known as Stewart's Ballroom. It had a fairly small stage, and on this occasion, due to the sizeable bill, there was an exceptionally large amount of equipment with no place to house it. 'Magazine and Bauhaus had already soundchecked,' says Allan Campbell, 'and the doors were about to open, but there was barely enough room for Josef K's gear. Paul couldn't play guitar because there wasn't room for his amp. Time was running out.'

Demonstrating an impressive line in prima-donna tactics, Murphy's mob rejected the band's request to create a few feet of space. With typical presence of mind, Campbell sought a solution and approached Magazine's sound engineer to ask about adapting the sound, given that they had one guitar out of commission.

'What kind of sound *is* this?' the engineer asked.

'I said, Do you know Television?' Campbell recalls, 'and he replied, I did some work with Television, I know exactly what you're looking for. Given the circumstances, he did a fantastic job. But that was a constant problem. Josef K were doing something with a very particular edge and it was difficult to get the sound right. But when it worked, it was hair on the back of the neck stuff.'

In June, the band had another high-profile engagement, supporting The Cure on two dates: first at Glasgow City Hall on June 18, and then two days later at Edinburgh's George Square Theatre, a show organised by Campbell. Those who witnessed the Glasgow show claim to have seen Josef K at the absolute peak of their game.

'It was the middle of the summer and light was streaming in through the windows,' recalls fan Hugh Mulholland. 'It had the feel of an outdoor gig. The stage was huge as it would normally have space for an orchestra, so the band looked tiny. Josef K were amazing, but my abiding memory is of being chased by a local hard man on Castle Street as I headed for home.'

It seems there was more than a whiff of violence in the air that evening. Malcolm Ross recalls the band themselves experiencing a similar confrontation. 'My memory involves Jake Black [later of Alabama 3].

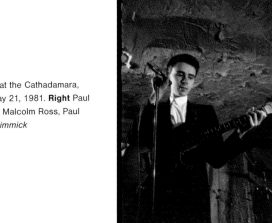

Josef K live at the Cathadamara, Glasgow, May 21, 1981. **Right** Paul Haig. **Below** Malcolm Ross, Paul Haig. *Alan Dimmick*

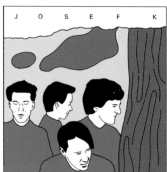

Above Josef K in full flight, live at Valentino's, Edinburgh, August 16, 1981. *Alastair McKay* **Left** 'Sorry For Laughing' single artwork. **Below** Portraits of the band. *Jordi Maxwell* **Opposite** Record sleeves, *clockwise from top left*: 'Chance Meeting' (Postcard version); 'Radio Drill Time' (picture sleeve); 'Radio Drill Time' (Postcard sleeve); *The Only Fun In Town*; *Sorry For Laughing*; 'Radio Drill Time' (picture sleeve reverse).

Amsterdam, 1981. **Main image** Malcolm lighting a ciggie. **Inset** The teams that meet in caffs (*left to right*: Haig, Ross, Weddell, Torrance); strolling around the city. *Fran van der Hoeven*

JOSEF K

BEURSSCHOUWBURG
08/04/1981 20.30
CONCERT·VIDEOS
220 FB/PHC-TTT:160 FB
22 RUE ORTS STRAAT
1000 BXL TEL 5112525
KO-PRODUKTIE/TION
BEURSSCHOUWBURG &
RISQUES DU CREPUSCULE

DESSIN JEAN-FRANÇOIS OCTAVE D'APRES FELIX ELIAS 1926/138/-JOSEF K·THE SCOTTISH AFFAIR·PART 1·80/-M·P·I703B17/01

ПИОНЕР

Original Material by :
Bauhaus-Membranes-Wally Van Middendorp (Minny Pops)-Billy Mackenzie (Associates)-Wendy Smith -Paul Weller (Jam)-Stuart Moxham (Y-M-G,Gist)- Joop van Brakel (Nasmak)-Colin Newman-Section XXV →Josef K.

POSTCARD RECORDS

"B" side

JOSEF K

50P

Josef k

Above Original Postcard promo photos.
Opposite Poster for a gig in Brussels; punk
fanzine *Pioneer* #2, featuring lyrics to 'Sorry
For Laughing' and an illustration by Malcolm;
Japanese promotional postcard; the Postcard
Brochure, 1981. *Courtesy of Mike O'Connor*

The final show at Maestro's, Glasgow,
August 23, 1981. **Left** Ronnie Torrance.
Right Davy Weddell. **Below** Men in black,
facing away from one another: Malcolm
Ross, Paul Haig. *Derek Louden*

He had formed a band, The Dialectics, but I'm not sure if they ever actually performed. They were rough and scary guys. We got out of the car at the entrance to the venue and one of them, known as Parky, grabbed Paul by the scruff of the neck, demanding, We better be on the guest list tonight, so make sure you take down our names! We had to apologise, saying, We're sorry, we'd have been glad to do that, but we've been told we can't get anybody on the guest list. One of his mates shouted, Parky, leave 'em alone, they cannae do it! Events like that were pretty common, to be honest.'

Highlights of the show included a smouldering version of The Doors' 'Crystal Ship'. Backstage, The Cure were happy to chat and offer encouragement, expressing admiration for the band's performance. At the same time, however, Robert Smith attributed blame for his band's tour bus breaking down on the way to the gig to Haig & co, insisting the ill fortune they had encountered to be a direct consequence of Josef K taking their name from Kafka's persecuted protagonist. If that sounds weird, it was an even greater surprise to hear that Alan Horne was uncharacteristically bowled over by their performance. It was one of the few times he expressed even a modicum of admiration for the band.

Seeing Josef K supporting The Cure at Glasgow City Halls that night changed the life of young Douglas McIntyre, aspiring guitar-slinger of Article 58 and future author of *Hungry Beat*. 'It was a total revelation. They appeared otherworldly, emanating wit, charm, and intelligence. I saw every Josef K live performance in Scotland thereafter.' Indeed, McIntyre's band would be invited by Josef K to support them on a UK tour in the Autumn. 'I was a fan first and foremost. I was a fan with a guitar in my hand. Article 58 only made one record, but when we toured with Josef K, it was amazing, watching your favourite band every night. And they were incredible. One gig with The Fire Engines in Edinburgh sticks out as being particularly memorable. Both groups were burning up at this point. The sound and fury fused with white light and heat demanding total attention.

Their guitars were on a collision course with Venus, sparking electrical stimulation in their trail. The blank generation was left trying to decode the scrambled frequencies!'

McIntyre's love affair with Josef K opened up new possibilities, with Alan Horne offering to produce a single for Article 58. The end result was a single on Allan Campbell's label, Rational. Malcolm Ross even accompanied McIntyre & co to the studio in Strathaven to oversee the recording.

Other memorable evenings followed, such as the Tribute To Frank Sinatra event at Valentino's on August 21, 1980. There were four bands on the bill that night (Scars, The Associates, and The Fire Engines being the others). 'I made a terrible poster for it,' says Nick Currie, 'but to be honest none of the bands were at their absolute best. Generally, however, Josef K were incredibly exciting as a live act. They dressed like Czech waiters with their shirts buttoned up to the top. Paul Haig shyly kept his sunglasses on. There was a coiled intensity to their presence, which matched the abrasive guitar sound. They would do a big climax to "Adoration" then leave the stage, and never encore. Paul had some of the coolness and coldness of Lou Reed. I found him a bit scary. Malcolm definitely seemed much more approachable.'

The refusal to play encores was a principle sealed in blood—one of the fundamental articles of the Josef K constitution. 'I always used to find encores patronising,' Ross later told Simon Reynolds. 'The roadies would come on to pack up the guitars, but if you clapped loud enough the band would come on again. That was the kind of ritual that Postcard wanted to change.'

The brevity of Josef K's live shows would alienate some audiences—in much the same way as The Fire Engines or those Jesus & Mary Chain performances midway through the 80s. But the band had another problem to contend with when they travelled down to London in mid-November for a show at the London Lyceum. Paul was struggling with the flu.

The show had been organised by John Curd of Strait Music and featured The Teardrop Explodes, The Fire Engines, and The Thompson Twins (who, pre-'Doctor Doctor', were a completely different proposition altogether). 'It was a fantastic line-up,' insists Allan Campbell. 'Everybody drove down except Paul, who was really ailing. I think he flew down and spent much of the gig sitting down.' Davy Weddell's most vivid recollection was missing a few notes after spotting Kevin Rowland in the front row of the audience. The band played 'Sister Ray' for ten minutes, with Malcolm on lead vocal.

'We played a few instrumentals,' recalls Ross. 'Despite Paul's illness, we chose to perform because we wanted to get paid. The Thompson Twins were on the bill—they were a pretty grungy, indie-type band at the time. They had approached us beforehand and suggested they go on after us. They wanted to leapfrog us on the bill, but we told them *no chance*. There were about thirteen of them—they were like a big hippie collective. Joy Division were there in the crowd too. We had driven down except for Paul, who was always a bad traveller. He didn't like being away from home, and he didn't like driving, whereas I quite enjoyed driving, overnight sometimes. His dad bought him a plane ticket.'

Events such as the Lyceum show ensured Josef K's profile remained high, and their next single, 'It's Kinda Funny', proved to be a masterstroke. Stylistically, it was unlike anything else they had recorded.

You may be dumb
But the passage of time
Can change anything
Like the feelings we find

'The first line was about a girl who was dumb to my feelings for her,' remembers Haig, 'but the rest is definitely reflecting upon Ian Curtis's death. I mean, he was twenty-three and he'd gone so quickly. I wrote it just after that happened, and the bass line is clearly a Joy Division bass line. I was reading a lot of books, having a lot of existentialist thoughts. But it all blended in to make a song about how fragile life is. That's really what it's about in a nutshell. It was one of the quickest songs I'd ever written. It took twenty minutes. I was going out that night to meet someone in the Tap O' Laurieston, and I just had an idea—the bass line came first. I used to record demos with two tape recorders bouncing off one another. Really hi-tech! It produced a terrible sound. But it was a way to get two parts, so you'd play bass and then overdub voice and guitar. Anyway, it became a cheery little song about the human condition.'

Perhaps not so cheery, but undoubtedly one of the band's most celebrated songs. The quivering viola played by Ross, possibly in homage to The Velvet Underground, provides a haunting backdrop. The song manages to achieve a level of transcendence that's absent from much of their otherwise frenetically paced work. Momentarily, as verse leans into chorus, the rhythm threatens to accelerate, the monochromatic guitar breaking into a mild shuffle before adding some deftly angular lines and Syndrum pow-pows, but what emerges is a cool ballad revealing great restraint, suggesting a depth of character hitherto disguised by noise and pent-up emotion. Despite that, the band ended up disappointed with the version Postcard decided to release, and sporadic rumours have circulated that foul play was involved.

'A couple of days after we'd recorded "It's Kinda Funny", Orange Juice were in at Castle Sound Studio to record "Simply Thrilled Honey",' recalls Malcolm Ross. 'I went along to that session as well, played a wee bit of piano and synth on it. After the session, we said that we'd listen to "It's Kinda Funny", then the mood kind of changed. There was a collective sense among the Orange Juice members that our song sounded better than what they had just done. And perhaps a feeling that I was making sure that the Josef K song sounded better. There was a bit of banter, but I could sense the hostility. The records were mastered at the same time, but when ours came out, the way it was mastered was bass-heavy. But I wouldn't claim it was sabotage or anything. All the same, Alan Horne said to me, If you're not happy with how this sounds, it wasn't me who wanted the extra bass put on it.'

Some rivalry had always existed between the two bands, precariously balanced with a fragile sense of brotherhood. Horne could quite easily upset the delicate equilibrium with a crude or dismissive comment. 'Alan was and is in the habit of making grand statements,' notes Jon Savage. 'Perhaps the Glasgow/Edinburgh thing had something to do with it. I thought Josef K were the perfect foil for Orange Juice, the one putting their goofiest foot forward but being quite serious and vice versa. I thought Josef K's rather austere demeanour was rather lightened by the fast tempo and lightness of the music.'

Despite those tensions, Ross recalls the band 'trying to present a united front to bands outside of the label. Alan nurtured a rivalry between Josef K and Orange Juice on the one hand, and the likes of Altered Images and Positive Noise on the other.' But while Orange Juice were in no rush to lose their pre-eminent position as Postcard poster boys, or even more importantly as press darlings, 'Simply Thrilled Honey' was never a match for 'It's Kinda Funny'.

A concert at Mick's Club in Carlisle in August brought the situation to a head. 'Allan Campbell had organised it, so naturally we presumed Josef K would headline,' recalls Ross. 'But Steven and Alan Horne weren't happy about that, believing that Orange Juice should go on last. I put my foot down and said no. Edwyn pretended he wasn't bothered, but I think secretly he was. Steven said something along the lines of, Well, we just want to do what's best for you, because we'll go down better than you. My recollection is that we went down much better than they did.'

The music press had come full circle too because Josef K had come full circle. There was near-universal praise for the band's new song. Dave McCullough wrote about both of the new Postcard 45s in the same *Sounds* review of November 29, 1980: 'Both records are so utterly brilliant in conception, so teasingly familiar yet distinctive in style and form . . . "It's Kinda Funny" makes Jilted John as tenderly emotional, as GENTLE as the Cambridge rapist. Stern and silent [they] remove the Successors To Joy Division crown for two and a half minutes and muse misty-eyed toward infinity, asking only WHAT IS LOVE?'

As a taster for the forthcoming LP, 'It's Kinda Funny' certainly whetted the appetite. Allan Campbell hailed the song as 'very mature. The thing that was distinctive about Paul was his kind of torch singer aesthetic: *The Face* magazine; that cool jazz aesthetic. He definitely had that. His distant demeanour. It definitely worked on stage, if not in person. He was a very charismatic guy.' Paul Morley concurred, later writing in the liner notes to *Entomology*, 'It sounded exactly like the singer in a group called Josef K should sound. It sounded like Josef K himself would sound if he slipped into this world and lurked behind the eerie modernised disguise of a pop song.'

For a brief beautiful moment, the whole world—and the inkies *were* the whole world to a generation of young people—was digging Josef K, and there were many writers who were eager to take advantage of the uplift. Chris Westwood talked up the Edinburgh scene in *Record Mirror*, although in his interview the band expressed some wariness about the possibility of being exploited by the London music-biz moguls, citing the experience of Another Pretty Face, who had very recently recorded an album that was rejected by Virgin. They were swiftly jettisoned by the label thereafter. Josef K were aware of the challenges traditionally faced by Scottish bands, who were accustomed to being overlooked by the parochialism of the UK record industry. Groups such as The Beatstalkers and The Poets had enjoyed a fair measure of success locally in the 60s without making significant inroads down south. That had been a long time ago, but there had been recent reminders too. Only a few years earlier, Wishaw band The Jolt had burnt out quickly after signing with Polydor. These instances would undoubtedly have had some bearing on the direction Josef K would take and possibly strengthened their inclination to stay with Postcard.

As well as Westwood, by now Paul Morley had become an ardent supporter of the band, regularly giving positive reviews in his inimitably loquacious prose. The band welcomed the reviews, but always with a pinch of salt. 'With Paul Morley, you couldn't take it too seriously,' smiles Haig. 'You just had to laugh at it, or else you would lose your mind. He was saying outrageous things: *Is this man [Haig] too cool to live?* [Actually from an *NME* review by the late Gavin Martin.] What could you say to that? It was nice to have that exposure, but I tried not to take it too seriously. Even at that time, you knew next week it would be someone else.'

Immediately prior to the Lyceum show, the time had come for Josef K to enter Castlesound Studios to record their debut album. Everything pointed to a modern classic.

9/15 | HIGH TIMES / LOW COUNTRIES

*Maybe [Europeans] had a greater appreciation and understanding
of the Kafka reference than people back home?*

DAVY WEDDELL

With recording sessions for the album completed, Josef K headed to the
continent to spend the last day of 1980 in the unlikeliest of locations.
Brussels. They were booked to play alongside Orange Juice at Plan K,
a bohemian establishment located at 21 Rue de Manchester. The event,
arranged by Allan Campbell, was promoted by local journalists Michel
Duval and Annik Honore. Honore's brief but intense relationship with
Ian Curtis had led in part to the Joy Division singer's suicide in May. The
couple had recently set up their own label, Les Disques du Crépuscule, and
Duval and Honore had offered to record something by Josef K while the
band was in Europe.

It seemed decidedly odd that a bunch of Scots would be spending
Hogmanay in Belgium. But it was an evening that would live long in the
memory. This was the first time Josef K had played outside of the UK, and
it would prove to be a pivotal moment in their career.

Things almost came undone before they had even reached the venue.

Simply getting to the Belgian capital proved a farcical experience. In order to save money, the band hired an old Luton van. Everyone (the members of Orange Juice, roadie Paul Mason, Campbell, and Horne, as well as Malcolm and Davy) squeezed into the death trap, taking turns to slum it in the back, where crumpled sleeping bags could barely relieve the discomfort caused by the absence of light and ventilation.

Paul and Ronnie, meanwhile, decided on an alternative strategy. To hell with rolling about the floor in the dark doing everything within your power not to heave your guts up. Instead, they opted to take the train. But this arrangement proved to be even more disastrous. As the train sped furiously southward toward its destination, the pair had been given strict instructions upon their arrival in Dover to look out for a white, windowless vehicle, but, after wandering around the ferry terminal for what seemed like an eternity, they were unable to find any trace of it. Unbeknown to Haig and Torrance, their Brussels-bound companions were still crawling down the M11 and had yet to reach the old port. Trains, it seems, travel faster than Luton vans. What today, in the technological age, would be a simple problem to resolve proved back then to be almost impossible.

To complicate proceedings, Allan Campbell had retained Paul and Ronnie's passports for safekeeping, meaning the pair didn't have the necessary documents to board the ferry. Before long, the bewildered, slightly suspicious-looking duo were detained and grilled by border guards. Following a few phone calls home to their respective parents, they were released and somewhat forlornly made their way back home to Edinburgh. As their train rattled northward again, the remaining passengers arrived at the ferry terminal. Campbell immediately called the Haig household and was informed by Haig's father of the mix-up, before reassuring him the passports were being kept safe at the ticket desk for the two, by now dog-tired, adventurers. When they arrived home, they barely had time for a cup of tea before booking tickets for the next train south.

'Ron and I had a hell of a time getting there. We travelled for two full days and were totally exhausted,' Haig recalls ruefully. To rub salt in the wounds, after finally arriving in Brussels, the pair had barely a moment to tend to their empty bellies. They managed to spot a Turkish restaurant near the venue. Ronnie ordered a burger and salad, while Paul was served up a platter of sheep brains. 'I tried to explain to the waiter that I was vegetarian,' he recalls. Unfortunately, his polite request got lost in translation, and after the offending article was taken back to the kitchen, 'they brought them back hidden under a pile of coleslaw!' Ronnie managed to tear a few chunks out of his overcooked beef before the pair sprinted to the venue, making it with minutes to spare.

Plan K was a highly unusual venue, regularly populated by hardcore anarcho-punks and skinheads. Tonight was no different. 'It was a big multimedia event in a four-story warehouse,' says Ross. 'Films were being shown. There were art installations and chill-out rooms. There was a weird hardcore punk element in the audience. There were older, arty-type people there too, but there was a bit of friction between them and the punkier crowd.'

The omens weren't good, and the band felt relieved that Orange Juice were scheduled to take to the stage first. 'Orange Juice went onstage while we were in the dressing room, but it had a window so you could watch what was happening onstage from there. Unfortunately, they didn't go down too well. They were heckled really badly. I think they were just too jingly-jangly for the audience, and everyone started to get agitated, pogoing and jumping around and shouting, before a plate of chicken and rice hit Edwyn in the face. It was all over his hair and dripping all over his guitar and everything. It was awful and must have been mortifying for him.'

As Orange Juice headed back despondently to the changing room, Josef K brushed past them heading in the opposite direction, the rush of adrenaline obliterating any lingering nerves. In the midst of the fracas,

Haig and Ross thought it wise to rethink their approach. 'As we were on next, we decided we'd have to give it total attitude just to survive!' admits Ross. Abandoning Plan A for Plan K, it became—ready, aim, fire—Josef K's Manchester Free Hall, *play fuckin' loud* moment. 'We thought we had better be as punk as possible so that we didn't get lynched. But it worked. The audience loved it.'

Alas, the volume and energy merely aggravated the situation, and before long a serious fight—involving around twenty-five speed-fuelled misanthropes—had broken out in the middle of the dancefloor. 'Eventually, we had to stop playing and head offstage,' adds Ross. 'It had turned into a proper riot!'

The band barely had time to recover their senses the next morning before booking into Little Big One Studio, where the voices for *The Adventures Of Tin Tin* had been recorded, to cut the planned single for Les Disques du Crépuscule. It would be a re-recording of the title track from their soon-to-be-released debut album, *Sorry For Laughing*. Recording for another label before Postcard had released their debut LP probably seemed to the casual observer like a strange move, but it illustrates the fly-by-night nature of the Glasgow label. There were never any firm contractual agreements. In any case, Horne was probably tickled pink that his protégés were releasing a record on an arty European imprint. *K* for kudos. Finally.

As soon as they arrived back home, the band performed a number of live shows, including a key date playing alongside The Blue Orchids, Cabaret Voltaire, The Passage, Basement 5, and Dislocation Dance at the ICA Rock Week Showcase in London on January 4. Their performance drew lavish praise from the *NME*'s Barney Hoskyns, who wrote, 'Josef K have style. A scant humouring smile stays permanently on singer Paul Haig's pink lips: he picks up a guitar halfway through the set and throws in straying, sarcastic solos over Malc's intent discontent rhythm. Josef K songs are intelligently fashioned, but not inflexible: they're sexy, shrewd, smart—Magazine without the Formula or the science. So much goes on, there's so much to go on. Enlightened go-go music.'

Jon Savage and Johnny Marr saw them in fine form at Rafters in Manchester the following month. '[They were] very speedy and blurry,' says Savage. 'They began with "Fun 'n' Frenzy", which was a terrific set opener. I liked their intensity and their clothes. I think Paul Haig was wearing one of those early 70s modernist shirts. It was over fast.'

—

In March, John Peel announced that the band's radio session would be broadcast on his show. However, as Ross explains, the tracks played that evening were not recorded specifically for the show: 'Radio One were doing this *Broadcast From Scotland* theme and trying to feature Edinburgh bands. For some reason they thought we had already done a session for Peel, but we hadn't. So, they got in touch with Alan Horne and asked for material. Horne offered what he described as out-takes from the *Sorry For Laughing* LP. So, we went up to the BBC studio and we met John Walters, who produced Peel's show. He invited us to take a seat, but we were in a rush because we had tickets to see Pere Ubu that night! They were playing with The Red Crayola. John Peel briefly appeared and asked if we wanted to stay and chat, but we said, *Nah*. I mean, it was complete confusion. No one had told us we were supposed to be doing an interview. We should probably have done it in order to promote ourselves, but we didn't really ever enjoy doing that kind of thing, and going to see Pere Ubu seemed like it would be much more fun than sitting around trying to talk about ourselves.'

Peel's patronage prompted Haig to pen a thank-you letter. 'After he received it, he phoned me at home, but I was out,' Haig recalls. 'I remember my mum being a bit starstruck. But that was really nice of him. He actually carried on playing my stuff for a wee while after I left Josef K.'

A second session—this time to be recorded especially for the show—was scheduled for June 15, for broadcast a week later.

The first Peel session was broadcast the same week as the release of 'Sorry For Laughing', one of two tracks the band had recorded during their New Year rendezvous in Belgium. Paired with 'Revelation', it finds Josef K at the absolute peak of their powers. It could well be the 45 that defines them. Most curious then that it was their first non-Postcard release since the debut single. With its bouncy, lopsided riffs, the deliciously infectious A-side is, on the surface, Josef K's most joyous song. On 'It's Kinda Funny', Josef K had out-Orange Juiced Orange Juice in a 'Velvets third album' kind of way. Now they had out-Orange Juiced Orange Juice in an Orange Juice kind of way.

The lyrics to 'Sorry For Laughing' have been the subject of much mirth and controversy. In an interview Haig gave at the time to Johnny Waller in *Sounds*, he explained that the song was 'about two cripples having a relationship. It's not a sick song, it's a happy song. They have a really happy relationship because they slag one another off. One guy's got wooden arms, the other's got no legs, and they're really happy together. In the last verse, the cripples get their own back, and slag off the macho people like Charles Atlas, because they can't do the thing that cripples can, like tumble down the lane and roll about. So many people don't want to know about cripples. They're taboo, but they are people with their own feelings and thoughts—that's what the song is about.'

Despite the somewhat archaic terminology, Haig's ruminations were clearly well-intentioned and were possibly borne from his own experience at the time. 'I was reflecting on my own frailties,' he says today. 'I was so thin and I didn't feel like I was like a *normal* person. Maybe I was like other people with physical or mental disabilities. I was fading away, but I was doing it for my art, which was crazy. At the time, people might have envisaged Charles Atlas as the epitome of a strong-bodied person.

So, I created two characters who weren't able-bodied but who were happy. They would rip the piss out of each other but had a strong bond. Their perspective would be that they were having more fun than anyone else. They were able to laugh at one another as well as the so-called *normal* people of this world.'

By contrast, the AA-side, 'Revelation', was totally relentless—a clattering cataract of noise, simultaneously airborne and earthbound, featuring a scything instrumental break that substituted for a chorus. At four minutes long, its gulping bass and ferocious percussion make it an exhausting listen. 'I didn't write many choruses actually,' says Haig. 'I liked the middle section or guitar break on "Revelation". Ronnie's drumming was brilliant—over time, it's become so apparent that he was an amazing drummer. He was intricate and light of touch. I often asked him to make things light and skippy, quite jazzy, and I think a lot of indie music which came afterward completely nicked from that. Maybe it all started with Ronnie?'

The single received glowing reviews upon its release in April 1981, particularly from Paul Morley in the *NME*. 'Their songs are contracted, summarily ambiguous squirts of romantic drama, impertinent and curious, swept along with a fleeting tone of irony. At first hearing, influenced by The Velvets, T. Rex ("By The Light Of The Magical Moon"), The Fall. On second hearing, all their own work, the bearer of myths. "Revelation" swells up towards the end and sounds real wild—its marbled anti-rock production [something] they failed to achieve on their unreleased LP.'

A few weeks later, Paolo Hewitt reviewed the flip side, although he was a tad more ambiguous. 'Jesus this is harsh. Frantic guitars burst into action and never let up, an Ian Curtis-type voice enters with dense vocals and occasionally the bass pops up to say, *Buuurrrrmmmppp*. This is either absolute crap or the best single I've ever heard. I'll come back to you on this one.'

In between the two Peel sessions, the band—despite their well-documented travel phobia—returned to Europe, as agreed, to play a string of live dates in the Low Countries. They found that European audiences were even more enthusiastic than those in the UK. Nevertheless, before one Dutch show, they were labelled as 'Depressi-wave'—a description that had Haig in stitches. They received a rapturous ovation from the audience at the Melkweg (Milky Way) in Amsterdam, although Ross remembers being attacked by a group of 'karate-practising teenagers who thought we were weird punks' before the gig. Meanwhile, on another Amsterdam date, Malcolm had to fill in on drums for Ronnie, who had gone AWOL for three days, familiarising himself with some of the city's other attractions—although, it should be said, nothing that involved drugs. To the end, Ronnie was the only band member not to dabble with drugs. Alcohol was fine. In his absence, the young Amsterdam intelligentsia gathered at the dressing room door to discuss the meaning of existence with their Scottish friends. Curiously, that type of interaction made Haig feel even more anxious. Though it provided affirmation that people were taking his lyrics seriously, he was unused to that kind of scrutiny back home, so he felt there was something not quite right about it happening in Holland either.

The band's typically combustible half-hour performance at the historic Beursschouwburg Arts Centre in Brussels on April 8, 1981, would later be released as the live album *The Scottish Affair (Part 2)*. During the same visit, they also recorded a bizarre video for the Belgian TV show *Generation 80*, which began with a lump of Slime © (all the rage!) being stretched across the midriff of an unidentified feminine form, slowly evaporating to reveal our sharply attired heroes miming 'Sorry For Laughing'. The studio set, the lighting, everything else here screamed *Top Of The Pops*, and it would have fitted in perfectly onto a 1981 show. Sadly, that is something that would never happen. The video is of particular interest as it constitutes one of the few remaining pieces of film featuring the band.

—

There was another reason the band extended their stay in mainland Europe. By now, everyone had agreed that the album they recorded at Castlesound wasn't fit for purpose. So, while in Brussels, they stepped back into the studio to speedily re-record it, rechristening it with a fresh title in the process. Some songs appeared, others disappeared, reflecting the ongoing evolution of their sound. When it was complete, it was time to return home. Haig spent most of the return journey vomiting in a paper bag on the hovercraft crossing the Channel, while Ronnie stocked up on Johnnie Walker Red label.

In Belgium, Haig—minus Josef K—had also recorded a song for Crépuscule. 'Mad Horses' would appear on a forthcoming label sampler. 'I felt I'd been let loose to do what I wanted—in a four-track studio with Wilf Smarties—and that seemed amazingly good fun, to be honest.' But perhaps of even greater significance was the liaison upon his return to Edinburgh with Metropak's Steve Harrison to record a 45 under the moniker Rhythm Of Life. The clean optimistic burst of 'Soon' pointed in a completely different direction from Josef K. For keen observers, the signs were hard to ignore. It seemed that Haig already had one eye on life beyond Josef K.

Shortly after their return from Europe, the band gave a revealing interview to Johnny Waller of *Sounds*. It's an important one in that it helps one better understand who the members of Josef K really were as people. It also invites speculation about how its contents may have shaped the ensuing critical fallout—not because they said anything outrageous but possibly because they didn't. And, despite the occasional lapse into dubious taste from Ronnie, they never would. At all.

The pop world was expectant of its stars. It wanted them to be flamboyant, to be outrageous, like Bowie and Bolan had been a decade earlier. Punk might have poked fun at that sort of thing, but popular music is cyclical. Long live the new princes of pop. Could Haig match them? By 1981, being a pop star required a huge amount of self-confidence and copious amounts of narcissism. In the company of Marc Almond, Duran Duran, Steve Strange, Adam Ant, and Japan, Josef K probably seemed relatively unglamorous. And they were far too inhibited for their own good. While they were four very different personalities, they weren't necessarily 'different enough' as far as their marketability was concerned. Torrance aside, they were shy and introverted, and while they were hardly unsure of themselves and their abilities, they had always been somewhat suspicious of anything that smacked of rock stardom. Being respected was more important than being on the front pages. In fact, to some degree, they were anti-rock'n'roll. They had always eschewed the laddish culture that accompanied that. There were no groupies queuing up outside the dressing room, and nor should there be. Although Ronnie may have entertained the odd friend, the others were determined to avoid any such 'chauvinistic' shenanigans.

Dave McCullough had labelled this aesthetic 'New Puritanism', and while today they would be lauded as 'woke' and 'progressive', in 1981 they may have come across as quite unremarkable and even a little boring. They were even occasionally targeted by the odd misanthrope. 'I remember once sitting quietly in the corner of a pub,' Haig told Paul Lester in 2007, ' and this guy came up to me and said, Are you Josef K? Do you suffer for your art? And he threw a pint of beer over me. I was really annoyed, so I picked up another one and threw it back. He was speechless.'

Waller took the unusual step—evidently at the group's request—of interviewing each member separately, firstly heading off to Edinburgh Zoo with Malcolm, then sharing out a packet of Revels with Davy Weddell on a guided bus tour of the city, before interviewing Ronnie and Paul in local cafes. Some excerpts from the interviews give a flavour of proceedings:

MALCOLM 'Syuzen, my girlfriend, used to really like us, but now she thinks we're rubbish. I honestly think Postcard is the best label around—it's got a very high standard of releases. Alan Horne doesn't really like Josef K. He never has done. The thing that really annoyed me was when we were away on tour and him and Edwyn did a radio interview slagging us off.'

DAVY 'When I left my job, my parents said they wouldn't have anyone in the house who was on the dole. I think my dad is quite proud of me now, but my mum is a bit more reserved. She thinks it's only going to last a year at the most. It could only last a year!'

RONNIE 'I like screwing—when I can—drinking as much as possible, just having a good time living it up. I was out with this gorgeous chick I met a couple of hours after we arrived. I went back to her hotel room and spent most of the next three days with her— seeing movies, shopping, drinking, eating, having a good time. I'm an exhibitionist. I love people watching me on stage. Hopefully, eventually, I'll do some modelling for *Vogue*.'

PAUL 'I just hate encores. We build up a really good momentum at the end of the set. You can't reach that height again. We feel it's pointless coming back after giving everything we've got. It would be such an anti-climax.'

As well as illustrating how different they were by nature, the interview exemplifies an inability or unwillingness to declare or even articulate their *raison d'être*. It brought back memories of their first ever radio interview with Colin Somerville, who asked the band what the songs were about. 'Oh, just about everyday life, really,' mumbled Ronnie, only to be quickly corrected by Paul. 'Actually, Ron, they're about a bit more than that!'

Josef K were never going to storm the charts through the force of their personalities. They were too self-effacing—some might even say too humble—for all of that. They were far too grounded. Perhaps it was a defence mechanism. *What if everything falls apart? Maybe we should be ready for that?*

This propensity to avoid engaging in idle claptrap and making empty vacuous promises exposed them as being too ordinary to make front-page news. Even in the music weeklies. They wanted to let the music speak for itself. They were idealistic but naive. How can you be stars when you don't want to look or act like stars? Perhaps it's not enough simply to make brilliant music.

Nevertheless, as spring flowed into summer, there was reason for optimism, and the second session for the John Peel Show came along at exactly the right time. June 1981 was a make-or-break moment. The re-recorded album was in the pipeline, there were a few live dates planned, with a full UK tour to follow in July and August, and they were about to record their second (first proper) Peel session. Nobody could have foreseen that ten weeks later it would all be over.

The four songs the band committed to tape for Peel on June 16 (before outclassing Scars at the Venue later that night) capture a dazzlingly brilliant and immensely gifted group of musicians playing the last new music they would ever record together. 'We had so little experience of studios and were learning as we went along,' says Ross. 'The first LP captures us as we were, but we had changed by then. That Peel session, as far as I'm concerned, was the best recording we ever did.'

The future was theirs.

10/15 | ART OF THINGS / DOUBLE VISION

Josef K are a band with identity, with verve, with foresight,
with belief, with a future. A dancing ground for the new age . . .
the kind of band fairy tales should be written about.

CHRIS BURKHAM, *SOUNDS*, MARCH 1981

It's very simple really. Josef K should have released their debut LP, *Sorry For Laughing*, exactly how and when they had originally intended at the beginning of 1981. The album had been pressed up as a white label, with Robert Sharp capturing the elusive essence of its creators with his ghostly monochrome shot of the foursome on Calton Hill, the shot bookmarked as the album's front cover. The post-punk scene was in flux, undergoing such rapid transformation that no group could afford to procrastinate. But procrastinate they did. Their indecision was decisive—it cost them, and they missed their moment. By the time *The Only Fun In Town* finally appeared, in July, they should have been releasing their second album.

Sorry For Laughing had been recorded the previous autumn, but it sounds perfectly built for 1981; conversely, *The Only Fun In Town* sounded a whole lot more like 1980, or possibly even 1979, than it should have. In 1981, six months was a long time. *Sorry For Laughing* could and should have been the album to spearhead the new pop movement of the 80s, but by the summer of 1981, the critical consensus was gradually shifting away from feverish discord and jagged abstraction toward a preference for smooth polished production and clean straight lines. Suddenly, hi-fi > lo-fi. It seemed that, virtually overnight, *Melody Maker* went pop and the *NME* soul daft. Lipstick, suits, briefcases, and coiffured hairstyles were everywhere.

Josef K had the suits, but the scratchy angular sound of *The Only Fun In Town* seemed out of step with the new *zeitgeist*. Glamorous new bands (Haircut 100, ABC, Soft Cell, Heaven 17, Duran Duran) were popping up everywhere, just as others (Swell Maps, Buzzcocks, The Slits, Throbbing Gristle) were gradually disappearing from view. Smartly dressed and radio-friendly, the new faces leapt off the glossy pages of *Smash Hits* and *Record Mirror*, while other more 'serious' bands underwent a radical facelift. The Human League's sound metamorphosised from the eerie spaciousness and metronomic pulse of *Reproduction* to the glam rush of *Dare*—disposable, irresistible—in a little over twelve months. In time, others such as Simple Minds would create the luxurious shimmer of *New Gold Dream*, which seemed as far removed from the sub-Roxy/Magazine pastiche of their 1979 debut *Life In A Day* as it's possible to imagine. Similarly, The Associates would discard the trench coats and dry ice to gild the ballroom with the elegant romantic tumble of 'Party Fears Two'.

Within twelve months, 'Party Fears Two' had stormed the charts. Their contemporaries all seemed to be on board. So, why weren't Josef K?

Perhaps, being too busy agonising about whether or not to release their debut album, they failed to notice the changes taking place all around them. But it is probably likelier that the band were too fiercely independent—and notoriously insouciant about the critics' perception of them—to care. Whatever the truth, the result was that *Sorry For Laughing* was first delayed, then shelved altogether.

Conflicting explanations exist for this strange decision, but in almost every instance the shadow of master manipulator Alan Horne looms over proceedings. In his history of Postcard, *Simply Thrilled*, Simon Goddard argues that the decision to reject the album was entirely down to Horne. He claims that while Horne acknowledged *Sorry For Laughing* was 'a good album'—maybe as good as Echo & The Bunnymen (NB: he didn't like Echo & The Bunnymen)—he strongly insisted it wasn't up to Postcard standards. It was a strange position to take, considering Postcard had never released an album before.

If the album's gestation was brief, it was also an uncomfortable experience. From the very beginning, Horne was determined to be at the centre of proceedings. His involvement wasn't always welcomed, and that set some nerves on edge.

'Almost every morning I would drive to Castlesound Studios, and Alan was always in the back of the car,' remembers Haig. 'He just kept ranting on and on, and I kept thinking, *Is there any possibility you could just shut up?* When the pair arrived at the Pencaitland-based studio, just southeast of the city, Haig would be mentally exhausted. It was hardly the ideal preparation for the day ahead.

Haig had recently acquired a synthesizer, which he brought to the studio. 'My parents had got me an old cheesy entertainment organ for my Christmas,' he says. 'Really nice of them, but it was an old-school rhythm box, which was for someone about forty years older than myself. But they let me take it back to the shop, and I got a Yamaha synthesizer instead. That meant I could add all the whooshing sounds and so on.' Employing his new toy with songs that were already well established was a risk.

Perhaps tellingly, producer Calum Malcolm—who went on to produce successful albums for many other artists, including The Blue Nile, Prefab Sprout, Orange Juice, Aztec Camera, Hue & Cry, and Wet Wet Wet—has only the vaguest memory of the sessions. For reasons that will become clearer later, the experience was underwhelming for everyone involved, to say the least. Despite that, all four members of Josef K recall Calum's steady hand and sage advice during the recordings. He also seemed to be a person who could possibly open doors, as Davy Weddell recalls: 'I remember Calum telling us that someone connected with David Geffen had called him about Josef K, so there was definitely a moment at which we thought, *Maybe we can make a real go of all this.*'

'Calum was reserved, restrained, helpful to us, professional,' confirms Ross. 'I remember asking him to listen to the bass on a particular record—I think it was something by The Pop Group—and we were wondering why their bass sounded far more powerful than the bass on our records. He pointed out that a bass drum was playing every beat that the bass was playing, and he pointed out that we weren't doing that, so we learned little things like that from him.'

Davy Weddell recalls the excitement of the process, though he also harboured a few concerns. 'It was great coming into the studio each day, particularly when it was just us and Calum. But maybe there was too much technology. I remember fighting to get the bass turned up louder. Calum would say things like, If you guys just want to disappear for a while, I'll set up the basic track: then you can tell me what needs tweaked.'

The band were pleased with how the sessions went. They then concentrated for a spell on other ventures, including a high-profile engagement at London's Lyceum. But as they waited for the final mix to ferment, some anxiety began to creep in. 'When you're nineteen, three months is a long time,' suggests Ross. 'We had to wait a couple of months between the recording and its release. We had really short attention spans. By the time a record came out, we were usually bored with it, so after recording the album, we decided not to listen to it again.'

Instead of listening to the album, they listened to Alan Horne, but Horne himself was beginning to experience a crisis of confidence. 'He went down to London and came back up with a test pressing of the album.

He said, Oh, do you know what? I'm really not sure about it at all. I don't know if it sounds that good. Like us, he would have heard it when it was first completed, but those seeds of doubt were cast. To be fair though, we had kind of moved on ourselves too. We had recorded some new songs as well, and the sound of the group had changed, so, when we heard it, we felt really disappointed. We had mixed "Sorry For Laughing" with a lot of reverb—it slows down and speeds up very badly—and Alan reassured us that we didn't have to release it.'

'When we heard it back, it felt flat, blanded out,' admits Haig. 'We expected a really trebly sound, but it wasn't there. We didn't think it sounded right, and Alan went along with that.'

It is hardly surprising that Horne elected to exercise caution. A self-styled perfectionist, he felt the first album on Postcard had to be immaculate. It needed to fit the narrative he'd already written in his head. The album was going to be so fantastic that the music magazines would run out of superlatives. None of that mattered to Josef K, but it mattered a great deal to Alan Horne. 'What annoyed me about Alan and Edwyn at times was they believed what the *NME* thought about anything to be the be-all and end-all of everything,' says Ross. 'Orange Juice were press darlings, whereas Josef K often got bad reviews, so we didn't care.' As things transpired, the press, eager in its anticipation, watched as the band stumbled, their heads and hearts drifting elsewhere.

'I wasn't there when the album was recorded,' laments Allan Campbell. 'Everything today is so well thought-out and carefully considered. There are business plans and so on. It's quite hard to imagine things as they were back then. I mean Josef K were just so incredibly idealistic. Paul and Malcolm have spoken subsequently about mistakes being made with the album, wanting it to sound rougher and more *live*. They weren't focusing on selling albums, only upon what was *true* to them. Playing live was so important. For lots of people, live is where the magic happens, whether you love Television or Iggy Pop or whoever. For Josef K, maybe that was true as well.'

Calum Malcom felt a little let down when the band decided to reject the album. 'He was a little upset,' remembers Ross. 'He suggested doing some remixes at a reduced rate if we weren't happy with it, so he was more than fair with us. We had to assure him it wasn't his fault. On the final mix of the song "Sorry For Laughing", he put quite a lot of reverb on the snare. It makes the snare too prominent. That was the thing when I first heard it—the timing wasn't great. We hadn't really played the song that well.'

'We were really tired,' adds Haig. 'It wasn't the mastering glitch that some people thought it was.' They had recorded four takes of the song but somehow contrived to choose the one with the sloppiest playing.

—

Sorry For Laughing never appeared. No one apologised. No one laughed. The album was never reviewed in the music press. Only a few dozen test pressings had been manufactured, although (false) rumours spread that thousands of copies had been consigned to the furnace. However, some high-profile gigs—in Brussels on New Year's Eve and at London's ICA three days later—would reignite the band's confidence and provide the catalyst for a new and 'improved' debut offering.

The Only Fun In Town (Postcard 81-7) would be recorded at Little Big One Studios in Brussels during the band's second trip to the Low Countries in April 1981. The studio was significantly smaller and less sophisticated than Castlesound—sixteen tracks compared to twenty-four—but that suited everyone. In a little over six days, alongside engineer Mark Francois, they hurriedly thrashed out the songs from start to finish. 'We re-recorded the album to give it a live feel, so it seemed more like what we were about,' says Weddell.

'While I prefer the original version now, at the time the re-recording was certainly more of the sound and character we were trying to achieve,' admits Haig. 'We wanted it to capture the essence of a live performance. But I was stupid in insisting that the vocals shouldn't be too high in the mix, so they were almost drowned out. I've barely listened to it since.'

The sleeve, with its gold lettering and graphic imprinted on a jet-black background—a nod to *White Light/White Heat*—was designed by Krysia Klasicki, who had also provided the calligraphy for the *Postcard Brochure*, and modelled on a 1961 picture book entitled *This Is Edinburgh*, illustrated by Czech artist Miroslav Sasek. Inside, there were various photos of the band, Horne, and various family members, such as Davy's father with a pipe. Assembled by Syuzen Buckley, it gave the impression of a united front.

Ross insisted at the time that the re-recorded album had more of a soul feel. It is a view shared today by many others, including Douglas McIntyre. 'In that early period, they were always changing, but then they scrapped the album,' he says. 'I used to meet some pals in the Bay Horse in Hamilton—hardly an existentialist pub—and we found out through hearsay that the album wasn't coming out. We were totally shattered by that, but I still insist that it was absolutely the right call. To me, *The Only Fun In Town* is far more representative of what Josef K were all about, and I think it is a much better album. Over the years, the band have revised their position on why *Sorry For Laughing* wasn't released, but I think it was the right choice. It's much closer to what Josef K were all about, more than the scrapped album, and it was also the album they were touring with at the time.'

Any hopes of a positive reaction in the press would be quickly dashed. Dave McCullough and Paul Morley were the first to put the boot in. 'That was a shocker,' admits Haig. 'We hadn't expected that. It was the early days of a leaning toward shiny pop music, and *The Only Fun In Town* was a black, dark, scratchy, misty, indie thing. We thought it had captured the sound and energy of a Josef K live performance, but it wasn't fulfilling the potential he [Morley] had noticed, and it seemed to him like a betrayal. It was quite an impact to see those reviews coming out. We hadn't foreseen that, but I can see what he was saying.'

In retrospect, perhaps they should have been better prepared. *Sounds'* Dave McCullough had already slammed their most recent 45. Now, with the album on his turntable, he let rip, calling it 'an incessant tinny racket. What do Josef K do with their excellent songs? They make them into an LP's worth of over-guitared, over-posed and over-American(a)ed dryness. . . . The de-codifying of the songs into clatter rock puts the listener in a rut instead of raising his senses . . . their forensic intensity . . . deprives the listener of air. . . . Josef K have made a laboured album that mistakes realism for reality. Kafka would be ashamed, not to say laughing.'

If they thought *that* was bad, worse was to come. Morley's review in the *NME*, subtitled 'A Postcard from Scornland', was scathing.

I should be talking about it in the same love-breath as *Empires And Dance*, *The Affectionate Punch*, *Kilimanjaro*, if not *Real Life*, *The Scream*, *Unknown Pleasures*. Instead, I can barely talk about it AT ALL. . . . They needed to fulfil their purist-punk idealism and represent their static-changing songs as impartial surrealistic variations on a 'Spiral Scratch' / 'Rebellious Jukebox' theme. They've ended up up-ended, ruining the poignant greatness, sad cheer and awkward grace of their songs with a grief-grey and stubborn dependence on the now useless premise of independence. The fundamental problem, the basic mistake, the overall stupidity of *Fun*, is that it does not GO FOR IT! The power of starkness, the chaos that can rule, the sound of the heavens—it is all denied in favour of canned guitars ringing out the hull of dead and suppressed laughter. Within grasp is the great magic, the tempting power of sensuous derangement, but JK cannot be bothered to grasp and make do with a pleasant painless canter through their miniature fairy tale world. This *Fun* is a period piece . . . Josef K have cheapened themselves and cheatened [sic] the world. Not bad for a first LP.

Despite their self-professed disregard for critical opinion, the poor reviews led Ross to reflect once again upon the reasons for scrapping the original album. Speaking to *Melody Maker*, he lamented, 'I don't think we gave [*Sorry For Laughing*] enough thought. We just went, Oh, we've got enough songs, so we can do an LP. I must admit, it turned out really badly. We put in too many things—gimmicky things—slamming doors, background shouts, that kind of thing.' Despite that, he admitted that 'from the point of view of our *career*, we should definitely have put it out. Things were moving so quickly.'

Too late. *The Only Fun In Town* appeared in its place and was duly slated. Unlike his idols, the young Douglas McIntyre was furious with the reviews. 'I totally disagreed with what they said. Historically, we can see they reflected the changing face of pop music. The whole new pop thing and having to compete with the charts and so on. The music papers—your weekly carrier pigeon—were so important, and they sold so well, so the writers had a huge influence. So, from being absolute press darlings to taking such savage beatings when *The Only Fun In Town* came out, must have just caused them to look at one another and think, *What's that all about? Are we supposed to sound like ABC now?* Good reviews ultimately don't matter too much. It's nice to get good reviews, but bad reviews tend to get under your skin, no matter how much you try to put up a shield. It probably had more of an effect on them than they would care to admit. If you are signed to a record company and you are reading negativity about yourself in the music press, it will be quite dispiriting however much you try to brush it off.'

The only fun in the music press came from Ian Pye in *Melody Maker*, who hailed the album as 'one of the few significantly original and captivating pieces of European music to find the light this year. . . . Josef K must have locked themselves away somewhere to conjure their delicately brittle magic because they cut through new psychedelia and dressed-up funk with the clean flash of a scalpel . . . Haig's vocals are mixed well down giving his voice a distant oblique quality that rides in cold contrast against the nagging treble high rhythm guitars.'

Given the benefit of another forty years' reflection, both Haig and Weddell are today convinced that the album should have been pitched midway between *Laughing*'s crisp polish and *Fun*'s tinny scratch. Despite the negative reaction of the press, Ross maintains the re-recorded album is the better one, while accepting that the band shouldn't have stalled on the first.

'It was art, not commerce,' he says in *Hungry Beat*. '[*The Only Fun In Town*] has more character. It's more of the complete thing. We should have put the first one out and then put a second one out. The second got completely slated by the journalists who'd loved us. By the time it arrived, that whole idea—Heaven 17, ABC—had begun to germinate, the musician as a businessman with suit, tie, briefcase, infiltrating the capitalist system and destroying it from the inside. You know, Paul Morley saying how disappointed he was we had made a "punk" album.'

'I didn't care about the press,' adds Ross today. 'It didn't really bother us. Our reviews were never that good. One person would give us a good review, and the next would slate us. Anyway, it *did* sell—it got to number two on the indie charts when it came out.'

Simon Reynolds, author of *Rip It Up*, today takes a different view. 'I prefer the unreleased scrapped first version—it's clearer, brighter. The retake seemed already behind the times when it came out—a Swell Maps-type record amid the new pop moves of Orange Juice, Scritti Politti, ABC, and Altered Images. On the scrapped and glossier first version, you can hear the tunes and Haig's voice better. Also, the track listing is different, with "Sense Of Guilt" and "Endless Soul" on it. Those are my two favourite Josef K songs.'

It is worth emphasising that despite their attempt to reproduce a live sound, ultimately Josef K were still recording an LP in a studio. 'I still love *The Only Fun In Town*,' Allan Campbell says in *Hungry Beat*, 'but what lives on, having seen Josef K so many times, is being in a club and feeling that wave of guitar sound and rhythm. That's what lingers on at the back of your mind, much more so than perhaps the record.'

As Ross points out, the album sold well—ten thousand copies in the first two days alone, around eighteen or nineteen thousand in total—and Rough Trade organised a national tour with Article 58 in support. Ross felt vindicated as he encountered some of the band's fans on tour. 'When we spoke to some of them, quite often they said stuff like, When we saw that Paul Morley review, we knew the album would be great! There was just that weird idea about the power of the *NME*. Paul Morley was funny, I liked him, but he could be so pretentious. All of that was very important to Alan Horne. Edwyn too. When the first Orange Juice album came out, it got I'd say, fairly mixed reviews, but Edwyn was just completely in despair about it all—*We'll have to change our style*—because the *NME* didn't like it. I mean, we didn't really give a fuck. We were pretty insular anyway.'

While the album sales were reasonably strong, stalling on the release still seemed to come at a cost of lost momentum, although not everyone agrees. 'The scrapped album had been followed by an incredible single,' remembers Douglas McIntyre, 'so I am not sure that argument holds. It felt like, at Crépuscule, there was a different kind of appreciation of the band. But sometimes it's just to do with timing. McCullogh and Morley were moving things forward in a different direction. Possibly, the music Paul made with Island might have been the way Morley hoped they would go, but thank God they didn't because it wouldn't have been Josef K any longer. But "Sorry For Laughing" is another exemplar of why *The Only Fun In Town* is a much better album. The version recorded in Brussels is infinitely superior. And the whole experience of being somewhere else, and working with other people who are possibly more sympathetic, taught the band that everything didn't have to be about Postcard. It was a stepping outside of that, with a cool graphic of the band on the cover and not just the label's kitten logo.'

The single in question was 'Chance Meeting'. As things transpired, it would prove to be the last 45 for Postcard (phase one). It was another re-recording, much to Haig's frustration, and an occasion that possibly pushed him closer to the exit than anyone realised. After a speed-fuelled night with Alan Horne lodging at his parents' house, Malcolm emerged with a new vision for what had been the band's debut single. Without Ross, it would probably never have happened. He ached to transform the song into something new and bright and accessible. Haig had not been keen on the idea—it felt too much like going backward—and he, being most inclined to embrace the future, wanted only to move in the opposite direction.

Haig was becoming more interested in electronic sound but was always more attuned to the opportunities provided by technology than his bandmates. He remembered being transfixed—as almost every impressionable young teenager was—watching Kraftwerk being introduced on *Tomorrow's World* in 1975. 'I'd been listening to Stockhausen and electronic music from the age of twelve or thirteen. I was perhaps more interested in Kraftwerk than Malcolm, and he didn't really like Throbbing Gristle, for example. I liked industrial stuff, Cabaret Voltaire. Malcolm probably wasn't as keen on that kind of stuff. If Josef K had kept going, I would probably have been the one who embraced new technology, pushing the production and so on.'

It seemed Haig and Ross were on different pages, but Malcolm held his nerve. On the new version of 'Chance Meeting', he added autoharp and invited his brother Alastair to perform too. Speaking to Simon Goddard, he recalled, 'Paul was in a huff, and I was running around putting down all these guitar parts and my wee brother was there on trumpet. We double-tracked him to try to make it sound like a full brass section.'

The song today is often accompanied on YouTube and other channels by a video recorded on 16mm film in 1980 by Glasgow DJ Nick Peacock. At the time, Peacock was undertaking a photography course at the city's College Of Building & Printing. As part of his final submission, he approached Alan Horne with a view to making a promo film for Josef K. Horne was quick to suggest Peacock film Orange Juice instead:

'Why Josef K?'

'Because I like Josef K.'

'Well, *I* don't like Josef K.'

Peacock was a regular attendee of the band's gigs—a regular Josef K nut. He asked the band what they would like to do. 'At the time, pop videos were new, and they were often very elaborate, like Ultravox with their smoke machines and so on,' he recalls. 'Paul suggested that I might want to film someone chasing someone else through a house with a knife. My instinct was to do a Beatles-type thing instead. Use some recognisable locations. Calton Hill. Some of the squares off the Royal Mile. The band had a reputation for being pretty solemn, and I thought it would be good to catch them being a bit silly instead, doing cartwheels, being a bit more fun. The live clips—filmed at the Venue the night before—were slotted in. It was all done over a few days.'

Peacock has out-takes from the session, too, but these have yet to see the light of day. 'We had great fun that day,' remembers Torrance. 'It's one of my abiding memories of being in Josef K. Plus, it's such a great song.'

Torrance wasn't wrong. 'Chance Meeting' (mk2) is one of the greatest singles of the era. Everything about it is perfect but, inexplicably, no one told Dave McCullough. 'Josef K have apparently decided to turn their combined guitar-sound into the musical equivalent of Shredded Wheat,' he wrote in *Sounds*. 'It's all tinny and tiny and a little self-consciously aimed at being one feels, A Different Angle. Maybe they are afraid of being a great pop group. Postcard sleeves are boring me and Alan Horne's pathological determination to break the charts is becoming a pain in the backside.'

Steve Sutherland was equally unimpressed in his *Melody Maker* review. '"Pictures" owes vocal royalties to loopy Lou Reed and instrumental debts to the Gang of 4, while "Chance Meeting" smartly nicks brass from The Teardrop Explodes' pocket. Neither is as abrasive as past outings. Both start the way they finish and do very little in between. Can, must, and undoubtedly will, do much better.'

Only Vivien Goldman at the *NME* had ears for the thing, although why she opted only to review only the B-side, 'Pictures', remains a total mystery. 'More of those ringing distorted sweeps of guitar that mean NEW Psychedelic, or is it New Romantic . . . at any rate the effect is of noble young profiles silhouetted against stormy skies, poised—posing—on a windswept mountain crag. Josef K sound like they are attracted by the nobility of agony, as exemplified by Franz Kafka's hungry anguished mug shots. So many Jimmy Deans. What a feeling!'

On this occasion the critics were spectacularly wrong. 'Chance Meeting' is one of the finest singles of the era—charming, romantic, ambitious, perfectly conceived and executed. The new arrangement was a total triumph, but there was something about the production that left the critics wanting. It sounded matte, they had ordered gloss. They expected a return on their investment, and they felt let down. Not only that, but the reworking caused such ill feeling within the band that it meant all the recycling had come at a cost. The cracks were widening.

11/15 | IT'S KINDA FUNNY / WE DON'T TALK ANYMORE

Everything is within you, gold and mud, happiness and pain,
the laughter of childhood and the apprehension of death. Say
yes to everything, shirk nothing. Don't try to lie to yourself.

HERMAN HESSE, 'RAINY WEATHER' (1920)

Bob Dylan turned forty in 1981. Paul McCartney, Mick Jagger, and Keith Richards were still in their thirties. The feeling back then, possibly intensified by punk and its aftermath, was that they were fading stars, old codgers, way past being interested in. Pop music was a young person's game. Things moved incredibly quickly. If you didn't keep up, you were kicked into touch and forgotten about. It's amusing to think about that nowadays, when all of those mentioned above are still making records in their eighties. In 1981, however, it was generally understood that being a pop star wasn't a lifelong pursuit. You were meant to crash and burn. One day you would grow up. No point in rushing it. Time would come for you soon enough. In retrospect, it was short-sighted to expect that as a given. Had no one yet figured out that audiences and artists were growing older alongside one another? That forty-year-olds didn't *really* want to die before they got old, and that they might want to 'Be-Bop-A-Lula' a little longer?

One more time for the road. And then some more. And so it has transpired ever since. A flurry of reunions. Encore, encore. Again and again. You only live once.

The year 1981 was a turbulent one, and not just for Josef K. It was one of the most violent in post-war British history. Thatcher's Conservative government was in the process of tearing apart the nation's soul through its monetarist economic policies, simultaneously opening avenues to instant prosperity for the privileged few while orchestrating the managed decline of heavy industry and making huge public spending cuts, strengthening the conviction of many that working-class communities were being systematically dismantled. With poverty and unemployment booming, the New Cross house fire in January accelerated the sense of disempowerment, sparking a series of inner-city riots, first in Brixton, then in Bristol and Liverpool, the likes of which had never been seen in Britain. At the same time, Irish Republican prisoners had gone on hunger strike in the Maze prison in Belfast in a bid to achieve political status. In both cases, the PM revealed herself to be impervious to the gathering storm of protest, holding firm in the face of vociferous opposition, cultivating an unmistakeably ruthless persona from which she would from thereon rarely deviate.

In the midst of the political turmoil, the Royal Wedding might have seemed like a slap in the face. With inner-city riots and unemployment spiralling out of control, here was the final insult, its pomp, opulence, and distraction a predictable charade, triggering that tenacious but bewildering stream of obsequiousness that has long been the preserve of the British working class. If it briefly gave people Ordinary Joe something to cheer, it was about as effective as putting a sticking plaster on a heart attack. The scars were running deep, and it wasn't long before murmurs of discontent began to be heard on radio and television, with The Specials' 'Ghost Town' becoming—spiritually, at least—the bleakest chart-topper of all time.

But 1981 proved to be Josef K's *annus horribilis* as well.

EDINBURGH, AUGUST 22

RONNIE *It's Saturday night. Smartest shirt on. Busier than usual in here. I hope Paul's not been waiting too long. Can't seem to see him. Ach, he's used to me being late. Might not get a seat now. Ah, there he is. Better get the drinks in . . . shite, he looks fucking miserable. I knew I should have got here earlier. When was the last time I saw him smile? Can't mind. That last rehearsal was a nightmare. He usually brings a song idea or two. Nothing. He wouldn't have done that before. He always loved rehearsals. He was always buzzin' with ideas. And now he's spending much more time away. The weirdest thing is, he's hardly saying anything at all. He was always such a good laugh. When was the last time we went to the pub with Malcolm and Davy? Ach, maybe he just needs a breather. Everybody needs a bit of headspace sometimes. He'll probably come round soon. It couldn't be that album review in the* NME *they were all talking about? I thought he couldn't care less about all that shite. Anyway, we'll have a blether.*

PAUL *Okay then!? Is that all he has to say? There was me getting all worked up about it as well. I'm stunned he seems so indifferent? Maybe I was right? Maybe he's not that bothered either anymore. No protest, no cross-examination, no attempt to change my mind. So, this is really it. Maybe he didn't hear me right? I meant* for good, *Ronnie. Okay?! Maybe he knows why I feel the way I do? He must have noticed something! They all must have. Were they fucking blind? Surely someone noticed. Or maybe they just couldn't care less. Och, well, I've said what I had to say.*

'Maybe you could say to the others, Ron.'

'Of course, Paul.'

The ashtray is filling up quickly. A few pints are swiftly sunk.

Did that go well? Was that easier or harder than I imagined it would be? I don't know anymore. I really could do without tomorrow night though. If Ron doesn't get a hold of the others tonight, then I'll speak to them before the gig.

GLASGOW, AUGUST 22

MALCOLM *Three hours sleep. Jeez, Alan just doesn't know when to shut the fuck up. I wish he wouldn't keep going on all the time. I feel absolutely knackered. How am I going to keep going 'til tonight? Still, at least I don't need to travel through from Edinburgh. Better check with Davy and see when they'll be here. Can I use your phone, Alan?*

Ronnie told you that? So, Paul makes decisions on his own now? Well, do you know what? Fuck him.

Forty-odd years have blurred or softened a lot of memories, but Ross in particular recalls the band's final moments most vividly. 'I was walking down with Syuzen for the soundcheck, and we met Edwyn in the street and told him Josef K were splitting up,' he recalls. 'Edwyn immediately asked if I wanted to join Orange Juice. So I did!'

It is impossible to overstate how much Haig's decision would have felt like an insult to Malcolm. It hardened him, but the blow ended up being softer for him than for Ronnie and Davy, for when he woke up the following morning, he was the new guitarist in Orange Juice.

Few know with any degree of certainty the reason Haig called time on Josef K. They thought they knew. Only Kafka himself knows what really happened to the protagonist of *The Trial*, for the novel was never completed and remains an existentialist riddle, open to myriad interpretations. The book's enduring appeal lies in its psychological depths, the subconscious human fear of horrors recognisable only to ourselves. Analogous to this, the truth surrounding Josef K's demise has remained something of a mystery to everyone outside of the band, but, curiously enough—in one sense at least—as time has passed, it has become ever more of a riddle to the members of the band themselves.

A short time after the split, Haig's 'explanation' was a straightforward if pithy one. He was, he told Johnny Waller, 'pretty depressed for a week, because it was the end of an era. We didn't really get on all that well towards the end. We didn't have anything in common, so there were no jokes, no happy feelings. It was just down to doing a job. Josef K weren't that famous anyway. We've split up, so what? Everybody changes.'

Was he faking indifference? Or was he trying to disguise a reality he found too difficult to accept, to nurse a wound too painful to heal? The most frequently cited explanation for Josef K's demise is that Haig, unwilling to tour and perform live any longer, opted to bail out. It contains a kernel of truth, but the singer has revealed subsequently that this was merely 'an excuse' he used to make the break. In truth, there was a concatenation of factors, of which here are some of the more significant ones.

Josef K made a few bad decisions during their career, but two in particular stand out as being particularly ill-judged. It now seems patently obvious that the decision not to go ahead with the release of their debut album was commercially a disastrous one. It was a mistake which would haunt them. All the momentum they had built up was stopped in its tracks. It is easy with the benefit of hindsight to point to this as *the* pivotal moment, but it is also important to remember that, collectively, they felt they were doing the right thing. Even today, they vacillate when comparing the two albums' respective merits. One wonders if this change of heart, like many other decisions, was made, if not under duress, then certainly as a consequence of less-than-subtle persuasion by Alan Horne.

'Not releasing that first Josef K album was a terrible decision,' admits Ross today. 'For building the label, for any kind of commerciality, it was just such a ridiculous decision to make. Horne wanted the first Postcard album to be an absolutely brilliant album, but would he ever have found that? Once Alan had enough financial stability to say, I'm not sure that's good enough to release, it became a bit like Brian Wilson with *Smile*, trying over and over again to make the perfect record. He always decried that he had neither the money or the infrastructure to make hit records on

Postcard, but he had that with Swamplands and still didn't have any hit records, even though he had the artists he wanted.'

The decision to bin the album hammered at least one nail in the coffin, if not the final one. But it did something else. Despite their apparent apathy, it made the band question themselves and their goals. 'When you read a review, no matter what you might think of it, there's usually an element of truth in it,' says Haig. 'You can't help but pick up on these things, and I probably began to think some of it was accurate.' He sensed, as many others did, that their contemporaries had moved beyond them. A bright shiny future beckoned for pop music. The signs would soon be everywhere. Compare *Life In A Day* with *New Gold Dream*, *Reproduction* with *Dare*. Josef K weren't quite ready to trade existentialist philosophy for this new world full of lush arrangements and love action. Re-recording the album to make it sound more like the past and less like the future came at a cost.

Horne's involvement in this key decision offers a microcosm of what was probably a much deeper problem. The clash of personalities between certain members of Josef K and their label boss perpetuated a ubiquitous sense of doubt and uncertainty within the group, possibly even a feeling of homelessness. They were like lodgers living in the attic, while Orange Juice had the lounge, kitchen, and ensuite to themselves. Josef K might be synonymous with Postcard Records—in much the same way as the Cocteau Twins are with 4AD or The Smiths are with Rough Trade—but one questions whether it was the right label for them. They didn't have the same lust for glamour and fame as Horne, nor the deft, occasionally arch demeanour to charm the press that Orange Juice possessed in abundance. They were forever the outsider at Postcard, always on trial, encumbered by their slightly awkward personalities and sombre worldview.

Signing with Postcard had come about through a moment of serendipity, almost as if it had been written in the stars, but few have given serious consideration to the possibility that Postcard (and Horne in particular) were, in fact, Josef K's ball and chain. Back then, with Horne lurking in the shadows, they probably wouldn't have been willing to admit it. Yet, for a group whose ego could be fairly fragile, signing for a bigger label (Virgin, Arista, or Polydor, say) might have suffused them with the necessary confidence to propel them on to greater things. Of course, it could quite as easily have backfired. It would have been a risk.

More financial backing could have allowed for a greater degree of freedom and experimentation in the studio. And perhaps they might have been appointed a shrewder, more empathic manager. Allan Campbell could have been 'that guy', but he was elbowed out. In part, that was due to a lack of finance at Postcard (Horne never had any money, and the band couldn't foot the bill themselves), but also due to what Horne perceived as a conflict of interests. Campbell had his own record label, and Horne was suspicious of his motives. That Paul and Ronnie appeared to trust Campbell more than him probably heightened his concerns. Suffice it to say, it was never going to work well with two 'managers', so one had to go. One wonders if the wrong one was jettisoned. Without Campbell's steady hand, Josef K lasted less than a year.

For some time, Haig had been struggling to articulate how he really felt. The doubts that plagued him—probably in the main due to the pressure he felt performing live and the expectations others had of his role as lyricist—manifested themselves in an eagerness to make music away from Josef K. By 1981, his musical vision had shifted, in parallel with his increasingly awkward relationship with the others. It was evident that, for some time prior to the split, the individual members weren't connecting with one another in the same way.

Strangely, there hadn't been many arguments or disagreements—no grievances aired, no outbursts, complaints or fisticuffs, no conference to examine the reasons things weren't right. Everything was left unsaid. This is hardly insignificant. Pop stars are usually fairly comfortable expressing their points of view. Indeed, some groups end up being little more than a tangle of egos. Perhaps one needs to be Scottish, or at least to have a rudimentary understanding of the Scottish psyche, to recognise this lack of expressiveness, this bottling up of emotions and feelings. If less so today than in the past, perhaps, it remains a distinctive characteristic shared by many Scots. There are many reasons for it, but it is borne in part from deep-rooted Calvinist theology, centuries of national subjugation, and a miserable climate. Intrinsic to it is a common understanding that dictates that people oughtn't become too big for their boots. Rather, they should stay grounded in their communities, enduring patiently, remaining stoic in the midst of difficult circumstances. One should toil and accept, not boast and complain.

Alongside those principles of duty, industry and sobriety, some might even argue that Calvinism is a philosophy of negation, with a track record of extracting every ounce of joy and fun from life. At the same time, its Scottish Presbyterian expression especially emphasised the democratic principle over and above the hierarchical system proposed by its Catholic predecessor and counterpart. That Pope's a bit of a pop star, isn't he? Definitely too big for his boots. Even if none of the four members were religious, despite Ross being a son of the Manse, the characteristics of Presbyterianism have been embedded deep in the Scottish psyche. If one marries these traits with the anti-establishmentarian principles of punk, the end result might amount to a reticence and inhibition that many construed as mealy-mouthed and fearful. In interviews, their apparent moroseness and reservedness didn't help their cause at all; they were so anxious lest they appear as false, egotistical, or, worst of all, 'sell-yer-soul-for-a-pound' glory hunters that they sometimes came across as taciturn, possibly at times even dull. More on point, they couldn't even bring themselves to speak to one another when things weren't working out. They were too polite, too anxious to rock the boat.

No rock cliches and no laddishness was all well and good. But no prima donnas either. Perhaps they needed one. They were reluctant to exercise judgement about one another, and even—fatefully—about their own music. 'Nearly everyone ignored Josef K, including, ultimately, Josef K themselves,' concluded Paul Morley.

This idea raises an inevitable question: was Josef K too democratic? Were its members too nice to be really successful? It is fairly natural that, among such a gang of close friends, people can be reluctant to insist on their own way. Paul was the lead singer and a great frontman, but it never felt like he was the leader or that there was any 'leader' as such. Josef K didn't have a Mark E. Smith or an Edwyn Collins—someone with the necessary resolve and ambition to drag the others along in a particular direction, even against their will. And there were certainly differences in the aspirations of each member. What would success have meant to each of them? What was success anyway? Who determines that? For Ronnie, it was money and fame; for Davy, it might have meant job security, a living; for Malcolm and Paul, maintaining integrity and credibility, although to varying degrees.

The extant clearly defined fault line—Paul and Ronnie vs Malcolm and Davy—undoubtedly hastened the disintegration of the collective relationship too. But ultimately, as Haig reflected later, the relationships drifted through the increasing sense of apprehension they felt when they got together: 'The truth is we didn't know how to speak to one another. I met with Malcolm a while back, probably when the film [*Big Gold Dream*] was coming out, and he was keen to get one or two things off his chest, mainly a comment he'd made about me in the press years ago which he regretted (that he was pissed off about me not wanting to tour anymore). At the same time, he said, If only we'd spoken more at the time, if we'd been able to do that more freely, things may well have been different.' Alas...

Regarding the touring excuse, Haig was unquestionably less keen than Malcolm and Ronnie about what had become an all-consuming undertaking. 'Playing live was a way of making money, but Paul was definitely less enamoured with doing that than the others,' insists Allan Campbell. 'He found it too much and wanted to try different things.' At heart, Haig was a home bird, whereas Malcolm didn't mind travelling. He was used to it. He had moved around a bit when he was a child so was better conditioned to travelling and visiting new places. Paul preferred recorded sound to live sound, and he was happier to flirt with technology, to experiment with new ideas. He had been one of the first musicians in the UK to acquire an 808 synthesizer. That meant he could now work at home, and that felt like a total liberation. He preferred being in the studio—and at home—to sitting on the tour bus listening to the wit and wisdom of Alan Horne. And he almost always felt very nervous singing in front of an audience.

Unlike Paul, Malcolm enjoyed the adrenaline rush of being onstage and the experience and opportunity touring provided. While he was equally introverted, Ross was far more at ease in other people's company. He enjoyed chewing the fat with everyone, exchanging opinions, meeting new friends, seeing new things, being part of the gang. He and Davy also had rent to pay, so touring provided a valuable source of income. They were never inclined to turn down any opportunity to do that.

Haig had other concerns that he found very difficult to articulate at the time. These brought everything to a head, but it is only now that he has felt able to discharge his mind about them. 'The whole thing about not wanting to play live was really made up,' he says. 'It was an excuse so that I could leave. I remember telling Malcolm that I didn't want to play live anymore, but that wasn't the real reason. Alan Horne really needed something to say by way of a press release. I didn't really know how to say what I wanted to say. All those other things. The way things had gone. The fact we weren't chummy anymore. We were no longer socialising. That was because of drugs, really, and some of the other band members' social and recreational pursuits. Things I wasn't involved in. That was such a divisive issue. There was no longer a connection anymore. I became increasingly isolated, and that made me pretty miserable. There was no fun being together anymore. We were just going through the motions. It was such a big thing. I wasn't happy for a while. It took a very long time to get to the decision. I hadn't been happy for a long, long time, and there were other things I wanted to do.'

Back in October 1980, in a conversation with Paul Morley for the *NME*, Haig had dropped a clue as to the status quo: 'We just have to make sure we come through the other side unscathed. I am sure we will.'

Clearly, his discomfort had been growing for a while. 'All through the last year of Josef K, I had been doing lots of stuff myself at home—experimenting with different sounds and ideas, synthesizers, keyboards, drum machines, and so on. I didn't have a clear sense of direction, but I enjoyed having the freedom to work by myself without having to run it by anyone else. I could just do what I wanted. So, one of the reasons for the split was definitely that I wanted to pursue my own musical ideas. But, at the same time, it was terribly upsetting and depressing to end it. I did suggest the band carry on without me, but nobody wanted to do that. It just wasn't good anymore, and I had to get out of it.

'I was so miserable by the end. I couldn't explain my reasons for leaving to the others, and I didn't want to get into an argument about it. I was pretty sure they wouldn't have understood what I was talking about. I didn't want to offend anyone. I couldn't stand confrontation. But it seemed to me that the drugs had taken over to a huge extent, and I felt really alienated by that. I didn't want to watch them taking speed and dropping acid. I probably felt sufficient peer pressure to try things for myself, but I quickly found out that those things were not for me. A lot of time was being taken up with the others' recreational drug use, and I wasn't included anymore.

They had started using drugs before me, and I possibly felt I should try to join in, but it just strengthened the divide, which was already growing. I couldn't relate to them anymore, and actually it pissed me off a little. I wasn't in any position to tell them how to live their lives, but how the fuck did they not notice? I must have seemed completely pissed off. Plus, drugs didn't seem like a Josef K thing.

'The musical connection wasn't really clicking anymore either. There was no discussion. I would go away and write and come back with the next song. There was no collaboration, really. It's always bugged me that I had very valid reasons for leaving. I was so uncomfortable and I felt dragged down by it all. Have you not got any new songs, Paul? they'd ask. It seemed a bit easier for them. Then, there were other hangers-on who started to appear. One guy in particular suddenly started appearing during rehearsals, tugging on the others' sleeves, whispering in their ears. I just thought, *Who is he and why is he always hanging around?* He had pockets full of drugs and it used to creep me out. So, it was those things, it wasn't about not wanting to play live anymore. Yes, I didn't want to play live with Josef K anymore because it wasn't fun with Josef K anymore.'

It can take decades to process traumatic events. A few years after the split, Haig was much more guarded when he spoke to *Melody Maker*. 'We'd been together for quite a while, and we'd done two major tours—major tours for us,' he said. 'But at the end of that, it got a bit played out. We'd been doing the same thing for two years and I decided to leave. When I talked to the rest of them, they felt the same way. Malcolm especially was feeling a bit played out and he wanted to move in a pop direction where he could get records in the charts.'

It is important to point out that Haig's perspective differs significantly from the others' recollections. It is possible that, over time, memories become skewed or softened. It is interesting to contrast Haig's explanation with Malcolm's suggestion in *Record Mirror*, which reported the split in

September, that the group was disbanded because Paul hadn't turned up for a band meeting.

In time, Ross would colour the blank corners of the canvas: 'We had been in each other's pockets for two years. While Davy and I were happy just to go around Europe in a smelly wee van, staying in cheap B&Bs, touring and playing, Paul and Ronnie didn't like that. Ronnie would have preferred better transport and nice hotels. Travelling made Paul ill—he couldn't help that. We weren't teenagers anymore; circumstances were changing. I had a girlfriend. I didn't want to spend all my spare time just hanging out with the band. I wanted to spend more time with her. We had lost the gang feeling. Davy and I were sharing a flat. We needed money to pay the bills, and so we'd book gigs. Ronnie and Paul had started to roll their eyes when we booked gigs. But we had never wanted to be in Josef K in our thirties. From the beginning, we had always admired The Velvet Underground—how their lifespan was short and their legacy and influence lengthy. Maybe we could split up and people will talk about us years later. We had the idea that bands only make two good albums. I still don't like more than three albums by any band. Maybe Talking Heads was an exception to that rule? The thing is, we were never planning to be The Who. It was like you were running downhill really fast. You were never sure if you could stay on your feet.'

Elsewhere, I have alluded to pop music (no longer) being a young person's game. But in 1980, the chances were that it would all be over in a flash. Ironically, Postcard was all about the moment, but that insight failed Josef K when it came to releasing the first album. It is conceivable that Postcard was often on the verge of becoming everything it set out to oppose. Horne's wildly oscillating interest levels in his charges didn't help. He was always looking for the next superstar. Someone to make him a millionaire. When he 'discovered' Roddy Frame, Collins would no doubt have felt slighted, while Haig felt the chink in the armour widening. His eggshell confidence couldn't stand another blow, but with Frame and Aztec Camera's arrival, Josef K went B-list, despite Horne's attempt to compare each of his four bands to a different phase of The Velvet Underground. Horne swooned over Roddy Frame, at the same time playing Orange Juice and Josef K off one another in an attempt to inject an extra edge to their competitiveness. Ultimately, Postcard barely existed at all—Horne bluffed his way through it all, making it up as he went along. It could have crashed and burned at any moment, but the label's very amateurishness, its slapdash charm, inspired others to follow the same pattern.

Horne was desperate for chart success, yet Josef K were too reticent, too sombre to be pop stars. Perhaps being or seeming 'independent' meant a whole lot more to them than it really should have. Independence is a state of mind, and it's always been difficult not to conflate the term with being signed to an impoverished record label.

'I remember Allan Campbell saying Virgin Records were interested in signing us, but we were adamant we were staying with Postcard and remained independent,' Ross recalls. 'That seemed so important to us at the time. Maybe that's one of the reasons we split up. We had no money coming through. We only made money from gigs. Looking back, I'm just quite fatalistic. What happened, happened. If we had really wanted to have commercial success, things might have been different.'

Haig concurs, while hinting at another troublesome reality—a lack of financial reward. 'Royalties? We didn't see any publishing money at all. That was pretty annoying. We got some cash through the distribution deal Postcard had with Rough Trade, but there was no accounting, and it seemed like there was no control over the finances. Oh, I'm sure there was money generated, but we didn't see any of it. Nobody had a clue what was going on. But at least I got enough through Rough Trade to enable me to purchase the first 808 drum machine ever in Scotland. At least I got *that* out of it all.'

In the introduction to this book, a comparison was made between Josef K and The Beatles. It might have seemed absurd to make one at all. But while Josef K were never going to be as culturally or musically significant, like the Fabs, they came undone by the gradual untangling of the bonds of friendship. In Peter Jackson's wonderful television documentary *Get Back*, the viewer becomes attuned to the foursome's subtle passive-aggressive gestures and expressions, in the full knowledge that the Beatles are coming apart at the seams. Now consider how the Fabs felt as individuals, how much was at stake, how many people depended upon their continued success. Ultimately, however, the desire to get the fuck out of there won out.

The members of Josef K had comparatively little to lose, but one can sense the same shadows of indifference flickering on the walls of the attic at Colinton Road during those last few rehearsals. Watches being anxiously checked, the sense that time was being wasted, not won. In that sense, the split was like the end of any intense friendship. Life would go on, much like before. But now it would be without the others. Paul and Malcolm were different personalities, but when you are teenagers and you make a connection around music, those kinds of obstacles can easily be overcome.

'I think it was a slow growing apart,' says Nick Currie, who had grown close to the band toward the end of things. 'Paul had more ambition—Paul Morley had labelled Haig the *fifth boy, the face and sound of 1982*. There was always the tug of ambition versus solidarity. Then the band were never happy with the album. Alan Horne could be quite scathing about them as well. It was turning into what Paul Morley described as a new folk music, which in those ways was a very bad thing to turn into. So, Haig went off to do the suave crooner with electronic backing, an interesting move, but he covered things like "Send In The Clowns"—things he was embarrassed about, and which have yet to see the light of day. He was taking a leaf out of the Subway Sect textbook—Vic Godard had already begun to lean toward more cabaret/lounge material. He became a bit slicker later on.

I remember hearing his remake of "Heaven Sent" with the Alex Sadkin production and it sounded like something from the future.'

There seemed to be a Kafkaesque inevitability to it all. By the end, the four members could barely speak to one another. Josef K, post-punk's classiest pioneers, procrastinated sufficiently long enough to find themselves suddenly playing an impossible game of catch-up. Those who had followed them from the start were puzzled and saddened by what seemed like an unsolvable conundrum—such promise unfulfilled, a bright star burning itself out in front of their eyes. A story that surely deserved a happier ending. But perhaps even the hardiest soul knew destiny would intercede. It was written in the book. The delight and the freshness had leaked out of it all. There was blood on the tracks, but something far worse in its place: the complete evaporation of any empathy between them. Plagued by doubt, they needed something to believe in, but ultimately, they didn't believe in one another, nor perhaps even in themselves.

In the end, the question of who or what Josef K might have become hardly matters. And the more time passes, the more of a miracle it seems that they *were* at all.

12/15 | HEAVEN SENT

JOSEF K & POST-PUNK

They had some great tunes, but the overall vibe is not as sweet as Orange Juice and Aztec Camera. A more sombre mood. Angst, doubt, guilt, unease—this was the palette of emotion, rather than Orange Juice's romantic longing.

SIMON REYNOLDS

Josef K enjoyed a brief if unspectacular period in the spotlight and received a fair amount of attention compared to many other bands who were consigned to remain beneath the radar. Yet theirs was hardly a Clash-style cavalry charge into the public consciousness. Instead, Josef K were one band among many, jostling for position in a post-punk landscape newly congested with numerous other abstract and oddly skewed figures. At first, it didn't seem too obvious, but each group's sound was readily identifiable and distinctive. What they did have in common, however, was the same reckless thirst for invention.

Punk's sonic onslaught was over, but its attitude would prevail. Determined to avoid every convention, the new generation was handed a new palette upon which to mix new and vibrant colours. The blank canvasses they faced seemed devoid of memory. A *tabula rasa*. Appalled by punk's strict privations, they began to resemble the dumb man who has learned to speak, the deaf man who suddenly hears. Punk opened the floodgates, but its lasting legacy wasn't safety pins and gobshite, not even Jamie Reid's epochal artwork, but rather what came afterward. It hadn't only given a green light to enthusiastic young wannabes but had inspired in more nimble minds a desire to reach further and try new things. The sense was growing that social and economic division were always going to be there, but that musically, at least, anything was possible.

It was the beginning of a period of fearless experimentation in British popular music—possibly its most creative and fertile period ever. It coalesced with the beginnings of the independent scene, with small labels springing up across the country. It was a time to celebrate idiosyncrasy and diversity. At the same time, it shared one similarity with the 60s Beat and Blues booms, in that it brought a number of naturally 'independent' artists into the mainstream. Alongside mavericks who operated at least initially in underground circles—Martin Hannett, Tony Wilson, Geoff Travis, Bob Last—the more conservative wing of the industry—the major labels, the money men, the unscrupulous A&R representatives, and so on—were keen to take advantage. They barely spoke the same language but sought to profit from the potentially lucrative new markets opening up. But they were unable to disguise their separateness from the mindset of the artists.

Some bands would sign to major labels and reap the rewards. There would have been little chance of getting the type of exposure they now enjoyed a few years previously. But unlike those 60s 'scenes' where excessive deviation from the formula might have resulted in total extinction, the independent labels of the early 1980s possessed sufficient confidence to allow their artists genuine freedom of expression. The outcome of that was that there were several bands who were spiritually in accord with one another while having little in common musically.

For the general public, weaned on Radio One; for lovers of 'the song', as well as for punk purists, many of these new post-punk upstarts were awkward, contrary, virtually impossible to love. Were they being self-consciously difficult? Sometimes the accusation seemed fair—think Throbbing Gristle or This Heat—but mostly it had to do with a natural aversion to sounds that were authentically original and often challenging. Here was the real 'progressive' rock, the new sonic revolution. Are you ready? Many were.

For the more discerning music fan, the years between 1979 and 1982— that is, the years of Josef K's brief existence—were a godsend. Albums like *Metal Box* and *Fear Of Music* had rewritten the index of possibilities. They were infinitely more sophisticated than anything punk had to offer, even if the underlying principle—to revolutionise and transform—was essentially the same. They proved that to be courageous didn't mean one needed to make primitive and abrasive noise. You could leave spaces, be cerebral and expansionist.

'Post-punk was all about the creeping back in of degrees of subtlety. Giving the song a chance to breathe,' Alan Rankine of The Associates later told Simon Reynolds. Equally, the new music didn't have to say anything political—and determining not to do so was political in itself. By and large, post-punk inclined toward the apolitical rather than the polemical, although there were notable exceptions (most notably Gang Of Four). But there was certainly a feeling that you could keep your cards close to your chest, that you didn't have to shout any more. You could be more subtle and ambiguous about what you felt. The music would do the talking.

Musically, post-punk was a bricolage of sources—African and new age, neoclassical and disco, electronic and Krautrock, dub and Tropicalia. Songs could be long, songs could be short, songs did not need guitars, songs didn't even need to be songs. There was no longer any reticence when it came to dabbling with the avant-garde, with what today one might call genre-hopping, or even with utilising technically gifted musicians. Talking

Heads, Joy Division, Wire, and PiL were the innovators. Post-punk became a melting pot of spiky, abrasive guitar, lushly textured soundscapes, dub fx, scratchy funk, industrial, ambient, and quirky rhythms. The bands who inhabited its landscape could never have existed before 1978, although—paradoxically—they were more likely to reference pre-punk than the class of '77. They were absolutely and perfectly a product of the era.

Josef K had sufficiently classicist sensibilities to allow them to transcend the present. This is one of the reasons they remain so vital today, adding to the mystery of their demise. The band's primary influences were and always remained The Velvet Underground, David Bowie, Television, Talking Heads, and Pere Ubu, but they also absorbed some of the strangeness and inventiveness of their contemporaries and were always listening to and learning from them. They socialised occasionally with their fellow Edinburgh bands while remaining resolutely independent from them in a creative sense. In turn, they inspired those other bands, propelling them forward by virtue of the sheer innovation of their own sound.

Their closest cousins were undoubtedly The Fire Engines. Malcolm Ross and Davy Henderson were good friends and remain so today, but the reciprocal influence was evident from the beginning, when they were plain old TV Art and The Dirty Reds. It had hardly been the friendliest of introductions. 'It was at the Wig & Pen we got to know Josef K,' Henderson recalled in *Hungry Beat*. 'There was a bit of acrimony between us initially because they were so great and we were so jealous—well I was. They could play anything and when they played at the Wig & Pen with Scars, we exchanged unpleasantries. I think there might have been some fists involved, very small ones, teenage fists. But then we became great friends with them through a shared interest in Lucky Strike cigarettes and other American tobaccos.'

It is hard to imagine one band creating the sound they did without the existence of the other. From their earliest days, The Fire Engines (as

The Dirty Reds) had shared bills with Josef K, both locally and even during some higher-profile concerts, such as at the Lyceum in London in November 1980. The two bands' careers seemed to overlap at times, and both would have kept a keen eye on the other. Vitally, they shared a similar sense of rhythm and discord—a frantic, dislocated, desperate urgency. But the musical similarity went further than the mere desire to produce a finger-shredding racket. In the first instance, there was a charm and mystique about both lead singers, even if Henderson's performances were usually more volatile and expressive than Haig's. Haig's cool, reserved, often motionless figure conveyed an identical impression—that he didn't give a fuck.

The reality was something else entirely—Haig, particularly in the early days, was bathed in discomfort when he fronted the band, remaining rooted to the spot—but the overall effect could sometimes intensify the exhilaration of the audience. By the latter performances, he was more inclined to express himself. 'I started moving around more freely onstage when I was playing less guitar,' he says. 'I had become a bit more relaxed. I had always wanted to go a little mad—but it would usually be a little stop-start because I was just too inhibited. People probably thought my actions onstage pretty strange. It was never a preconceived thing, just a spontaneous action.' At the same time, Fire Engines guitarist Murray Slade had a comparable playing style to Malcolm Ross, although he undoubtedly drew more from the convulsive rhythms of the Magic Band and the jerky stop-starts of no wave than Ross, who was in some ways a more nuanced and sensitive musician.

The Fire Engines could well have ended up as Josef K's labelmates, had Alan Horne been quicker off the mark. He would forever be tormented by the feeling he'd let them slip through his fingers. Had they joined the Postcard 'roster', who knows what that might have meant for Josef K? Perhaps they might have felt more at home, less out on a limb. Instead, Henderson opted to set up his own label, Codex Communications. One of the first people he consulted about their choice of debut single was

Malcolm Ross. Ross suggested 'Discord'. Henderson disagreed, opting instead for the spasmodic annihilation of 'Get Up And Use Me'. In some people's eyes—those who saw in Josef K only the live noisy angular racket, The Fire Engines outpunched them. But, in truth, Josef K had greater range. Perhaps that was their undoing.

Scars too had possessed a similarly twitchy anxiety, particularly at the beginning, with scratchy, often ferocious guitars upfront. There was a comparable sense of existential dread in the lyrics, although with Scars it did not seem quite as subtle. The bands knew each other well and hung out together with The Fire Engines at the Tap O' Laurieston. 'You could have Scars, Fire Engines, Associates, Josef K, all mingling around on the one night,' says Haig. 'I know that sounds like an English press myth—*just go up to Scotland and you'll catch all the Scottish bands on the one night*—but you actually could for a while! We'd all come out of punk at the same time. You could relate to the others whom punk had affected. It was a sense of us against them, the bond firmly strengthened by being shouted at regularly in the street.'

As each band developed, a little competitiveness began to creep in between them. One gig in particular—at the Venue in London on June 16, 1981—marked a significant transition in relations between the Josef K and Scars. Josef K were second on the bill, Scars having released their debut album, with Josef K's still a few weeks away. But Scars' perceived 'seniority' counted for nothing.

'When the curtains opened, there was just this huge roar,' remembers Ross. 'The place was packed. I liked the Scars but there was a bit of rivalry between us. By the time they were halfway through *their* set, people were drifting off. There was definitely a sense at that moment that we had overtaken them.' With bitter irony, by the same time the following year, neither band would even exist.

As for Orange Juice, some assumed that they and Josef K were living in each other's pockets—that Postcard was a happy family of ultra-hep cats who lounged around cafes drinking milkshakes in the afternoon, bought the same Penguin paperbacks, and shopped for smart second-hand threads to impress audiences during their evenings' work. But aside from the fact that they were labelmates—and regularly shared the same bill—they didn't really have that much in common. Their musical mindsets took odd detours from one another, even if both took The Velvet Underground as their chief inspiration. To put it somewhat crudely, Josef K absorbed the 'Venus In Furs'/'White Light/White Heat'/'The Murder Mystery' Velvet Underground more than the 'Sunday Morning'/'Pale Blue Eyes'/'Candy Says' VU preferred by Edwyn & co.

Orange Juice possibly heard the Velvets in a similar way to how Jonathan Richman heard the Velvets—The Velvet Underground wrote love songs with real depth, unflinching in their honesty, deceptively tender and often misunderstood. By contrast, Josef K were possibly hearing what Echo & The Bunnymen or Joy Division were hearing: The Velvet Underground were an avant-garde bunch of genius misfits, fearless and ultra-modernist. While that may be a tad over-simplistic, there is no doubt that Orange Juice were a more conventional pop group, preferring melody over discord, songs over atmosphere and experimentalism. 'It's Kinda Funny' was probably the closest in style to Orange Juice that Josef K ever came, and, as mentioned previously, it was likely the catalyst for some combativeness and antipathy between them. Stylistically an anomaly in Josef K's canon, it remains the song many people remember most fondly.

Josef K probably shared more in common with Simple Minds than they would care to admit. People often forget just how forward-thinking Simple Minds actually were at the turn of the decade, once they had shaken off the temptation to mimic Roxy Music. The records they made between 1980 and 1982 were incredibly adventurous. They reinvented themselves following European tours that nurtured a fixation with classical European art and iconography and motoric, mildly industrial soundscapes. Even so, the two bands did not sound at all similar—Simple Minds' shimmering synths and chiming, ethereal guitars differed from K's jagged discord— but both were equally likely to experiment with sound and texture at the expense of composing love songs, as Orange Juice did. Take Simple Minds' own 'Love Song', for example—a doggedly emotionless thing— and compare it with something like Josef K's equally linear if much more furiously paced 'Revelation'. Structurally, even spiritually, they are one, even if the overall effect contrasts sharply. Like Josef K, Simple Minds were less likely to follow convention—songs possessing verses, choruses, middle-eights—than Orange Juice, who never really shook off their pop classicism, nor would they have wanted to. It's one reason Orange Juice were more successful than Josef K. The others? 'Ambition and Edwyn,' says Jon Savage.

Another spiritual cousin was The Associates, with whom the band became close friends. Paul Haig and Billy Mackenzie developed a very close bond that continued until the latter's untimely passing. Like Simple Minds, The Associates' early music was mechanised, disorientating, a touch Teutonic, and often arrhythmic. Before long, they would add to those sensibilities a glossy synthetic sheen, and with that 'New Pop' was born. The result was their 1982 masterpiece, *Sulk*: Scott Walker or Frank Sinatra sung in a haze of pink, purple, and turquoise, a million miles removed from Josef K's serrated edges but still defiantly European.

Something like *Sulk* possibly nudged Haig in that direction, but his stage-shy persona meant he was more comfortable experimenting alone with technology in his bedroom or sitting by the window, nose-deep in *Hunger*, whose nameless narrator at one point states, 'I felt pleasantly empty, untouched by everything around me and happy to be unseen by it all.'

A lot of experimental music of the early 80s, and particularly German artists such as Harald Grosskopf, drew inspiration from Bowie and his Berlin phase. In the UK, his influence often manifested itself more in the face paint and star quality than in the music itself. None of that New Romantic music—Japan, Visage, Duran Duran, et cetera—could have emerged without his influence. While Josef K were equally inspired by him, there is little if any sonic similarity to Bowie's music. And, just occasionally, Paul Haig—with his flirtatious charm and fashionable haircut—gave the impression he might feel more comfortable in the company of some of those new groups.

Of the many new British bands who emerged during this period, some were close in spirit if not necessarily similar-sounding. Josef K shared a bill with The Monochrome Set in May 1980 and there was a shared quirky inventiveness in both bands. Others were as decidedly anti-rock but expressed this in other ways, such as the dreamlike filigrees of Vini Reilly's Durutti Column, which borrowed from folk, ambient, classical, and even prog rather than punk. Reilly employed a more atmospheric use of space, making for a decidedly less nervy proposition. Fellow Mancunians A Certain Ratio, along with London outfit 23 Skidoo, employed avant-funk rhythms like Josef K did but married them to experimental, occasionally Afrocentric, soundscapes. Cardiff's Young Marble Giants were even more radical, reinventing the guitar altogether for their minimalist classic *Colossal Youth*, a throbbing masterwork of muted apocalyptic emotion.

Meanwhile, Throbbing Gristle seemed dead set on outraging the establishment, going beyond abstract, deconstructing noise to produce an entirely nauseating melange. Likewise, This Heat, with their turgid abrasive expressionistic sheets of noise, could never have hoped for a commercial return, but they typified the spirit of the age and the complete abandonment of all convention to a brave new artistic vision. The Raincoats' atonal rhythmic junkshop produced a cauldron of folk, modal jazz, avant-garde, and crooked reggae. Leeds' Gang Of Four and Delta 5 were closer in spirit musically, with their scratchy punk-funk hybrid, but their Maoist politics were alien to Josef K. Other bands such as Sheffield's Human League and

Cabaret Voltaire embraced modernism but sought to replace guitars with synthesisers—an alien concept, at least in 1980, to Haig and Ross.

Several of those bands appeared on the *C81* compilation, a cassette-only release of independent talent issued by the *NME* in collaboration with Rough Trade in January 1981. Josef K were on there too, the inclusion of 'Endless Soul' prefiguring its surprise omission from *The Only Fun In Town*. It was a fantastic collection, with Josef K rubbing shoulders with crossover acts such as The Specials and The Beat and other terrific selections from DAF, Cabaret Voltaire, Blue Orchids, John Cooper Clarke, Wah!, Pere Ubu, Robert Wyatt, and Scritti Politti.

On the other side of the Atlantic, there was a handful of bands who would have captured Josef K's attention, and who in some ways were even closer in spirit than their UK contemporaries. If the art-rock sound of New York was the band's chief inspiration, it is unsurprising that they identified as kindred spirits some of the new artists who emerged in the wake of Talking Heads and Television. There has been a resurgence of interest in the early 80s NYC underground scene, with its ingenious union of the slicing guitars of no wave with the energy and fizz of disco and the emergent new East Coast hip-hop sound.

One of the brightest new acts was Bush Tetras, who grew out of the ashes of The Contortions and made awkward and angular punk-funk. The discordant jag of 'Too Many Creeps' and 'Snakes Crawl' got them noticed, but on 'You Taste Like The Tropics' one can hear the resemblance to Josef K. It's not hard to imagine Malcolm Ross shuffling around the stage, even if Cynthia Sley's delivery was always decidedly more aggressive than Haig's. Josef K played alongside them at the London School of Economics in February 1981, part of a terrific bill that also included Delta 5 and The Nightingales.

Liquid Liquid, who formed shortly after Josef K, were another outfit sometimes labelled 'dance punk' or 'punk funk'. They created a state-of-the-art sound that was probably too hip for the time but yielded the colossal 'Cavern', reworked with enormous success by Melle Mel on the global smash 'White Lines (Don't Do It)'. Unlike Bush Tetras, Liquid Liquid were less well-known to Josef K, but they too embraced the possibility of fusing together funk rhythms and lean guitar lines. 'Optimo' is even funkier than Josef K, its percussion as furiously inventive as Torrance's. The overall effect is defiantly anti-rock—something Josef K always strove for themselves, but in Liquid Liquid's case accomplished via a sparer use of guitar. They were distant cousins who shared a similar understanding of what music could be and what it ought to sound like in the new decade.

Perhaps closest of all were The Feelies, whose most celebrated song, 'The Boy With The Perpetual Nervousness', should have been pluralised and trademarked as a band name by Josef K themselves. The feverish rhythms and intricate note-picking would have been very familiar to them, and *Crazy Rhythms* was an album they were hooked on following its release in April 1980. A useful touchstone is 'Original Love', on which Glenn Mercer's delivery bears an uncanny resemblance to Haig.

So where did Josef K really fit in, and did they even want to? It was always more important to do something uniquely their own. While the bands already mentioned were undeniably innovative and groundbreaking, Josef K arguably had more things in common with other bands who were able to cross over to the mainstream and achieve a greater degree of success. In that sense, it makes their commercial failure all the more puzzling. At the same time, insists Ian Rankin, 'There was something slightly standoffish about them. I could never quite my head around it. It's not that they were a difficult band—three-minute songs, not too complex, and they clearly could play well. The lyrics were always interesting. They were a literate band who wanted to be taken seriously.'

Of all their contemporaries, Josef K were most inspired by Joy Division. Enough has been written about Joy Division elsewhere, but Josef

HEAVEN SENT | 189

K certainly borrowed gallons of their existential angst ('*Here are the young men / The weight on their shoulders*'), stole from their wardrobe (those dark shirts and occasional raincoats, worn, said Haig, 'because it might rain'), and nicked from their sonic toolbox. Dark bass lines. Pow-pow.

Without denigrating the contribution of Mark Francois, one can only speculate about the outcome had Martin Hannett been invited to sprinkle his fairy dust on *The Only Fun In Town* instead. As well as augmenting Joy Division's second LP, *Closer*, Hannett had recently produced *The Correct Use Of Soap* by fellow Mancunians Magazine. The latter was a striking album—the band's third—and the perfect realisation of their fusion of Devoto's misanthropic genius with the quintet's ambitious soundscapes. Their futurist manifesto was anchored around Barry Adamson's bubbling geyser bass lines and John McGeogh's surgical guitar lines, everything given a thick sheen by Dave Formula's cinematic synth washes. Fellow Scot McGeogh was one of the most inventive guitarists of his time, and Ross—equally industrious—was an avowed admirer. Josef K had been offered a support slot when Magazine played the Astoria. It could have been the type of occasion to unnerve them, but by then they were by then accustomed to opening for the odd big name.

Another memorable support slot involved opening for Echo & The Bunnymen at the Grangemouth Hotel. The Bunnymen provide a good indicator of what Josef K could have become. The difference? Supreme self-confidence. Stylistically, Mac & co were probably marginally more indebted to The Doors and Love than The Velvet Underground. If they looked backward for inspiration, the big production on their records elevated their heady mix of post-punk rhythms and neo-psychedelic guitars to something with universal appeal. And, in Will Sergeant, they possessed the greatest guitarist of the generation, endlessly inventive, technically brilliant. Ultimately, the Bunnymen were considerably more ambitious. They wanted to be famous and so they were.

In an interview conducted by *Stand & Deliver* fanzine shortly before the band's breakup, Ross acknowledged a similarity—at least idealistically—to The Fall. However, looking back now, he considers Wire and Alternative TV to be more like kindred spirits. 'I liked The Fall, but they just weren't musical enough.' Through sheer bloody-mindedness and an unparalleled capacity for reinvention, Mark E. Smith was able to circumvent the various shifts in fashion throughout the 80s and indeed into the twenty-first century. Ross and Haig admired aspects of their sound—the angular kineticism—but stood at a distance from the garage and rockabilly sludge. Unlike Smith, they didn't teach the music press what to say about them (the press seemed unusually obedient in Smith's case). In stark contrast, Josef K barely told them anything.

A closer comparison than The Fall would be The Pop Group, who undoubtedly caught the attention of Haig and Ross, as well as members of The Fire Engines and Orange Juice, when they supported Patti Smith at the Edinburgh Odeon in August 1978. Their late frontman, Mark Stewart, later claimed that this performance was as much a catalyst for the future direction of the Scottish post-punk scene as seeing Subway Sect that famous night a year earlier. The Pop Group deconstructed funk with their throbbing rhythms, but the scar and bite of John Waddington's guitar sound made for a different kind of dance. Stewart could be suave but equally could surrender his poise to an almost unhinged hysteria, redolent of the berserk theatrical showmanship of Nick Cave with The Birthday Party.

Ultimately, though, there really was no other band like Josef K. The truth is, comparisons, while interesting to make, are invariably inadequate, for Josef K did not fit in with anyone or anything, not on a personal level nor on a musical one. For they were unique.

'[They were] like no one else,' says Jon Savage. 'That was a big part of their appeal.'

It is also one reason they disappeared through the crack in the wall.

13/15 | MISSIONARIES / ENDLESS SOUL
THE LEGACY OF JOSEF K

*Josef K were the perfect band. Everything about them: the look,
the sound, the songs. Paul Haig's voice, that incredible white
funkiness coupled with soul. No one sounded like them before
or after. . . . Shine bright, burn fast, Josef K certainly did that—
their music still sounds so fresh today, like no one else.*

STEFAN KASSEL, MARINA RECORDS, *HUNGRY BEAT*

Josef K had everything. After all, Paul Haig was the coolest man alive. So
claimed Paul Morley. It was true. FACT1981. The blackout VU shades
and charity shop threads steered a path midway between 60s bohemia
and the emergent new romanticism. A perfect model for the new bright
future promised by the 80s. Haig, like a post-punk Sartre, sang how Lou
Reed might interpret Frank Sinatra, or conversely how Sinatra might
have tackled 'I'm Waiting For The Man'. Every box was ticked. The
poet. The philosopher. The intellectual. Supercilious. Fresh-faced. Cute.
Stylish without drawing attention. He drew others to himself through his
apparent indifference to everything. Sentences were short, statements non-
existent. Less is more. Every action and gesture magnified the mystery. Not

only that but he was an extremely talented guitar player (an attribute that is sometimes cruelly overlooked), and he could pick up any rhythm and melody just by using his ear.

Haig had—and still has—an insatiable appetite for creating music. He was always bursting with ideas. He was painfully shy but—though he would probably deny it—a magnet for the girls. He could have been the biggest pop star of the 80s, up there with Prince or George Michael or Morrissey, and it baffles some as to why he wasn't. 'I liked the enigma and his cryptic quality, the beauty of his voice and definitive nature of his appearance,' said Morley. 'He was my kind of pop star. He looked like he read Beckett but listened to Diana Ross and The Supremes ... the perfect hybrid.'

Malcolm Ross was one of the most brilliant and creative guitarists of his generation, up there with John McGeogh, Johnny Marr, and Will Sergeant. He has proved subsequently to be also one of the most versatile, dabbling in country & western and film music, among other genres. His guitar playing was unimaginably brave—always adventurous, oftentimes thrilling. But while he could wring improbable shapes from his instrument, he was capable of great subtlety too. 'I loved his style and approach,' says Marr, while Jon Savage adds, 'I rate him very highly. He never got the props he deserved. He was very individual, melodic and percussive.'

Ross possesses an intelligent ear for arranging music and can play several other instruments. Postcard was home to three Scottish bands in the early 80s, and Malcolm was so highly respected that at one time or another, he played in all three of them. No one else can make a similar claim. On a personal level, he possessed the kind of spirited and convivial temperament that meant he was always able to fraternise with anyone. He remains a person of principle, driven by a keen sense of justice. Like his co-pilot Haig, he was hardly a fan of confrontation but was unafraid of being truthful. And the truth hurts sometimes. It is unlikely you will hear anyone utter an unkind word about him, so much do they admire his integrity.

Davy Weddell was the quickest learner in pop. Few recognise him as the most innovative musician, but in retrospect, he was the glue that held the band together. Perhaps Josef K would have imploded even earlier, had he not taken up the challenge to play bass. Despite his initial desperate anxiety at being thrust into the spotlight, as Nick Currie has pointed out, Weddell went on to make a truly unique sound with his instrument. He was an essential ingredient in the mix. And, in any case, there are few things more thrilling than a super-fan being thrust into the spotlight with an unfamiliar instrument dangled under his nose. And having the balls to make a success of it.

There is a case for Ronnie Torrance being the greatest post-punk drummer of all, not only because he had the superhuman levels of energy necessary to propel the speed-fuelled ferocity of songs such as 'Drone' and 'Revelation' but also because his style was highly unorthodox. Live performances were particularly impressive, given they were almost always delivered after consuming a full bottle of whisky (his minimum daily intake).

All the pieces were in place, so who was listening and learning? In 1990, *Melody Maker*'s Simon Reynolds penned a glowing review of the retrospective collection *Young & Stupid*. It was the second compilation album to feature that title. Reynolds's analysis was typically brilliant, but the piece contended that Josef K had left 'no progeny … unless you include The June Brides.' An acute observation, but one that barely raised an eyebrow. What seems strange, however, is that a quarter of a century later, Josef K are regularly cited as one of the most influential post-punk bands of all.

Perhaps it is because few bands since have sounded like Josef K. That they were simply too much of a one-off to inspire copyists. Who else could do what they did? Yet arguably their influence has been vastly underestimated. Some might point to a few other bands who owe them a significant debt, even if they rarely cite them as a primary influence. Indeed, there have only been a small handful of artists in the intervening period who have mentioned Josef K as a key influence. And there have been periods of time when they have failed to register any sort of interest.

'There was virtually a decade—from around 1989 to the late 90s, maybe 1996 or 1997, when we had been more or less forgotten about,' says Ross. 'No one mentioned us at all.' It's interesting that Ross picks out those years, as this was a period that saw the emergence of hip-hop and electronic dance music on a global scale. Guitars temporarily went on vacation, returning with three chords in a Parka and a pair of trainers.

One could make tangential comparisons with other artists whose influence was slow to ferment, such as Big Star and Nick Drake, neither of whom got much of a look-in between the mid-70s and the mid-80s. It was only then their music really began to attract greater recognition. Even the influence of The Velvet Underground was a gradual 'trickle down sonics', unlike Bowie, the Pistols, The Clash, and Joy Division, all of whom were surrounded by armies of instant imitators.

Certainly, for a time at least, Josef K were the very definition of *au courant*. They came from punk but they embraced the future. It is beyond question that they had an immediate influence on their contemporaries. Haig was stylish and savant, the Martin Frys and Glenn Gregorys of this world would have had one eye on him as they modelled their own images. Their bands offered up the kind of sophisto-pop that Haig would go on to make on his own (and, it may be argued, he willed for Josef K). Indeed, as Ronnie Torrance points out, in many ways, Josef K created 'a bridge between punk and New Romanticism'. Those shiny groups bore little resemblance to Josef K musically, but they recognised in Haig a credible and stylish pop star—and reckoned that they too could be taken as seriously. Perhaps *they* would be the faces of '83 and '84.

However, pop music has a nasty habit of leaving people behind, and as those bands took centre stage, Josef K faded from view. It seemed only a few bands picked up the mantle. But Josef K's legacy goes much deeper than what at first might appear obvious. Indeed, one is tempted to argue that a great deal of mid-80s music drew from Josef K as much as, if not more so, than Orange Juice. The conventional/consensus view—and this is probably what Reynolds was thinking in 1990—is that Josef K influenced The June Brides and possibly The Wedding Present, and that was about it. But one influence that's largely overlooked is a portion of the line-up on the *C86* cassette.

'Often, people think of *C86* itself as a *genre* itself these days,' says Douglas McIntyre. 'It's associated with that kind of shambling anorak sound, but a lot of the bands on that compilation were quite angular-sounding. The bands that were signed to the Ron Johnson label, like Big Flame and The Mackenzies, for example. The Mackenzies were massive Josef K fans, so there's a direct link there to the Ron Johnson bands. They would have been influenced by The Fire Engines too, but The Mackenzies would definitely have been more influenced by Josef K.'

The more obvious and oft-quoted influences are mentioned routinely because Phil Wilson (June Brides) and David Gedge (The Wedding Present) confessed to them. 'It would have been John Peel who first made me aware of Josef K,' says Wilson, who saw the band perform at the ICA on January 4, 1981. 'I liked them a lot on first hearing, but not quite as much as I adored their Postcard labelmates Orange Juice. My friends and I longed to see Orange Juice live, and, as we were living in London, we didn't have to wait too long. There was an added bonus as Josef K would be supporting. During the concert, my view of them changed completely. Orange Juice were terrific, of course—joyous, anarchic, fun. But Josef K were a total revelation. Great songs, aggressive noise, plus the coolest lead singer in the world. They leapt ahead of Orange Juice in my estimation. I didn't just admire Paul Haig, I wanted to *be* Paul Haig. Got the suits, got the haircut, got the band.'

An even more significant influence, and one that almost always gets overlooked, is The Smiths. Johnny Marr was an avowed admirer. He was too original a musician to be in anyone's debt, but he absorbed from a whole variety of sources. For certain, the young guitarist found the spirit and dynamism of Josef K infectious and appealing.

'They seemed to be part of a new time and a new approach, which for people of my age was pretty exciting,' he says. 'There was some promise there, throwing off the old paradigms of punk, which is ironic given that punk was supposed to be a throwing away of things. I thought they sounded a bit like Cabaret Voltaire with guitars. I think we shared a similar attitude about what we didn't want to be and what was new, musically and aesthetically. We'd all grown up loving the guitar, but what had come in the years directly before us had become outdated and obvious, unrelatable. It felt like, *We have to try something different because everything is different now.* That's how I was seeing it. Although our approach to songwriting was different, the very early Smiths had a similar sound to Josef K—stripped down with no obvious trappings of *production*. Bleak. Almost dystopian.'

Marr also observed that Josef K seemed committed to looking as anti-rock as possible. 'A lot of the guitar bands at the time still looked like very rock'n'roll . . . American . . . or new wave, or like The Velvet Underground at best, whereas Josef K looked like they were from the Bauhaus, and they played unusual guitars for the time. Fender Mustangs high up. That in itself was a break from the past. The only other person I'd seen doing that was Rob Symonds from Subway Sect.'

It was ultimately Marr's love of Chic and his Fender Twin Reverb that gave The Smiths their unique sound, but there is a suggestion in songs such as 'Hand In Glove' and 'This Charming Man' that he was able to marry that to the freneticism of post-punk, in particular the toppy urgency of Josef K. 'I've said it before,' Marr adds, 'but to me bands like Josef K and The Smiths were the letter A in the new lexicon after punk, which I felt was the letter Z in the old one. They seemed to have a collective agenda— something they'd thought about. That was impressive and seemed current.'

Josef K's influence is also discernible in the more ravishing and exhilarating music-makers that followed in the late 80s. Of special note would be That Petrol Emotion, who grew out of the ashes of the Undertones. Listen to the frenzied discordant guitars and the lopsided rhythms of their first album, *Manic Pop Thrill*. Now that's an album title handmade for Josef K. Consider too the likes of My Bloody Valentine and Sonic Youth, both of whom shared Josef K's rush of ecstatic discord, albeit in less brittle and angular form. Haig has only recently explored Sonic Youth's records, noting immediately that they employed Jaguars and Jazzmasters. Speaking of Josef K's aesthetic, he acknowledges a tendency to 'do away with guitar solos and instead employ guitar breaks ... we wanted to create a noisy scratchiness where the guitar solo should have gone. It felt avant-garde. Make a noise with chords you don't know.'

Haig's description could quite easily fit the music of Sonic Youth, who first performed together shortly before Josef K's break up in June 1981 and became one of the most startlingly original bands of the late 80s. Ross remains less convinced. 'Some composers really just use their ears rather than their brains to arrive at the sounds that they want to make. Sonic Youth used strange tunings—we never did that at all—but it was a matter of trying to find the right sound, and so even if we used more unconventional chord changes, we didn't employ strange tunings like Sonic Youth.' There was nothing funky about Sonic Youth either, but it's tempting to join the dots in any consideration of the evolution of the post-punk sound, where multiple secondary influences are absorbed tangentially and discernible in subtle ways.

Even if Josef K's profile dipped for the best part of a decade, as Ross suggests, there were disciples and dabbling dilettantes who pinched from them at will. At the turn of the twenty-first century there was a 'revival' of sorts, with the emergence of a new group of bands who borrowed heavily from the post-punk period, particularly from Gang Of Four, Joy Division, The Fire Engines, and Josef K. British outfits such as Bloc Party and American bands like The Strokes and Interpol seemed determined to recapture the sonic aura of 1980. 'You would occasionally hear things sometimes and be reminded of Josef K,' notes Ross. 'Other people probably stumbled upon the same things we stumbled upon, so it's hard to say with any certainty who we've influenced directly. My younger son Stan thought "Sorry For Laughing" sounded like The Strokes, although it's not really a typical Josef K song. But maybe Josef K's sound, which evolved via Talking Heads, the Velvets, and Television—a very New York sound—was simply drawing from the same range of influences as The Strokes would later draw from.'

It would be another band—from Edinburgh no less—who would bear Josef K's influence more markedly than any other. Even the band's name dropped a hint. Franz Ferdinand. A European name. From history. Iconic. Not fictional, this time, but evoking the same mystique.

'I first heard Josef K when someone lent me a recording of their Peel sessions at some point in the 90s, when I was in my early twenties,' says frontman Alex Kapranos. 'There was a proper darkness to the music and lyrics, yet the energy was an electrical fire. Even the name. Naming yourself after a Kafka novel. *That* Kafka novel. So knowing yet naive simultaneously. Or not. There is a stark simplicity in naming yourselves after the anti-hero of a book like that. I'd loved *The Trial* as a teenager, the isolation, alienation, and futile resistance articulated how I felt about the life I had. This music also articulated some part of how I felt when I heard it, too. That's what makes us love music, isn't it? When it communicates what we feel but cannot find the words for ourselves.'

Kapranos was instantly entranced. 'The laconic deep delivery of the vocal was cool. Velvets kind of cool. Then there was the rhythm. It was the kind of music that I wanted to dance to. In the abstract, the same type of arrangement as the JBs or Chic, where the guitars are thin, rhythmic, and repetitive; the bass is prominent and has a melodic hypnotism to it; the drums taking the hi-hat sixteens and eights to the fore, rather than the heavy sludge beat of rock or punk. But it seemed from another planet next to those bands—a planet that was more like the one I lived on. I didn't live in Detroit or NYC. I lived in Glasgow, and my girlfriend was in Edinburgh. I do believe that the landscapes of a band's environment cast shadows across the music. I could feel that familiar Edinburgh winter wind biting through the atmosphere of their sound. The short days and 3pm nightfall. Or was that the projection of my own eager imagination? I didn't care. The arrangements were smart, unique, and inventive, yet there was a feeling that it was about to tumble into a fatal crash, like watching an athletic child ride a bike for the first time, where the confidence, ambition, and natural prowess shake and wobble as the limbs overreach into doing it for the first time. It sounded sophisticated but raw, and seemingly unafraid of its flaws.'

Franz Ferdinand would enjoy a level of commercial success unimaginable to Josef K. That possibly irked Haig, who in an interview shortly after their emergence as chart stars was fairly scathing, claiming Kapranos & co had ripped off Josef K's sound. The band's hit smash, 'Take Me Out', had a swaggering self-confidence and verve, going on to storm the charts and setting the scene for a 2004 debut album that sold over three million copies (compare that to around twenty thousand of *The Only Fun In Town*). However, from the outset, Franz Ferdinand were always a far more commercial proposition. They possessed a similar if less abrasive urgency but lacked the dark existentialist gloom characteristic of Haig, although the vocal stylings were sometimes similar.

'Josef K sound little like Franz Ferdinand,' claims Kapranos. 'Yes, there are obvious parallels from the geography of our inception to the literary awkwardness of our oblique take on the dancefloor. I may be wrong, but I felt there was a degree of self-destructive anti-commercialism within Josef K. They would never have played *Top Of The Pops* even if they were asked. I felt like that when I was twenty-one too. The bands and music I made then said *fuck you all*, but I was thirty-one when the first Franz Ferdinand LP came out, and by that time I was more mellow, and the idea of playing *Top Of The Pops* became more amusing than appalling. I'd had over a decade of living on the breadline because of the music I made, so when a degree of commercial success arrived, I didn't sabotage it in the way I would have done if I'd been a few years younger or if I was in Josef K. I was sick of Safeway Saver beans. It was time for some Heinz.'

As someone with a great respect for both bands, Douglas McIntyre remains a more neutral observer. 'I think Franz Ferdinand were definitely influenced by Josef K, but I wouldn't agree with the idea that they stole all of their ideas from them. They weren't ripping anybody off, and from where I'm sitting, the influence is not all that audible.'

Haig himself would later soften his views somewhat, telling Paul Lester of *Record Collector*, 'They've said "Sorry For Laughing" is one of their favourite songs; they've worn their influences on their sleeve. If they hadn't said the things they've said and done the things they've done, our album [*Entomology*] wouldn't be coming out on [Franz Ferdinand's label] Domino. It's brought our music to a younger audience. If Josef K existed now, we'd probably be like Franz Ferdinand. If we'd had that exposure—because at the time there was no MTV, none of those vehicles for promotion—we'd have been quite successful in the mainstream. Would we have been up for that? Probably not. We weren't as commercial or accessible as Franz: even though they're arty, they're also quite jolly. They lack the mystery and darkness of Josef K.'

As well as appealing to contemporary musicians from their home town, Josef K's fingerprints can also be detected today in a handful of Canadian artists, most notably in the jittery rhythms and serrated guitars of Jon Varley (in particular his work with NOV3L), the jarring rumble of Ought (pitched midway between The Fall and Josef K), and Pottery ('Spell' from the *No. 1* EP is an uncanny recreation of K's freneticism and panache).

There are also young artists in the UK who have picked up the mantle, most significantly jazz-punk innovator Archy Marshall (aka King Krule), who has spoken frequently about Josef K in press interviews, commenting in *Narduwar* that they created 'intelligent music . . . coming from a pure place.' Marshall's disorientating take on urban blues occasionally produces rushes of scintillating guitar work reminiscent of Josef K (say on 'Emergency Blimp' or 'Hamburgerphobia'). Overall, there is a similar spirit of adventure, even if Marshall draws from a wider range of genres and styles.

It is undeniable that Josef K's name, their style, and most of all their music has become synonymous with a kind of post-modernist cool. 'In terms of what people pick up on, it's probably that fast-funk feel— the frantic and slightly flustered boppy post-punk groove,' says Simon Reynolds. 'A scratchy and scrappy take on Chic.'

'They have become part of the canon of artists,' says Kapranos. 'It's an unspoken canon, but everyone knows who is in it and who is not. Sure, some drift in and out over the years, but there are some who are steady, like The Velvet Underground, Roxy Music, or Bowie. Josef K are in there. It's like having an entry or two in the *Norton Anthology Of Poetry*. You're just there. Andrew Marvell or Philip Larkin. "Sorry For Laughing" or "Pale Blue Eyes". It's just there. Everyone who knows, knows.'

'I am glad people are still talking about them over forty years later,' adds Jon Savage. 'They were one of the more outstanding groups I saw during that period.'

We live in a furiously paced, hi-tech world—one constantly high on anxiety. Everywhere and in everything, our senses are becoming increasingly deadened, suffocated by a kind of hopeless narcolepsy in the midst of the relentless babble of useless information. The music that many enjoy in these times often reflects the need to recalibrate, to seek refuge and balance, but it must be said that Josef K's music—with guitars that 'trilled like bells and trembled for dear life', per Paul Morley in the liner notes to *Entomology*—offers a more realistic approximation of the psychological/ emotional state of the world today.

14/15 | THE RECORDS WERE LETTERS

AN A–Z OF JOSEF K SONGS

Josef K were Postcard's cutting edge—spiky, insouciant,
sardonic, existentially loaded and debonair. And,
throughout, their melodies remained pop at heart.

MARTIN ASTON, *MOJO*, AUGUST 2004

If one excludes *The Farewell Single*, Josef K committed a mere twenty tracks to vinyl (including various re-recordings of the same songs) while they were active. That's one song less than the total on the first Wire album. However, due to the glut of reissues and special editions that have appeared over the intervening years, many other songs have come to light, alongside several live recordings.

Listeners may be fairly limited by what they can access on streaming services today, and collectors might be expected to pay over the odds for physical material that's no longer available. Here is a critical lowdown on all of the songs that have been officially made available to the public in some shape or form since the band's inception. For those that have appeared in both studio and live form, our examination will be confined to the former, unless there is special reason to do otherwise.

'ADORATION'

At least two versions exist of this song, which began to feature as the band's set closer in the spring of 1981. '*I'm sick of wearing these sunglasses*,' quips Haig on the earlier recording (available on *Crazy To Exist: Live*). By then, it wasn't the only thing he was sick of. The melody is pleasingly upbeat and infectious, with marvellous twangy tremolo bending over the bridge. Weddell's bass probes, Torrance's drums are muffled, and as the song reaches its climax it builds with a sustained, frantic, cacophonous ringing-in-the-ears to much audience enthusiasm. Lyrically, it is classic Haig fare:

> *Why adore something you can't see*
> *Stay down here and talk to me*

'Yes, it's that Woody Allen scene in *Annie Hall*, isn't it?' Haig laughs. 'The scene where he meets the girl in the art gallery—and she complains about the absurdity of being alive in a godless vacuous universe.'

The second version, recorded at Valentino's only a week before the end, is slower in tempo and features a more trebly guitar sound, while the dirge is less controlled toward the end. 'This is the last song . . . and I'm not going to say anything else,' Haig announces, although few at the time would have understood the poignancy of what seemed like an innocuous remark. Valentino's was their second-to-last show, but it still showcased everything that thrilled about Josef K: melodies to undress you, lacerating performances.

'THE ANGLE'

One of those confusing Josef K songs with multiple variations of title. The original version was the last track on the first side of *The Only Fun In Town*. A work-in-progress at the time of *Sorry For Laughing*, it is lean and stripped back and features squealing guitars and a double-tracked vocal. It is Davy Weddell's favourite Josef K song.

Feel emotion and let loose my fear
See yourself from their angle
Don't move away until you know
A chance like this—can't let it go!

The first version on *The Farewell Single* ('One Angle') is cleaner and more pronounced. The guitars chime rather than squawk, the backing vocals possess a haunting choral effect, the bass line is taut but purposeful, and the beat remains steady and patient. 'Second Angle' is an instrumental version.

'APPLEBUSH'

A cover of the Alice Cooper song from 1969's *Pretties For You* LP. 'I remember first going out with Malcolm and noticing that album tucked away in his record collection,' recalls Syuzen Buckley, Malcolm's wife (then girlfriend), who performs the lead vocal on the track.

'There was a gig at the art college one night, and we had covered it then,' remembers Malcolm. 'Paul liked Alice Cooper too. We both had the albums. I mean, there's some real shite on there as well as some brilliant songs, but that was one we both really liked. We performed it at the Venue as well, the night we supported Scars—that was the first night I thought, *We're a success.*' There's no need to replicate the harmonica from the original version. Instead, we are treated to a mild-ish *no wave* breakdown. It's less edgy and angular than is customary for Josef K, but the curly licks and Syuzen's cool, professional delivery make the whole thing rather charming.

'ART OF THINGS' aka 'PICTURES' / 'PICTURES (OF CINDY)'

This evolved from a murky rather unremarkable TV Art demo into a tune in two distinct parts. The spontaneous outbreak from its scouring, fingernails-on-the-chalkboard intro into something more blissful and transcendent (those twangy chiming guitars again) makes it sound almost bipolar. Melodically, it is a precursor to The Wild Swans' legendary 'Revolutionary Spirit' or The Lotus Eaters' 'First Picture Of You'. Davy's bass bubbles up a relentless rhythm, jarring with Ronnie's unorthodox textured percussion, leaving little space before the whole thing jerks into convulsive *Doc At The Radar Station* rhythms with agreeably cushioned hihats. It's a decidedly odd construction, ending on the downhill—irregular, arrhythmic, lopsided. It feels a bit like a work in progress, except that it was both an early TV Art demo—ill-defined, keyboard-based, unremarkable— as well as a band favourite after its re-emergence as 'Pictures' or 'Pictures (Of Cindy)'.

'Stuart Maconie raved about the guitar on this,' says Haig, 'although for some reason I think he credited it to Malcolm.'

'CHANCE MEETING'

In many ways, 'Chance Meeting'—a nod to the song of the same name on *Roxy Music*—defines Josef K. It is the song that bookended their career—their first ever release and the last 45 they recorded for Postcard. It also charts the trajectory of their development as a band, from sluggish amateurs to classy sophisticates.

The Absolute 45 was drawn from the TV Art demo. Compared to the later Postcard revamp, it sounds tired and a little pedestrian, but next to 'Take 2' from the same demo tape it's a fairly chirpy affair. The wonky Fall keyboard overwhelms the stoic rhythm section, while the guitars—scratching out little arcs in the background—are so discrete as to be virtually inaudible. It's an unimaginable distance from the classic and more familiar Josef K sound. Even if it breaks into a slow gallop after two minutes, it remains a subdued affair, although the melody is breezy enough to just about carry it off.

The Postcard re-recording was a divisive affair, with some accounts suggesting Haig stormed out in a rage after being forced to concede to

Horne's demands. In reality, the truth is that he was simply less keen than Malcolm Ross to rework extant material. He was always looking to the next thing and wasn't inclined to look back.

'If Horne had spoken to me the way Simon Goddard says he did, it wouldn't have ended well for him,' suggests Haig. 'At most, I might have asked why. It was *my* song. Why do you keep fiddling with it? But to be honest, Malcolm saw something in that song that I didn't. I didn't mind that at all, but Horne getting on board with him probably got my back up.'

'I remember Alan and Paul arguing over it,' notes Ross. 'We were back at Castle Sound studio. Their relationship was really bad by then. They were barely civil to one another. Alan was saying stuff like, We have to be aiming for hit singles. I recognised some commerciality in the song, and so did Alan. We thought maybe we could get something played on Janice Long and Kid Jensen. We chucked everything at it—even a Rickenbacker twelve-string in the fade out. It's not like Paul was against making a hit single, but he didn't see the point of using a better studio. Alan would snap, 'If you think that, why are you even here?' There was friction, but Calum Malcolm and I tried to just ignore it and get on with things.'

Despite Haig's reticence, Ross was right. He brought the guitars centre stage, with even the second rhythm more trebly, much cleaner. He added horns (courtesy his brother Alastair), which gave the song a touch of class, affording it a joyous optimism. Haig's register is higher on the re-recording. He manages to overcome any reservations to sound more emotionally involved than he does on the original.

'Malcolm's autoharp comes in during the last verses,' adds Haig. 'It sounds like a hundred mandolins playing.' The autoharp was inspired by Malcolm's (and possibly Horne's) fondness for The Lovin' Spoonful's 'Do You Believe In Magic?' 'My mum taught special needs children and she had brought it home from school and that's how I got to know that instrument,' Ross says.

Even better are the horn and strings in the outro—strikingly similar to the finale of 'You Set The Scene' on *Forever Changes*. In Ross's hands, it became an absolute peach of a single, undoubtedly superior to the earlier version. The second version was then utilised for the first John Peel session. The best of the various live versions to get a release is the Brussels recording, which finds the band at the height of their powers. 'Chance Meeting' could define Postcard—even more so than 'Falling And Laughing' or 'Blue Boy'—and what the label was striving for. To these ears, it compares favourably to anything Orange Juice managed before they moved to Polydor.

'CITIZENS'

One of four songs to appear on both the scrapped and released album, although this time in radically different form. The discarded *Sorry For Laughing* arrangement, with Joy Division synth swooshes and Torrance's richly textured insistent percussion, contains a hiccupping riff recalling 'Hair Pie Bake 2' from *Trout Mask Replica*.

'We used wind noises from a synthesizer I had got for my Christmas,' Haig says. The trumpet sound too is simply one note from the synth. 'I spent ages twiddling the knobs trying to get some kind of noise of it.'

There is a brief passage of restraint, but the nervous energy arm-wrestles the ennui out of existence to produce a thrilling racket. They would abandon this arrangement during their live shows and by the time of *The Only Fun In Town*, the transformation was complete. Despite the tinniness of the production, one hears an altogether different Josef K: confident, suave, Chic through a meat-grinder; lean, cool, deliciously funky.

'CRAZY TO EXIST'

It could have been the title of this book, and it could be Paul Haig's epitaph. Still, it made the title of the posthumously released live retrospective. On the earliest version (the B-side of 'Radio Drill Time'), we hear a Fall-ish skiffle, with tinny clunking guitars. The vocal sounds almost disconnected from the melody, particularly before the tempo slows for its fuzzy distorted coda. The mix on the aborted first LP holds firm to the rockabilly Fall rhythm, but the production is marginally cleaner, adding atmospheric wind noises that would be removed for the re-recording on *Fun*.

'DRONE'

Although reimagined as 'Forever Drone', this earlier version—envisaged for the first LP—is so distinctive and so good that it merits a separate entry. One of those insanely out-of-control fairground rides—round and round on the sticky wall, escape route cut off—that Haig seemed strangely keen to put to bed as soon as it was recorded.

'"Drone" had a kind of 60s-flavoured feel—the lyrics were really personal,' he says. 'It had a lot to do with a really bad acid trip I had. On that fateful night, I really felt like there was no support coming from anywhere in the world. I used the Yamaha synth and the bass and drums sound quite reduced. It's a very haunting sound: *I like to start | Fade away | Don't even catch | Just decay*. I was thinking about the artist suffering for his art. The lyric *Yellow poise | Street lights* was often misconstrued as *yellow boys*. Lyrics are always very visual to me. It's a dark trip on the one hand, but then there's a beatnik element too, as I was reading Kerouac at the time (*Drink some gin | Soak the action*). It's one of my favourite lyrics.'

'ENDLESS SOUL'

Arguably *the* most underappreciated Josef K song, 'Endless Soul' was abandoned, along with 'Drone', after the first shot at the album, possibly because it had appeared on the *C81* compilation in the interim. The trembling twin overlaid rhythms showcase everything modernist about Josef K's sound—the sound of ants scurrying around feverishly. Here is Josef K as spiritual heirs of the forward-moving rhythms of Neu! No beginning, no end. Endless. Paul delivers a vogueish delivery with smart wordplay, offering a brief diversion from the customary concerns ('*questioning the right to be*').

Moving to another town
While the week were standing still
Life pulsating all around
Where there's fear there's a will

Malcolm provides the deadpan accompaniment to a melody that momentarily twists on its axis before resettling once more into its linear momentum. With its trebly toppy squalls and lighter-than-air rhythm section, it is unquestionably one of the band's finest moments. Why on earth they stopped performing it live remains a mystery, and *The Only Fun In Town* is all the weaker for its omission.

'FINAL REQUEST'

Haig's reflections on the absurdity of existence defined him, but his lyrics were always intertwined with more personal concerns, and oftentimes he sounded angst-ridden, if not in acute despair. The words to 'Final Request' typify that sunless outlook:

To prevent a disaster
But first we'll talk
Like we've never talked
And grow so tired
And find no solution
Those golden moments
Must vanish forever

'It's about an actress who takes pills, basically,' says Haig. 'I was a huge Marilyn Monroe fan, and I used to always read stuff about her life and how she died. I was fascinated by that.'

Coupled with its frenetic car crash rhythms, 'Final Request' is a heady brew. It's the rhythm section here that makes it—Davy Weddell's speedball bass alongside Torrance's inhuman breakneck percussion. 'That's the speed you play at when you're twenty years old,' nods Haig.

'It's tight and acerbic,' says Ross. 'It couldn't have been by anyone else.' He's right.

'FOREVER DRONE'

It could be that the shift from the angular discord and hysteria of 'Drone' to this lighter jangly episode might puzzle the odd listener. Perhaps they were trying to sound a little brighter. Instead, they may have unwittingly invented the 'shambling' scene. The scratchy, amateurishness sounds a million miles away from the strange dark geometry of the original. There are three live versions out there; the two on the *Crazy To Exist* compendium vary the dynamics, with the later (London) version jamming on the accelerator.

'FUN 'N' FRENZY'

The opener to 'both' albums and to most of the band's live shows, 'Fun 'n' Frenzy' contains one of the great guitar intros—toppy, twangy, atmospheric, distant, mysterious—before it locks into a feverish discord and burn. There's a stabbing 'lead'—a flock of seagulls squawking—before it draws on a little Cramps-y fuzz to fade out. The version on *Fun* is pacier, but for both records it succeeds as a fantastic calling card for the band's sound. Barely two minutes in length, it remains one of the landmark songs of the era.

'HEADS WATCH'

'Heads Watch' finds Josef K at their thrilling, jagged best.

> *I stand and look outside*
> *At pseudo-punks and all the mindless*
> *I see what they think about here*
> *I watch the girls and watch the heads turn*

Haig casts a knowing sideways glance at his less-than-inspiring contemporaries and the vacuum created by the punk scene. The playing is racy and dextrous, featuring a little pointed exchange worthy of Verlaine and Lloyd. Overall, the closest reference point is probably 'Damaged Goods' by Gang Of Four, although it's a comparison that they would perhaps dispute (they were by no means fond of Gang Of Four). Clocking in at just over two minutes, the tempo is astonishing. It is hard to believe the rhythm is not mechanised, while Weddell's three-dimensional bass drop gives Hooky a run for his money. It contrasts sharply with the original demo, which, due to its near-minimalist arrangement, cannot conjure anything like the same energy.

'HEART OF SONG'

'*These words are so dull, yeah?*' When Paul Haig quipped that Josef K were 'a funny group', it is unlikely too that many would have taken him seriously, but this is that rare occasion where it suddenly seems blindingly obvious. He'd used this lyric before, on 'Radio Drill Time', but in this setting, one couldn't help but take them at face value. But this was different. The version of 'Heart Of Song' on *The Only Fun In Town* is brittle if funky— the descending chord sequence slows slightly, with a strange guitar break that sits uncomfortably with the rest of the song. The guitar clangs away, and the melody, while pretty, doesn't really dance, doesn't really move.

THE RECORDS WERE LETTERS | 213

However, the Peel session rendition is a mighty step forward—sharper, smarter, tighter, smoother, suaver, swaggering, melodious. The verses lure you in, but the hook remains tantalisingly out of reach until the homecoming chorus, which arrives prematurely, breathing done the neck of the second verse, where its descending guitar line drops into a blissful low end. It's as if they couldn't wait any longer, succumbing to an almost desperate rush to the climax, with the last 'chorus' caressing the sweetest g-spot. Dripping with style and finesse, it's the sound of love, of joy—a song to die for.

'Malcolm said to me fairly recently, You never wrote choruses,' Haig notes wryly. '*Have you just noticed*, I thought? If you listen to "Heart Of Song", it has a very epic—I suppose you would call it—refrain. But yes, it's definitely not a chorus!'

'HEAVEN SENT'

And, for a moment, perfect alchemy. The two guitars here—completely interdependent—succeed in making it one of Haig and Ross's greatest collaborations. Haig locks onto a solitary string for the rhythm, shifting up a fret two thirds of the way through, with Ross delivering all the angles. The overlapping rhythms and the wiry fluidity of the guitars prove that Josef K were truly a force to be reckoned with.

The solemn, quasi-religious imagery seems totally at odds with the buoyancy of the music. 'I'd been reading an anthology of Japanese literature and was imagining a deity–human relationship,' says Haig, who re-recorded the song solo for Crépuscule as an almost unrecognisable slinky synth-pop number two years later.

'IT'S KINDA FUNNY'

The single—which some felt had been tampered with in order to keep Orange Juice happy—was strangely omitted from *Sorry For Laughing* and did not make it onto *The Only Fun In Town*, for which they re-recorded a different version minus the viola, Syndrum, and Haig's 'one-two-three-four' introduction. It's a fuller sound, less stark, but like the remainder of *Fun*, the vocals are buried a little deeper. 'There was a dissonance between what was being sung and the delivery,' notes Franz Ferdinand frontman Alex Kapranos. '*It's kind of funny*. Sung with such a deadpan weariness. Nothing funny at all.'

To give some indication of the song's impact and legacy, Haig recalls that around 1994 or 1995, he was approached by Vic Reeves (Jim Moir) in a bar. Decidedly awkward and trying to gather his thoughts, he momentarily pondered what to say, but before any conversation arose, Reeves approached him with a wry smile and crooned—word perfect—the verses to 'It's Kinda Funny'.

'THE MISSIONARY'

'I had Malcolm's dad in mind when I wrote "The Missionary" in my bedroom, using my old two-cassette trick,' recalls Haig. 'When I was writing it, I felt all the best parts of Josef K music were represented in the song. We recorded a great version of it at the right time and managed to put it in a bottle and cork it.'

Along with Ross, Haig reckons it the greatest Josef K song, and it is easy enough to understand why. It's an extraordinarily complex creature, an inspired blend of jangle and angle—almost the apotheosis of Josef K's sound. It's also evident that their influence upon The Fire Engines was reciprocal, although the guitar licks here sound marginally more conventional. Miraculously, however, they navigate an obstacle course of crooked angles to procure a smooth rounded finish. Weddell's bass throbs and pulses artfully, Ronnie's beat is steady. It's smart and funky and almost has almost too many ideas for its own good. Haig sounds in complete control, despite the characteristic bursts of angst:

Passing through small towns that have no religion
Seeing the faces that make me so charming
Talk to the people that never stop singing
Ask 'em some questions and think about leaving

'When I got the guitar line—a riff or motif that stretched across the whole verse—I knew I wasn't going to be able to play that and sing at the same time,' Haig says, 'but I knew Malcolm could do that, so he got to play the best guitar line I'd ever written while I was just playing rhythm chords. It was written pretty quickly, although not as quickly as "It's Kinda Funny".'

Released as the band's swansong in early 1982, as the A-side of *The Farewell Single*, it prompted this gushing review from Barney Hoskyns in the *NME*, who called it 'the farewell single from the only one of those Postcard groups that really mattered. "The Missionary" is like a storming punk version of "What Goes On" with Paul Haig using his Lou Reed larynx as passionately as ever. A high-voltage guitar funk thrasher that really travels—welcome relief from the Orange Juices of this twee little world we inhabit. I remember when the *C81* cassette came out, the distance between Edwyn's "Blue Boy" and Paul's "Endless Soul" seemed almost immeasurable. Paul, please don't hide your love forever.'

'This is the way Josef K was heading,' says Haig. '"The Missionary" was the best song we ever recorded. I had absolutely no concerns about us being a spent force.'

'"The Missionary" is just fantastic,' agrees Jon Savage. 'Chic on speed. Just the two guitars and the demented disco drums. Nothing else like it. Shame it was their last release. I used to bash it in the first year of the Hacienda. Perhaps that's why there was no one there!'

'I like "It's Kinda Funny",' adds Johnny Marr, 'but "The Missionary" is my favourite. It's so original, and the sound is totally definitive, singular, and a great noise. It really reflects the times for me.'

'NIGHT RITUAL'

This early TV Art demo could quite easily be an outtake from *Live At The Witch Trials*. Decidedly shambolic and very much in the vein of 'Rebellious Jukebox' or 'Industrial Estate', it finds the band experiencing a final moment's hesitation before breaking free from the spluttering sludge of '77 Fall.

'NO GLORY'

'No Glory' is one of the best of the TV Art demos. The cyclical, skewered guitars, with their descending Television chords, mangle themselves in a gnarled *no wave* maelstrom before escaping again via the back alley. The bass is much higher in the mix than it should be, sounding like it might burst through the floor. The whole thing conjures up a mood of real dread. However, the melody and most of the lyric were abandoned for the reimagined version on *Sorry For Laughing*. Here, while the playing is superior, it's a scattershot jumble of rumbling bass, puffed-out hi-hats and anarchic guitar riffs, while the phrasing is a blatant steal from 'David Watts'. It is possibly one of the most confusing Josef K tracks, the only constant being Haig's typically assured delivery. It still comes across as a bunch of random, cut-up ideas, a sort of perfect sonic (non-jazz) accompaniment to some old beat novel like Kerouac's *Dr Sax*.

'RADIO DRILL TIME'

'Radio Drill Time' is a distinctive brew, reference points subtle enough not to be indiscreet, but it's also clear they are pushing beyond those formative influences. Their own voice is growing louder, clearer. Despite the fact that it was a pivotal moment for the band, heralding the most significant stylistic shift of their career, it was rarely performed live afterward.

'I think it still sounds great,' says Haig. 'It's very modern sounding.'

See also chapter 8.

'REVELATION'

Remember when you were ten years old, and you could run so fast it seemed like your legs were about to take flight? You stole a glance at them while you ran, and, provided you didn't trip over a stone and break your leg, they just kept on going. They could carry you into the wind if you wanted to. And you would never be out of breath. Ever.

That's 'Revelation'. The feeling of being young. And stupid. Frissons fast and free. Having said that, it's possible that all Paul Haig was able to see was the impending brick wall or iron fence in the distance. Approaching fast. No way out.

Forced to look at these pages
So many times exposed
Don't know I miss them
Gives the notion I'm not alone

'Revelation' was written sometime between the aborted LP and *Only Fun* and was introduced to the band's live sets before becoming the B-side to 'Sorry For Laughing', which makes it one of the greatest singles of all time—no exaggeration.

'There is controlled feedback from the beginning to the end,' says Haig. 'I remember sitting by the Fender twin reverb amp and turning the volume control up and letting this noise wander through the track.'

Perhaps a seldom-considered reason why they weren't happy with the first album was that they left this off. That was missing a trick. It had to be on the next one. It *had* to be. The gulping bass from Davy is fantastic, the tempo of Ronnie's percussion outrageous. If you want to know what Josef K could do that no other band could do, here's where to start.

'ROMANCE'

Haig's croon is sonorous, enigmatic. He doesn't sound romantic at all. In fact, the song is curiously sexless, mechanical over carnal, surface over substance. Crucially, that was the point.

> *Certain, certain place and time*
> *Somehow locked up in your mind*
> *Romance, living upon dream*
> *Future see it on a screen*

Two versions were recorded at the session, one containing a bubbling bass accompaniment that pulls from the quagmire only a faint melodic figure. The two guitars work at awkward angles—one is tingling, buried in the mix, the other intermittently slumberous then scything. There are injections of scissor-riffing producing lesions of feedback. The bass is almost three-dimensional, like a flattened outtake of John Cale's on 'White Light/White Heat'.

'Romance' set a template for future Josef K compositions, with verse and chorus curiously indistinct, creating an almost horizontal trajectory, a narrow channel opening like a wind tunnel through which they would begin to accelerate rhythms beyond human capacity, beyond reason. But as yet there's little sign of that. After three minutes, 'Romance' collapses in on itself, recalling some uninspiring Contortions dirge. There's nowhere left for it to go.

A brisker version was recorded at the same time. It sounds less controlled—more rock'n'roll—but has some equally scintillating guitar work.

'SENSE OF GUILT'

The original title of this song is one the band always wanted to forget. Guided by youthful instinct rather than an attraction to the grisly or macabre, there's little need to elaborate here, but they were certainly embarrassed by it. Probably due to those associations, they dropped it before re-recording the album. It was reasonably faithful to the earlier TV Art demo—virtually narrated by Haig, à la 'The Gift', minus Syndrum and viola.

The track itself is genuinely unnerving—not because of the associated subject matter but because of its brooding intensity and prickly aggression. Ross's haunted viola is genuinely terrifying, recalling the blood beginning to flow in 'Heroin'. The angles are sharper, and then those blood-curdling screams . . . one imagines Haig at his work in the medical records office, being confronted by all those faces, old faces, infected limbs and organs. What was this life? And to dust we shall all return. And some taken so cruelly and so soon, Smallpox, diphtheria, scabies, scurvy. Scurvy of the brain. Such a tender organ. Osteomalacia, rickets, Proteus syndrome. Those names: Arnold D. Dayton. Elizabeth Anne Corbett. Wilfred P. Hayburn. It fed into the music and the words, and probably the hyperanxiety.

> *My mind's a blank but for a faint reminiscence*
> *Was she real, or maybe a dream?*
> *I rested well apart from a recurring nightmare*
> *So when the homicide people ask me questions*
> *I'll tell them about my dreams.*

Here, Torrance's locomotive percussion drives the taut intro before the first guitar breaks loose. It is then suffocated by the second. When they clash together, it sounds like bullets ricocheting off the top of walls. The structure is tight, the tension sustained—it's bloody marvellous.

'16 YEARS'

'16 Years' made the cut for *Only Fun* and became a live favourite early in 1981. A slice of up-tempo scratchy funk, the twangy pick-ups are genius, and the rather jaunty melody is a little at odds with the lyric:

> *Yes, I stood by the roadside*
> *Saw many happenings there*
> *That's the place where the ghosts died*
> *When we were young and still could care.*

'The song is really about tough guys at school, who caused harm to people just to satisfy their own perverse pleasures,' Haig explains. '*Guys like me don't give an inch | They want to see you squirm and flinch.* It's what I saw on the faces of some of the bigger bullies at high school.'

'SORRY FOR LAUGHING'

The band's single for Crépuscule made up for the sloppy execution on the abandoned LP of the same name. It boasts a falling-down-the-stairs rhythm mixed with a bright jangle. It was playful, danceable, immediate, while the bass line is terrific, mirroring the first guitar. Ostensibly about disabled people having a laugh (see chapter 9), it's a song that contemporary fans will forever associate with the band due to surviving footage of them miming the track on the Belgian TV show *Generation 80*.

'I heard it while living in Melbourne in the early 80s and loved the mad tension of it,' says Australian musician Dave Graney, ex-Moodist and later collaborator with Malcolm Ross in The Coral Snakes. 'Paul Haig's vocal so controlled and cool, while the guitar, bass and drums all skittered about around and underneath it.'

'At T In The Park around 2009, I played a session with Edwyn and Malcolm,' recalls Alex Kapranos. 'I was overjoyed. I mean, here were two of my absolute heroes that I was singing and playing with. It was the first time I had met Malcolm, and I'm afraid I bombarded him with many questions. I hope I didn't freak him out. I remember saying how much I loved the guitar on "Sorry For Laughing" and I had been obsessed with it for years. How did you work it out? How did it come to you? He just sort of laughed and said, Ach, I just put my fingers there and it sounded right. The mystery is, there is no mystery. It just happens when you are not thinking about it too much.'

'TERRY'S SHOW LIES'

A one-track encapsulation of the unbridled invention of the era. A complete reinvention of the song on the TV Art demo, with its doddering keyboard and nervy *Talking Heads 77* vibe, it would become one of the key tracks on *Sorry For Laughing*. Now here's a song! A Pop Group-inspired agit-funk masterclass with superb glassy production. It's danceable, it has gallons of attitude, and the guitars are incredible.

> *Turn the hate on him*
> *Turn your hate on him*

'It's about talk show hosts at the time and in general,' says Haig. 'How the popularity of one is so high, then comes crashing down, and the audience turns on him. Then general paranoia takes over,' he adds enigmatically.

'TORN MENTOR'

A laboured, almost turgid track with little thrust or dynamism until three minutes in, when it is hijacked by a surprise 'Rock Lobster' guitar break. Even so, it settles back into the slow groove before petering out indistinctly. It feels a little like rough math work as Haig and Ross freely experiment with texture, tone, and technique, clearly still in awe of Television and the Voidoids, but overall, it's something of a pale copy of 'Little Johnny Jewel'. The most significant aspect of the song is that part of the lyric was reappropriated for 'Endless Soul'. The title was a play on the word *tormentor*.

'Your mentor is fucked up,' says Haig. 'It's about a mentor figure who is seriously flawed.' He does not specify the person he had in mind.

'Torn Mentor' is uncharacteristically lengthy by Josef K's standards. Those five minutes feel like ten, the airlessness relieved only by a sudden tempo shift.

'VARIATIONS OF SCENE'

A fantastic dose of *Third Man* noir, dazzlingly atmospheric with its solitary note piano riff, footsteps, flute, and Syndrum. Josef K's obsession with European existentialist fiction captured in a bottle. The understated guitar is brilliant, while the drum fills at the end are lifted from *Marquee Moon*'s 'Friction'. It inhabits its own world, where gravestones open and a sense of dread and cliffhanging suspense builds slowly but determinedly. It is one of Haig's most ornate lyrics—all marble and mosaic, statues and empires:

> *Let's cherish these galleries*
> *The echo and the noise*
> *We'll move right through them*
> *And all these bitter joys*
> *These colours they are rising*
> *And changing beyond*
> *The possibilities are reaching beyond.*

And, for a moment, the possibilities were endless. Haig sounds ready to rule the world.

15/15 | MEMENTO MORI

WHAT JOSEF K DID NEXT

It wasn't a band. It was a way of life.

PAUL HAIG, LINER NOTES TO *ENTOMOLOGY*

PAUL HAIG

Following Josef K's dissolution, Haig began a solo career, briefly relocating to Brussels before recording for Crépuscule. He made his first solo album with producer Alex Sadkin in New York. Later, he released material on Les Temps Moderne, Circa, and also under the moniker Rhythm Of Life, which became the name of the label he founded. In the mid-80s, he enjoyed various collaborations with other musicians, most notably Bernard Sumner of New Order. He has released twelve solo albums, and while he continues to make music today, live appearances are exceptionally rare. He lives in Peebles in the Scottish Borders.

I listened to a test pressing fairly recently, and I found that really difficult because it brought back so many memories. I could hear a lot of ghosts from the past, including the characters who inhabited those songs. I was the lyricist and therefore I had to vocalise what Josef K were all about. I had to tell others what we felt. I found that very difficult. I had to delve very deep down into the depths to find stuff to write about. Sometimes I think I got too close to it. But there are some people in the world who talk about Josef K the way we would have spoken about Television. And that feels like an achievement. There is nobody around today, who is today what Josef K were to yesterday. The equivalent of Josef K, the things that are happening now, are nowhere near as important as Josef K were at that time.

MALCOLM ROSS

Upon leaving Josef K, Malcolm joined Orange Juice, with whom he made two albums. Later, he joined Aztec Camera, touring with the band and playing guitar on their 1984 album *Knife*. Afterward, he formed The High Bees with his wife Syuzen and was part of the touring groups for Edwyn Collins and Paul Haig in the 80s. Ross has gone on to work alongside several other musicians, including Barry Adamson, Dave Graney, and Blancmange. He served as a musical consultant for The Beatles' bio film *Backbeat* and played guitar with Johnny Depp on the soundtrack to the film *Chocolat*. Ross recorded two solo albums in the 90s and subsequently played with the band Buckley's Chance, once again with Syuzen. Today, he still occasionally plays with friends in various line-ups, as well as driving a taxi. He lives in Edinburgh.

Josef K was one of the most happy and exciting times in my life. We were constantly on an upward trajectory, and it felt like we were a part of the new and inspiring cultural happenings. The four of us—together, united—created something whose sum was far greater than the individual parts. For different reasons, we were each so vital to the mix, but Paul was undoubtedly the greatest talent and main force in the band. I'm very proud of our canon of work, and knowing that people are still listening to our music today is evidence that we got at least something right. On a personal level, I got together with Syuzen during the band's existence, and that made it an even more special time. I'm proud of my time in Orange Juice, too, but the best thing I've done in my life— next to being a father and husband—was being a part of Josef K.

DAVY WEDDELL

Davy played on the 1982 album *The Man On Your Street* by The Happy Family, fronted by Nick Currie (aka Momus). He later teamed up with Metropak's Stephen Harrison in the short-lived band Heyday. After other musical projects failed to get off the ground, he worked in bars in London. He was briefly employed as a runner for a healthcare production company, during which time he learned how to edit videos. He has been involved in video production ever since. Weddell lives in Gibraltar, where he works for the local television company.

Those were great times. I was going to say memories, but I'm not sure of how much I can bloody remember. Still, I was so disappointed when the end came. I had been steadily improving as a musician. It just didn't work out for me in other bands afterward. It was every teenager's ambition to be in a band back then, so I'm very grateful for it all. Now everyone just wants to be an influencer. My daughter plays the records from time to time. I think they still sound like great songs.

RONNIE TORRANCE

Ronnie went on to play with Boots For Dancing, then reunited with Davy Weddell for a stint in The Happy Family. Following a brief spell—again alongside Davy—in Heyday, Torrance left the music business for good in 1985 and started his own property-investment company. After the financial crisis of 1992, he began working as a mortgage insurance broker, and he has been involved in financial services ever since. He lives in the Algarve, Portugal.

I have very fond memories. It was such an exciting time to be in a band, and Josef K was one of the coolest around. I loved living for the moment and having a taste of that rock and roll lifestyle—making music, being wasted almost 24/7, and meeting many nice ladies along the way. I must have been responsible for countless acts of stupidity and sometimes wonder if the boys had me in mind when they called that album Young & Stupid! We broke up far too soon—before we had reached our full potential—but life's too short to be plagued by regrets. I had no idea that Josef K would become so influential, so I am proud and feel privileged to have been part of that legacy.

EPILOGUE /
1980: MY FAVOURITE THINGS

More than forty years have passed since Josef K enjoyed their brief moment in the spotlight. Alongside hairlines, memories are receding fast. As eager youngsters, the band immersed themselves in the culture of the times. It was *their* era. They were well-read and equally discerning when it came to music and cinema.

At the same time, as self-styled modernists, they desired to escape the present and embrace the future.

For this exercise, each member of the band was asked to re-imagine what his nineteen-year-old self might have identified as 'My Favourite Things'.

PAUL HAIG

Book: *Hunger* by Knut Hamsun
Film: *The Shining*
Actor: Jack Nicholson
Album: *Remain In Light* by Talking Heads
Song: 'Are You Glad To Be In America?' by James 'Blood' Ulmer
Band: The Associates
Singer: Billy Mackenzie
Place: Edinburgh
Food: Vegetarian
Ambition: To write good songs
Describe your bandmates: Nutters

MALCOLM ROSS

Book: *Amerika* by Franz Kafka
Film: *Apocalypse Now*
Actor: Marlon Brando
Album: *Marquee Moon* by Television
Song: 'She Is Beyond Good And Evil' by The Pop Group
Band: Pere Ubu
Singer: David Bowie
Place: Edinburgh
Food: Chicken Kiev
Ambition: Success for Josef K
Describe your bandmates: Funny, intense, and supportive

DAVY WEDDELL

Book: *The Subterraneans* by Jack Kerouac
Film: *Alphaville*
Actor: Various, male and female
Album: Various
Song: 'Romance' by Josef K
Band: Josef K
Singer: Billy MacKenzie
Place: Edinburgh
Food: Cheese Beano
Ambition: Success
Describe your bandmates: Chums

RONNIE TORRANCE

Book: I don't do books. Being dyslexic has its benefits.
Film: *The Shining*
Actor: Steve Martin—he makes me laugh!
Album: *Unknown Pleasures* by Joy Division
Song: 'Love Will Tear Us Apart' by Joy Division
Band: Joy Division
Singer: Bowie. A creative genius who is truly unique.
Place: Edinburgh/Brussels
Food: French/Scottish. Amazing product and taste.
Ambition: To earn great wealth
Describe your bandmates: They're great guys. If I was to find fault, it would be with Paul. He's a Jambo!

JOSEF K ON RECORD /
SELECT UK DISCOGRAPHY

WHILE ACTIVE

'Chance Meeting' b/w 'Romance'
Absolute 45 / ABS001, November 1979.

'Radio Drill Time' b/w 'Crazy To Exist (Live)'
*Postcard 45 / Postcard 80-3, August 1980.
Issued with standard Postcard brown sleeve,
then as a folding picture sleeve with Orange
Juice's 'Blue Boy' b/w 'Love Sick' / Postcard
80-2 on the reverse.*

'It's Kinda Funny' b/w 'Final Request'
Postcard 45 / Postcard 80-5), November 1980.

Sorry For Laughing
*Postcard LP, unreleased. First officially released
as the second disc of the two-CD issue of The
Only Fun In Town and subsequently in various
other formats.*
'Fun 'n' Frenzy' / 'Heads Watch' / 'Drone' /
'Sense Of Guilt' / 'Art Of Things' / 'Crazy To
Exist' // 'Citizens' / 'Variation Of Scene' /
'Terry's Show Lies' / 'No Glory' / 'Endless
Soul' / 'Sorry For Laughing'

'Sorry For Laughing' b/w 'Revelation'
*Les Disques du Crépuscule 45 / TWI 023,
April 1981. Released under license from
Postcard / dual cat no. Postcard 81-4.*

'Chance Meeting' b/w 'Pictures (Of Cindy)'
Postcard 45 / Postcard 81-5, May 1981.

The Only Fun In Town
Postcard LP / Postcard 81-7, July 1981.
'Fun 'n' Frenzy' / 'Revelation' / 'Crazy To
Exist' / 'It's Kinda Funny' / 'The Angle' //
'Forever Drone' / 'Heart Of Song' / '16
Years' / 'Citizens' / 'Sorry For Laughing'

POST-SPLIT

The Farewell Single
Les Disques du Crépuscule 45 / TWI 053, 1982.
'The Missionary' // 'One Angle' / 'Second
Angle'

'Heaven Sent'
*Supreme International Editions twelve-inch
single / Edition 87-7, 1987.*
'Heaven Sent' // 'Radio Drill Time' / 'Heads
Watch' / Fun 'n' Frenzy'

Young & Stupid
*Supreme International Editions compilation LP /
Editions 87-6, 1987.*
'Heart Of Song' / 'Endless Soul' / 'Citizens' /
'Variation Of A Scene' / 'It's Kinda Funny' /
'Sorry For Laughing' // 'Chance Meeting' /
'Heaven Sent' / 'Drone' / 'Sense Of Guilt' /
'Revelation' / 'Romance'

Young & Stupid
Les Temps Modernes CD / LTMCD-2307, 1990.
'Romance' / 'Chance Meeting' / 'Radio
Drill Time' / Crazy To Exist (Live)' / 'It's
Kinda Funny' / 'Final Request' / 'Sorry For
Laughing' / 'Revelation' / 'Chance Meeting' /
'Pictures (Of Cindy)' / The Angle (One Angle)' /
'The Angle (Second Angle)' / 'The Missionary' /
'Heart Of Song' / 'Applebush' / 'Heaven
Sent' / 'Endless Soul' / Radio Drill Time (demo
version)' / 'Torn Mentor' / 'Night Ritual'

Endless Soul
Marina compilation LP / MA40, 1998.
'The Missionary' / 'Endless Soul' / 'It's Kinda
Funny' / 'Sorry For Laughing' / 'Heart Of
Song' / 'Revelation' / 'Chance Meeting' / 'The
Angle' // 'Drone' / 'Variation Of Scene' / 'Final

Request' / '16 Years' / 'Heaven Sent' / 'Heads Watch' / 'Radio Drill Time' / 'Adoration (Live)'

Crazy To Exist: Live
Les Temps Modernes CD / LTMCD-2319, 2000.
Tracks 1–10 recorded at the Beursschouwburg Arts Centre, Brussels, April 8, 1981; tracks 11–20 recorded live at the Venue, London, August 8, 1981.
'Fun 'n' Frenzy' / '16 Years' / 'It's Kinda Funny' / 'Crazy To Exist' / 'Forever Drone' / 'Revelation' / 'Citizens' / 'Chance Meeting' / 'Sorry For Laughing' / 'Final Request' / 'Fun 'n' Frenzy' / 'Heaven Sent' / 'Chance Meeting' / 'The Missionary' / 'It's Kinda Funny' / 'Heart Of Song' / 'Forever Drone' / 'Sorry For Laughing' / 'The Angle' / 'Adoration'

The Sound Of Josef K: Live At Valentino's
Rhythm Of Life CD, ROL 011, 2003.
'Intro' / 'Fun 'n' Frenzy' / 'Heaven Sent' / 'Chance Meeting' / 'Forever Drone' / 'Heart Of Song' / 'Citizens' / 'The Missionary' / 'The Angle' / 'Adoration' / 'Revelation' / 'Fun 'n' Frenzy' / 'Chance Meeting' / 'Terry's Show Lies' / 'Final Request' / '16 Years' / 'It's Kinda Funny' / 'Sorry For Laughing' / 'Romance'

Entomology
Domino compilation CD / REWIGCD30, 2006.
'Radio Drill Time' / 'It's Kinda Funny' / 'Final Request' / 'Heads Watch' / 'Drone' / 'Sense Of Guilt' / 'Citizens' / 'Variation Of Scene' / 'Endless Soul' / 'Sorry For Laughing' / 'Revelation' / 'Chance Meeting' / 'Pictures (Of Cindy)' / 'Fun 'n' Frenzy' / 'Crazy To Exist' / 'Forever Drone' / 'Heart Of Song' / '16 Years' / 'The Angle' / 'Heaven Sent' / 'The Missionary' / 'Applebush'

Sorry For Laughing & TV Art Demos
Les Temps Modernes double LP and CD / LTMLP-2549, 2012.
'Fun 'n' Frenzy' / 'Heads Watch' / 'Drone' / 'Sense Of Guilt' / 'Art Of Things' / 'Crazy To Exist' // 'Citizens' / 'Variation Of Scene' / 'Terry's Show Lies' / 'No Glory' / 'Endless Soul' / 'Sorry For Laughing'
Bonus CD: 'Chance Meeting (Take One)' /

'Terry's Show Lies' / 'No Glory' / 'Final Request' / 'Art Of Things' / 'Romance (Take One)' / 'Torn Mentor' / 'Night Ritual' / 'Heads Watch' / 'Chance Meeting (Take Two)' / 'Sense Of Guilt' / 'Romance (Take Two)'

The Only Fun In Town
Les Temps Modernes double CD / TWI-2305, 2014.
Disc 1: 'Fun 'n' Frenzy' / 'Revelation' / 'Crazy To Exist' / 'It's Kinda Funny' / 'The Angle' / 'Forever Drone' / 'Heart Of Song' / '16 Years' / 'Citizens' / 'Sorry For Laughing'
Disc 2: 'Fun 'n' Frenzy' / 'Heads Watch' / 'Drone' / 'Sense Of Guilt' / 'Art Of Things' / 'Crazy To Exist' / 'Citizens' / 'Variation Of Scene' / 'Terry's Show Lies' / 'No Glory' / 'Endless Soul' / 'Sorry For Laughing'

It's Kinda Funny
Les Disques du Crépuscule LP / TWI 022, 2016.
'Romance' / 'Radio Drill Time' / 'It's Kinda Funny' / 'Sorry For Laughing' / 'Chance Meeting' / 'The Missionary' // 'Heaven Sent' / 'Revelation' / 'Crazy To Exist' / 'The Angle' / 'Pictures (Of Cindy)' / 'Final Request' / 'Chance Meeting (The Absolute Version)'

The Scottish Affair (Part Two)
Les Disques du Crépuscule LP / TWI 019, 2019.
Live album recorded at the Beursschouwburg Arts Centre, Brussels, April 8, 1981; see also Crazy To Exist (Live).
'Fun 'n' Frenzy' / '16 Years' / 'It's Kinda Funny' / 'Crazy To Exist' / 'Forever Drone' / 'Revelation' // 'Citizens' / 'Chance Meeting' / 'Sorry For Laughing' / 'Final Request'

BIBLIOGRAPHY /
NOTES & SOURCES

Unless indicated otherwise, all quotations in this book are from the author's interviews 2020–2023.

Some of the source material comes from interviews and reviews first featured in the pages of the *NME*, *Sounds*, and *Melody Maker*.

In addition, the book has drawn from other journals—*Smash Hits*, *Record Collector*, and *Stand & Deliver* fanzine, as indicated, as well as from interviews conducted by Grant McPhee for his 2015 film *Big Gold Dream*. The following books, websites, and articles were also used:

BOOKS

Simon Goddard / *Simply Thrilled: The Preposterous Story Of Postcard Records* (Random House, 2014)

Knut Hamsun / *Hunger* (Leonard Smithers & Co, 1899)

Herman Hesse / *Wanderung: Aufzeichnungen* (Fischer, 1920)

Franz Kafka / *The Trial* (Gollancz, 1937)

Douglas MacIntyre and Grant McPhee / *Hungry Beat: The Scottish Independent Pop-Underground Movement 1977–1984* (White Rabbit, 2022)

Simon Reynolds / *Rip It Up And Start Again: Postpunk 1978–1984* (Faber, 2005)

Jon Savage / *England's Dreaming: Sex Pistols And Punk Rock* (Faber & Faber, 1991)

WEBSITES

josef-k.org

thenewperfectcollection.com

ARTICLES

John Clarkson / 'Josef K: Interview', *Penny Black Music*, November 26, 2006

Chris Connelly / 'Confessions Of A Hysterical Music Addict 1975', *Decibel*, October 26, 2011

Dave McCullough / 'A Postcard From Paradise', *Sounds*, August 30, 1980

David McLean / 'Loved Edinburgh Record Store That Was At Forefront Of City's Punk Scene In The Late 1970s', edinburghlive.co.uk, November 10, 2022

Kenneth O. Morgan / 'Britain In The Seventies—Our Unfinest Hour?' *Revue Française de Civilisation Britannique*, doi.org, 2017

Nardwuar / 'Nardwuar vs. King Krule', youtube.com, December 17, 2013

James Nice / 'Josef K Biography', lesdisquesducrepuscule.com (undated)

Ben Opipari / 'Colin Newman: Wire', *Songwriters On Process*, January 7, 2011

Taylor Parkes / 'I Went Much Further Than I Ever Thought I Could: Johnny Marr Interviewed', *The Quietus*, November 27, 2012

Alexis Petridis / 'Josef K: Entomology', *The Guardian*, December 15, 2006

Billy Sloan / 'Billy Sloan He's K-razy For Scots', thefreelibrary.com, October 1, 2006

Johnny Waller / 'Welcome To The Funhouse', *Sounds*, May 30, 1981

ENDNOTES

2 / 'Josef K was about the heroic ...' Simon Reynolds

9 / 'I don't dislike rock stars ...' Paul Haig to Johnny Waller

18 / 'It's kinda funny but ...' Leyla Sanai, NME, August 15, 1981

19 / 'I think Josef K is ...' Paul Haig to Johnny Waller

20 / 'I blame the NME ...' Alan Horne, NME, August 29, 1981

20 / 'We'd been together too long ...' Paul Haig to Johnny Waller

37 / 'I'd heard they were ...' Paul Haig, The New Perfect Collection, November 24, 2015

44 / 'The window [was] crammed ...' Chris Connelly

47 / 'shocked, uneasy. I remember ...' Malcolm Ross to David Pollock, Record Collector, October 2022

48 / 'We used to dye all our clothes ...' Vic Godard to Jon Savage

55 / 'I started off playing guitar ...' Ronnie Torrance to Johnny Waller

61 / 'We just didn't care about ...' Paul Haig, liner notes to Endless Soul (Marina, 1998)

63 / '[taking] the axe to rock'n'roll ...' Colin Newman to Ben Opipari

82 / 'As soon as I heard ...' Paul Haig to Simon Reynolds

82 / 'It was just a matter ...' Malcolm Ross to Simon Reynolds

95 / 'a credible boutique ...' James Nice

96 / 'I was reading an awful lot ...' Paul Haig to Grant McPhee, audio interview for Big Gold Dream (undated)

97 / 'It just happened the way ...' Paul Haig to Mark Brennan, Melody Maker, May 14, 1983

102 / 'Postcard had this quality ...' Paul Morley to Douglas MacIntyre and Grant McPhee

103 / 'Serious Edinburgh band ...' Melody Maker, February 23, 1980

103 / 'More wigs and hats ...' NME, March 1, 1980

103 / 'Josef K come clean ...' Sounds, March 1, 1980

110 / 'about as psychedelic as ...' Harry Longbaugh, Sounds, December 13, 1980

115 / 'Alan had this vision ...' Paul Haig to Simon Reynolds

119 / 'Josef K's very raison d'être ...' Paul Lester, Record Collector, October 9, 2007

123 / 'A loose attack on ...' Chris Westwood, Record Mirror, September 27, 1980

123 / 'Songs about the radio ...' Paul Rombali, NME, August 23, 1980

123 / 'The cruds who've pissed over ...' Dave McCullough, Sounds, September 6, 1980

123 / 'Scotland seems to have ...' Dave McCullough

124 / 'Josef K make me ...' Dave McCullough

125 / 'It was a great venue ...' Ian Stoddart to Grant McPhee, audio interview for Big Gold Dream (undated)

127 / 'I was in utter awe ...' Nick Currie, liner notes to Endless Soul (Marina, 1998)

130 / 'I always used to find ...' Malcolm Ross to Simon Reynolds

134 / 'Both records are so utterly ...' Dave McCullough, Sounds, November 28, 1980

134 / 'It sounded exactly like ...' Paul Morley, liner notes to Entomology (Domino, 2006)

139 / 'Josef K have style ...' Barney Hoskyns, NME, January 10, 1981

141 / 'about two cripples having ...' Paul Haig to Johnny Waller

142 / 'Their songs are contracted ...' Paul Morley, NME, March 21, 1981

142 / 'Jesus this is harsh ...' Paolo Hewitt, NME, April 11, 1981

145 / 'I remember once sitting quietly ...' Paul Haig to Paul Lester, Record Collector, October 9, 2007

145 / 'Syuzen, my girlfriend, used to ...' Malcolm Ross to Johnny Waller

148 / 'Josef K are a band with identity ...' Chris Burkham, Sounds, March 14, 1981

155 / '[It is] an incessant tinny racket ...' Dave McCullough, Sounds, July 4, 1981

155 / 'I should be talking about it ...' Paul Morley, NME, July 25, 1981

156 / 'I don't think we gave it ...' Malcolm Ross, Melody Maker, August 22, 1981

157 / 'one of the few ...' Ian Pye, Melody Maker, July 18, 1981

157 / 'It was art, not ...' Malcom Ross to Douglas MacIntyre and Grant McPhee

158 / 'I still love *The Only* . . .' Allan Campbell to Douglas MacIntyre and Grant McPhee

160 / 'Josef K have apparently . . .' Dave McCullough, *Sounds*, May 9, 1981

161 / 'Pictures owes vocal royalties . . .' Steve Sutherland, *Melody Maker,* May 9, 1981

161 / 'More of those ringing . . .' Vivien Goldman, *NME*, May 9, 1981

162 / 'Everything is within you . . .' Herman Hesse

166 / '[I was] pretty depressed . . .' Paul Haig to Johnny Waller

170 / 'Nearly everyone ignored . . .' Paul Morley, quoted by Alexis Petridis

172 / 'We just have to make . . .' Paul Haig to Paul Morley, *NME*, October 4, 1980

173 / 'We'd been together for . . .' Paul Haig, *Melody Maker*, May 14, 1983

180 / 'Post-punk was all about . . .' Alan Rankine to Simon Reynolds

181 / 'It was at the Wig . . .' Davy Henderson to Douglas MacIntyre and Grant McPhee

185 / 'I felt pleasantly empty . . .' Knut Hamsun

191 / 'Josef K were the . . .' Stefan Kassell to Douglas MacIntyre and Grant McPhee

192 / 'I liked the enigma . . .' Paul Morley to Douglas MacIntyre and Grant McPhee

193 / 'no progeny . . .' Simon Reynolds, *Melody Maker*, October 20, 1990

200 / 'They've said "Sorry For Laughing" . . .' Paul Haig to Paul Lester, *Record Collector*, October 9, 2007

202 / 'trilled like bells . . .' Paul Morley, liner notes to *Entomology* (Domino, 2006)

203 / 'Josef K were Postcard's . . .' Martin Aston, *Mojo*, August 2004

215 / 'The farewell single from . . .' Barney Hoskyns, *NME*, March 20, 1982

223 / 'It wasn't a band . . .' Paul Haig, liner notes to *Entomology* (Domino, 2006)

INDEX

ACKNOWLEDGEMENTS

First of all, thanks to my long-suffering family—my wife, Wendy, and my children, Anna, Ruth, Reuben, and Maria—for putting up with me disappearing for mysteriously lengthy periods over the last three years . . . you're the best.

To Tom Seabrook at Jawbone for showing faith in my idea and for his great patience, diligence, and skill in guiding me through to the book's completion.

To my longtime friends and co-founders of *The New Perfect Collection* blog, Terry Tochel and Paul Gallagher, both of whom continue to school me with their encyclopaedic musical knowledge. They, alongside my brother Peter, have been a very welcome source of counsel and encouragement throughout the book's evolution.

I owe a very special debt of gratitude to fellow *Shindig!* contributors and respected authors Greg Healey and Fiona McQuarrie, for taking the trouble to offer advice and guidance and for proofreading my pitch to Jawbone.

I would like to offer thanks to Grant McPhee, for his invaluable practical assistance and resource-sharing in the face of constant pestering; to Josef K superfan Mike O'Connor, for sharing his memories of watching the band and for his help in providing scans of band memorabilia; and to Jordi Maxwell, for her wonderful artwork.

Likewise, I am grateful to David Stubbs, for his sage advice and efforts to bring things to fruition. There have been many other acquaintances who have been delighted to help, and I'd like to mention in particular Paul Lester at *Record Collector*, as well as Chris Roberts and Marco Rossi, for their advice and encouragement.

I am especially indebted to Stewart Lee for volunteering to write the foreword to the book.

I would like to thank Derek Louden, Mike Lynch, Alastair McKay, and Fran Van der Hoeven for helping with finding suitable photographic material for the book.

To all those who have made themselves available for interviews or who have contributed in their own way. In particular, I'd like to thank Douglas McIntyre, Steven Daly, Allan Campbell, Nick Currie, Ian Rankin, Jim Lambie, Alex Kapranos, Johnny Marr, David McClymont, Phil Wilson, James Nice, Gary McCormack, Simon Reynolds, Jon Savage, the late Tommy Cherry, Innes Reekie, Tam Dean Burn, Nick Peacock, Alastair McKay, Syuzen Buckley, Marc Tilli, Dave Graney, Vic Godard, John Martin, Caroline Binnie, Hugh McLachlan, Calum Malcolm, Rich Cundill, Jon Mills, Andy Morten, Camilla Aisa, Jamie Atkins, Andrew Thompson, Rory Manchee, Hugh Mulholland, Richard Oxley, Phil Hubbard, Maartje Jansma, Steve 'Stig' Chivers, and Andy @Birmingham81. Also, thank you to my brothers, Martin and James, for their constant love and support; and to Ray, Stevie, and Stewart, for their generous companionship. Not forgetting Mum and Dad—miss you loads.

Finally, to Paul Haig, Malcolm Ross, Davy Weddell, and Ronnie Torrance: for their time, honesty, patience, and fine company. But, most of all, for the music.

ALSO AVAILABLE
FROM JAWBONE PRESS

Riot On Sunset Strip: Rock'n'roll's Last Stand In Hollywood Domenic Priore

Million Dollar Bash: Bob Dylan, The Band, And The Basement Tapes Sid Griffin

Bowie In Berlin: A New Career In A New Town Thomas Jerome Seabrook

Hot Burritos: The True Story Of The Flying Burrito Brothers John Einarson with Chris Hillman

Million Dollar Les Paul: In Search Of The Most Valuable Guitar In The World Tony Bacon

To Live Is To Die: The Life And Death Of Metallica's Cliff Burton Joel McIver

The Impossible Dream: The Story Of Scott Walker & The Walker Brothers Anthony Reynolds

Jack Bruce Composing Himself: The Authorised Biography Harry Shapiro

Return Of The King: Elvis Presley's Great Comeback Gillian G. Gaar

Forever Changes: Arthur Lee & The Book Of Love John Einarson

Seasons They Change: The Story Of Acid And Psychedelic Folk Jeanette Leech

Crazy Train: The High Life And Tragic Death Of Randy Rhoads Joel McIver

A Wizard, A True Star: Todd Rundgren In The Studio Paul Myers

The Resurrection Of Johnny Cash: Hurt, Redemption, And American Recordings Graeme Thomson

Just Can't Get Enough: The Making Of Depeche Mode Simon Spence

Glenn Hughes: The Autobiography Glenn Hughes with Joel McIver

Entertain Us: The Rise Of Nirvana Gillian G. Gaar

Read & Burn: A Book About Wire Wilson Neate

Big Star: The Story Of Rock's Forgotten Band Rob Jovanovic

Recombo DNA: The Story Of Devo, or How The 60s Became The 80s Kevin C. Smith

Neil Sedaka, Rock'n'roll Survivor: The Inside Story Of His Incredible Comeback Rich Podolsky

Touched By Grace: My Time With Jeff Buckley Gary Lucas

A Sense Of Wonder: Van Morrison's Ireland David Burke

Bathed In Lightning: John McLaughlin, The 60s And The Emerald Beyond Colin Harper